DISPLACED AT HOME

DISPLACED AT HOME

*Ethnicity and Gender
among Palestinians in Israel*

Edited by

RHODA ANN KANAANEH

and

ISIS NUSAIR

STATE UNIVERSITY OF NEW YORK PRESS

Cover photo: Singer Abeer in a scene from *Slingshot Hip Hop*, 2008, directed by Jackie Salloum. Courtesy of the director.

Published by
STATE UNIVERSITY OF NEW YORK PRESS, ALBANY

For information, contact
State University of New York Press, Albany, NY
www.sunypress.edu

Production, Laurie Searl
Marketing, Anne M. Valentine

Library of Congress Cataloging-in-Publication Data

Displaced at home : ethnicity and gender among Palestinians in Israel / edited by Rhoda Ann Kanaaneh and Isis Nusair.
     p. cm.
Includes bibliographical references and index.
ISBN 978-1-4384-3269-4 (hardcover : alk. paper)
ISBN 978-1-4384-3270-0 (pbk. : alk. paper)
     1. Palestinian Arabs—Israel—Ethnic identity.   2. Women, Palestinian Arab—Israel—Social conditions.   3. Palestinian Arabs—Israel.   4. Israel—Ethnic relations.   I. Kanaaneh, Rhoda Ann.   II. Nusair, Isis, 1967–

DS113.7.D57 2010
305.892'7405694—dc22   2010004945

10 9 8 7 6 5 4 3 2 1

CONTENTS

III. GENDERING BODIES AND SPACE

IV. MIGRATIONS

ILLUSTRATIONS

FOREWORD

Lila Abu-Lughod

In 1948 when Palestinians found that, as Honaida Ghanim puts it so well, a border had brutally crossed them, they could never have imagined how profoundly their lives would diverge. The new border known as the Green Line separated the minority who managed to remain in villages and cities within the new State of Israel from the rest of the territory that had been the home of Palestinians, and from the broader Arab region that would now house the majority who were made homeless refugees.

News about the Palestinian-Israeli conflict always seems to be about those outside "the green line." About those in the camps in Lebanon. About the Palestinians of the West Bank and Gaza, the territories occupied by Israel in 1967. In his sad meditation on the relentless expropriation and paving over of the hills and valleys of the beautiful countryside that illegal Israeli settlement-building after the occupation of the West Bank entailed, the writer Raja Shehadeh describes not just the destruction and danger that have confined him and made his beloved country walks from Ramallah nearly impossible, but also his crushed idealism. As a young man he had thought he could use the law to halt the redrawing of borders. Over time, he has come to feel that this cannot be done. The facts are on the ground now.

With the 1991 Oslo Accords that, in Shehadeh's view (shared by many others), undermined any capacity of the Palestinians to halt the settlements and curtail Israeli control over the rest of Palestine, he began to understand better his fellow Palestinians who grew up within the "green line." In his haunting book, *Palestinian Walks: Forays into a Vanishing Landscape* (Scribner, 2007), he describes the naive optimism of a new arrival to Ramallah who has come in with the PLO to set up the Palestine National Authority. When he takes her for a country walk near the Dead Sea, a walk that reveals Jewish settlements dominating the hilltops and highways carving up Palestinian land but forbidden to Palestinians, she seems unable to grasp the significance of what she is seeing. He finds himself for the first time identifying with the Palestinians he had disdained—those who had lived under Israeli military rule from 1948–1966 and who now live as uneasy citizens within a nation-state defined by its Jewishness, and thus their non-belonging. He writes:

For the first time, I felt like those Palestinians who stayed in Israel
in 1948 must have felt when they argued with us after the 1967 war.
They would tell us: "You don't know a thing about Israel. We can
tell you what is coming: land expropriations, biased zoning that will
strangle your towns and unfair taxation that will impoverish you."
And we would look with condescension at them and think they
had lived for so long under Israel that they had become colonized,
unable to think beyond their narrow claustrophobic reality. They
probably think Israel is the whole world, we would comfort ourselves.
Not only have their lands been colonized but their minds as well.
(Shehadeh, 2007: 109)

This is a book about the complex lives of these Palestinians whose
experiences differed from those who fled, whether to Beirut or to other parts
of Palestine outside the Green Line in a series of internal displacements
that no one imagined would end up being so permanent. It is also a book
by a remarkable new generation of women scholars who are all Palestinian
citizens of Israel and have turned their attention to the situation of this community—its social dynamics, its politics, its history, and its culture. Most are
products of Israeli universities, part of that minority of Arabs who managed to
get admitted to such institutions. None hold full academic appointments in
Israeli universities, as reflects the general situation of the Palestinian citizens
of Israel who indeed face systematic discrimination in employment. Many
have left the country for opportunities to study or to teach, some thinking
that they might return, others knowing they can't if they want some level of
personal freedom, decent lives for their children, or satisfying careers based
on merit, as Ibtisam Ibrahim's interviews with highly educated émigré women
indicate. They are different from Palestinians who grew up in the diaspora,
or even in the West Bank and Gaza, not only in the obvious ways such as
fluency in both Arabic and Hebrew, and a capacity to joke in Hebrew (as
I discovered when Isis Nusair and Rhoda Kanaaneh organized a workshop
in New York to bring them together), but because they know intimately
what it is to live in Israel as a Palestinian. This new generation of scholars
gives us clear proof that the minds of Palestinians within the 1948 borders
have not, as Raja Shehadeh had presumed, been colonized.

These critical, clear-eyed, and theoretically sophisticated social and
cultural analysts who have done serious social research and are not afraid
to talk about what they see have much to teach us. Not only does their
research teach us what the situation of Palestinians in Israel is or was in
the past but, more broadly, what the complex and contradictory impacts of
colonization can be on a population; how the power and fears of states can
interlock in deadly ways; what the relationship is between nation, ethnos,
and state; and what can happen to the social dynamics of gender and kinship under adverse economic and political conditions.

The studies in this book reveal the situation of Palestinians in Israel to be complicated, the internal divisions to be multiple, and easy generalization impossible. We find acquiescence under economic compulsion, sometimes colored by illusions born of marginality and wishful desire, as with Bedouins who join the Israeli army with motives of helping their families and claiming the rights of citizens but finding themselves part of a larger process aimed at sharpening ethnic division in the service of the state. We also find political and cultural resistance in various registers. A historian traces the clever legal maneuvering of men who attempted to form a political movement inspired by Arab nationalism in the late 1950s and early 1960s but were subject to surveillance and suppression. A cultural critic shows us the wide popularity of the hip-hop produced by young organic intellectuals from both the mixed cities and the Arab villages of Israel; these men and women rap in Hebrew and Arabic about police brutality, house demolitions, sexism, and Palestinian identity.

Perhaps most innovative in this collection is the sustained attention to women's lives and voices, and to gender issues more broadly, among Palestinians in Israel. Always half of the population and always intertwined with men, women rarely get equal attention in analyses of social worlds, especially in highly politicized contexts. Yet, as these essays show, asking questions about their memories of past events and political periods; about their political loyalties and voting patterns in the present; about their views of love, marriage, and residence; about their attitudes toward sexuality and experiences of their bodies; and about their educational and career aspirations provides enormous insight into the social and political contexts within which Palestinian life is lived within "the green line" and how this precarious but stubborn minority within the state of Israel attempts to reproduce itself and find a path.

Among the many divisions that mark the lives of Palestinians within the 1948 borders, like those outside these borders, are whether they are urban or rural; indigenous to the cities and towns in which they live or migrants to them; educated or not; have land or are forced to work in factories, farms, or the army; belong to strong families or weak; are men or women. The uniqueness of the situation lies in the extent to which these differences are forged in the shadow of and made significant in the mirror of the Jewish Israeli presence that structures the lifeworld of this set of Palestinians.

Among the insights that emerge from attention to women's particular experiences, narratives, and language is a strong appreciation of the importance of local communities not just as sources of identification and places of security but as ambivalent terrains of struggle. From the ways different generations of women talk about their worlds, one senses both the persistence of special localized visions and the heavy presence of the outside forces that frame local existence, from the surveillance of the Israeli state to the institutions that absorb and spit out individuals. Some of the scholarship in this book refutes Western and Israeli images of women, whether in revealing the pre-Nakba participation of women in agriculture and the flexibility of the divide between public and private, or in showing just how differently cohorts of women understand themselves, experience their possibilities, and claim the public sphere. Other scholarship challenges conventional Palestinian expectations of women, showing how the Israeli military system of control leads to families' increased surveillance of women's bodies, asking why women's loyalties to husbands' kin are uncertain, and pointing to the possibilities of alienation.

Breaking with the dominant paradigms of Israeli social scientific scholarship on Palestinians within "the green line," which depoliticize and obfuscate by labeling Palestinians a minority ethnic group and never acknowledging them as the real natives of the land, the scholars in this volume cast a critical eye on the unequal laws and the charged history and discriminatory practices of the Israeli state as these affect their Arab "citizens." They are also keenly aware of the way these larger political and economic structures interact with the more local structures of family and community that place special burdens on women and girls. They don't turn away from the consequences—whether in terms of violence against women or controls over their movements, sexuality, and even education—but they also don't blame "culture" or "tradition." They acknowledge that Jewish society in Israel provides a model of modernity and some new opportunities for education and independence, as well as creating the conditions for girls and women to be subjected to the all-too-predictable pressures to serve as defensive boundary markers for ossified patriarchal family and community forms.

Perhaps the most intriguing essays in the book are ones that question the most taken-for-granted aspects of daily life and political action. The intellectual daring is fresh even as the internal social risks of raising such questions must surely be formidable. One study breaks the taboos around sexuality, asking women about their sexual feelings and experiences and finding surprisingly wide variation, despite the ubiquitous recognition of the importance of a "line in the sand" that should not be crossed. Another essay suddenly renders queer the very ordinary custom of a woman moving to her husband's home and village—recognizing at once that this patterned movement could well be called internal migration, if one took women seriously, and that it represents a custom whose impact on women and basis in inequality may be worth challenging. Even in political terms we find this sort of strange daring to look at what is unspoken. Why, the essay asks, are Palestinian political activists of various persuasions silent on the Israeli policy of encouraging Russian immigration in huge numbers, even when the immigrants are not Jewish? Why don't Palestinians make demographic arguments the way Israelis do? What self-censorship is at work such that Israelis don't link the Palestinian right to return to their homeland to the official law of return that entitles all Jews to "return" to a place they have never been?

Reflecting on the scholarship in this book, one feels compelled to ask: "Where does this courage to ask critical questions of the Israeli state and of their own communities come from?" The Palestinian women scholars of Israel seem to have come of age, not just intellectually in their mastery of methodologies from oral history, archival work, close reading, to interviewing, but politically. They are part of a new future for Palestinians in Israel, and perhaps for Israel itself: they are looking hard at the way things are, open to global ideas and political visions, breaching the borders that used to confine them to claustrophobic enclaves, reflexively examining their own history as colonized and their own experience of being strangers in their own land. They are trained on the local without becoming parochial. The year 2008 saw the upbeat documentary about DAM, the most popular Palestinian hip-hop group from "inside" being screened to packed audiences in New York. The rappers are in touch with rappers from Ramallah and the wider Palestinian diaspora. One can't help thinking that they represent a new vanguard in the revelation of the injustice that is Israel and the potential of Palestinian protest. The generation of women scholars who contributed to this book may be part of another vanguard. They are intellectual pioneers who reveal the many layers of power and subordination in that strange place that is Palestine/Israel. Israeli discrimination and wider contact with Palestinians and non-Palestinians, including feminists from around the world, has made them not "self-alarmed by their own existence," as Kanaaneh and Nusair argue the state wishes them to be, but able to confront the basic contradiction with which they live: their existence in Israel is real but their inclusion is impossible in a state defined by the legal and political divide between Jew and non-Jew. Where does one go from there?

—Lila Abu-Lughod
Joseph L. Buttenwieser Professor of Anthropology
and Gender Studies, Columbia University

ACKNOWLEDGMENTS

The idea for this collection began at an informal gathering of five friends, all doctoral students or recent graduates and all Palestinians from "inside." We had gathered for lunch during the 2005 Middle East Studies Association meeting to catch up on each other's news and research. Our conversation was so interesting it seemed obvious that we should organize a panel together for the next MESA meeting. Drawing in several additional colleagues and friends, and with the sponsorship of the Palestinian American Research Center, we put together a double panel at the following year's conference titled Palestinians in Israel Revisited. The papers spoke to each other beautifully and, again, it seemed natural to consider publishing the articles as a collection.

The papers did however pose implicit challenges to one another and there were several questions left hanging from the MESA session. We needed a workshop to continue the conversation and wanted to add a few additional participants into the mix. We thank Janan Abdo, Areen Hawari, and Nouzha Rouhana-Khamees for helping recommend some of the wonderful contributors to this volume. We thank Rochelle Davis, Judith Tucker, and Penny Mitchell for trying to find us a venue and funding in Washington, DC. We were incredibly fortunate to have had the support and encouragement of Lila Abu-Lughod at that stage. We thank her, together with Rashid Khalidi and Penny Mitchell, for helping us make the workshop possible in June 2007. We thank the Columbia University Institute for Research on Women and Gender and the Middle East Institute for hosting and funding the workshop. Thanks to Astrid Benedik, Mirlyne Paulajoute, Vina Tran, and Page Jackson for their assistance with the workshop logistics. PARC was again key in supporting this stage of the project. We are particularly thankful to all the friends and friends of friends who generously opened up their homes in New York City to host the workshop participants: Issam Aburayia, Jamil and Reem Dakwar, Leena Dallasheh, Sandi Dubowski, Peter Mitchell, Sana Odeh, Lisa Ross, Aseel Sawalha, Randa Serhan, Karim Tartoussieh, and Eman. Both Eman and Lisa invited participants to stay at their homes without knowing the organizers and after reading only a one-paragraph description of the project. The workshop would not have been possible without the incredible generosity of all of the hosts.

The discussants at the MESA panel as well as at the Columbia workshop offered key questions and critiques that have significantly shaped this book. We are indebted to Lila Abu-Lughod, Lisa Hajjar, Sherene Seikaly, Ella Shohat, and Rebecca Torstrick for their insightful comments. We thank Rebecca Torstrick, who read a draft of the entire manuscript and gave us detailed feedback and suggestions. Three anonymous reviewers were also helpful in shaping the project. And our editor at State University of New York Press, Larin McLaughlin, shepherded this project with care and finesse. For help with the images, we thank Sharif Waked, Leena Dallasheh, Shira Robinson, Kamal Aljafari, Ibtisam Maraa'na, Ora Wise, Hannah Mermelstein, and the staff at *Slingshot Hip Hop*.

Rhoda Kanaaneh would like to thank the New York University Department of Middle Eastern and Islamic Studies for its support during the editing of this project. Isis Nusair would like to thank Denison University and PARC for providing research funds to support this project. She would also like to thank Alana Slezak for her editorial assistance, and Beth Jeffries, Anne Crowley, Joseph Wollard, Russell Sharp, and Brenda Ronk for their administrative and technical support. But most of all we thank the contributors to this volume for their hard work and dedication to the project.

Figure 1. Map of the region, prepared by Maisoon Nassar.

INTRODUCTION

Rhoda Ann Kanaaneh and Isis Nusair

Johayna Hussein worked hard for twenty-nine years in the Israeli Ministry of Health. She was recognized for her excellent job performance with a prize awarded by the director general of the ministry for best employee. Despite her qualifications, years of service, and dedication to her work, she hit the glass ceiling at the mid-level position of Regional Inspector of Family Health Clinics in the Acre district. Like many Arab government employees in Israel, Ms. Hussein played it safe.

Then the glass ceiling came crashing down on her head. She participated in what turned out to be a massive demonstration in the city of Umm al-Fahim in March 2008 against the Israeli military siege on Gaza. She allegedly told a reporter covering the demonstration that she was there to protest "the Zionists who are massacring our brothers in Gaza" (arabs48, February 12, 2009). By luck, her photo made it to the front page of numerous newspapers and was broadcast on Channel 1. When she arrived at work the next morning at the Ministry of Health, the office was in an uproar. She received an angry call from her boss in Nazareth demanding to know why she had participated in a demonstration. Hussein was under the impression that she had done nothing wrong by expressing her opinions when she was off duty. She was later called in by an investigator for state employees in Jerusalem, after which she was suspended from her job (*Yediot Ahronot*, February 12, 2009).

Johayna is fighting back by taking her case to Adalah, the Legal Center for Arab Minority Rights in Israel (Adalah, 2009b). The Arabic press adopted her as a cause célèbre, splashing headlines of her court battles on their front pages (e.g., *Panet*, February 12, 2009; February 13, 2009). Israel offers its Palestinian citizens participation, but often at the token level, as it defines itself as a state of and for the Jews. They experience it as a contradiction, simultaneously exclusionary but with a promise of inclusion, a democracy and a colonial power, offering both possibilities and their foreclosure. They maneuver and strategize in different ways around the restrictions the state imposes on them.

1

HISTORIES OF CONTRADICTION

What is considered particularly threatening about Johayna's behavior is her criticism of the state in solidarity with Palestinians in Gaza after all the state had "done for her" as an employee. When Israel was created in 1948 and during its early years, the majority of Palestinians, some 725,000 people, were expelled or displaced from the land in what is known to them as the Nakba (Catastrophe). The small minority who remained in the new state were eventually given Israeli citizenship, though of a second class.

The new state refused to recognize these remaining Palestinians as a national minority in its declaration of independence as is required by international legal norms (Rekhess, 2007). Yet it drew a clear boundary separating the minority and the majority and conferred different rights on each group (ibid.). It was created as a settler colonial society for Jews from around the world at the expense of the native population (Abdo and Yuval Davis, 1995). The state maintained and continues to maintain Jewish supe-riority and grants preference to Jews symbolically, structurally, and practically (Ghanem, Rouhana, and Yiftachel, 1998). Though formally included in the democratic electoral process, Palestinian citizens were regarded as a problem minority excluded from the state's definition of the "common good."

There is a fundamental disjuncture between nation and state: the Israeli state is defined as Jewish, Palestinians are not. This disjuncture is in part shaped by history and memory. In chapter 5 of this volume by Fatma Kassem, Palestinian women in the cities of Lydd and Ramleh recall how "the Jews entered and took us." Most of these women now live not in their original homes, but in houses abandoned by other Palestinians who could not return. From these haunted spaces, they often can see their old original homes nearby, now inhabited by Israeli Jews (Abu-Lughod and Sa'di, 2007; Slyomovics, 1998). This offers a glimpse into the state's Judaization policies that attempt to maintain a Jewish majority and to distribute and settle Jews as widely as possible in the country.

The Nakba entailed intense physical and psychological upheaval for most Palestinians. This was certainly the case for al-Birweh women (chap-ter 7) who were removed from their village by Jewish forces in June 1948. Some became refugees in Syria, Jordan, or Lebanon and some managed to stay within the new state as internal refugees in villages near their original hometown. Al-Birweh land was used to build two Jewish settlements, Ahihud and Yasur. The internally displaced refugee women Lena Meari interviewed had only one form of legitimatized access to their former land: as agricultural laborers for the Jewish bosses who now controlled it. Im Ahmad was one such laborer. When she took the liberty of filling a bucket with cucumbers for herself from land that had belonged to her family only a few years earlier, her Jewish supervisor called her a thief. Palestinians' connections to their pre-1948 lives were essentially criminalized in the new state.

Author Honaida Ghanim was raised in the small village of Marjeh near the 1948 armistice line. She grew up with stories of family members separated from each other by the new border that divided Israeli-controlled territory from Jordanian-controlled areas. In chapter 6, a mother and daughter would both pretend to go out to hoe the land in order to whisper news and greetings to each other across the Green Line that split their property and family in two. Previously routine actions—visiting relatives, harvesting crops, trading goods—became risky and dangerous. Ghanim argues that for the Palestinians inside Israel, the Green Line border drawn between them and their relatives, friends, or trade partners could not and would not be conceptualized as a normal fact or *fait accompli*. Though Israel imposed severe travel restrictions and attempted to control the movement and labor of Palestinians with military rule until 1966, Palestinians living under this strict military control and surveillance consistently attempted to cross the border. Visiting their families, harvesting their crops, and purchasing merchandise now were defined by the state as "infiltrating," "sneaking," "evading," and "penetrating."

Authorities attempted to sever these Palestinians' connections to their history and to other Palestinians now living under Jordanian rule in the West Bank or Egyptian rule in Gaza or as refugees in neighboring Arab countries. Yet this attempt to shrink the space around Palestinian citizens has never been entirely successful—as evidenced by the massive protests against the siege in Gaza held in Arab cities and villages inside Israel. Time and again, Palestinians in Israel reach out to transcend these boundaries and contest space (Peteet, 2005; Benvenisti, 2000).

Part of the state attempt to shrink the space around its Palestinian citizens involved their redefinition as somehow other than Palestinian or even other than Arab, as in the case of the de-Arabization of the Druze and Bedouins (Hajjar, 2005; Jakubowska, 1992), and as ethnic minorities (in the plural). Palestinian citizens are allowed to relate to the state not as a national group but as subdivided Muslims, Christians, Druze, and Bedouins, a framework that underscores the state's efforts to fragment and marginalize them (Lustick, 1980; Firro, 2001; Jiryis, 1976; Cohen, 2006). Any attempt to transcend this model of non-Jewish minority in a Jewish state is stifled, sometimes violently so. The al-'Ard movement, established in 1959, used strictly democratic and legal means within the Israeli system. However, as Leena Dallasheh argues in chapter 1, because it was pan-Arabist and Palestinian nationalist and rejected the minorities framework, the state repressed it, censured it, intimidated and imprisoned its leaders, and eventually banned it. This demonstrates the limits imposed on Palestinian citizenship in Israel, and Palestinian struggles against those limits from early on. Dallasheh argues that although Palestinians are allowed to participate in the Israeli system, they are forbidden from challenging its fundamentals.

Al-'Ard also reached beyond the shrunken space permitted it in Israel by appealing to the United Nations in 1964 to intervene to protect the rights of the Arab citizens of Israel. Its letter to the UN represents an attempt by the movement to break the silence enforced on it inside Israel by turning to international institutions. Reaching out internationally has been a strategy reflected in the general rise in the number of nongovernmental organizations among Palestinians in Israel, from forty-one in the early 1980s to over one thousand organizations (Ittijah, 2008) that have expanded the limited space for public action. These organizations have harnessed the use of international law and the universalist language of human rights to advocate for and establish mechanisms for social change inside Israel.

Other Palestinians in Israel use the strategy of identifying with the local rather than the national. For example, many invest more in municipal than in national elections (chapter 8), they identify with their villages and clusters of villages in spite of national borders that now dissect them (chapters 4 and 6) or military actions that displaced them from the villages (chapter 7). Yet others use the strategy of being "good Arabs" and try to conform to the state's requirements of them as disconnected from other Palestinians and from their past. Some go so far as joining the Israeli military to fight other Palestinians only a few miles away. They do gain certain advantages, limited as they are by the Jewish definition of the state. They remain nonetheless ethnified as minorities. Because the Arab soldiers whom Rhoda Kanaaneh (chapter 2) interviewed lived on land the state wants to remove them from in order to Judaize it, their homes are subject to demolition regardless of their dramatic demonstrations of loyalty to the Jewish collective.

Shafir and Peled argue that in the 1970s and 1980s, the tension between the ethno-nationalist republican discourse and the democratizing liberal discourse in Israel tipped toward the liberal because of changes in the global and national economic realities at the time (Shafir and Peled, 1999). They argue that government controls during this period relaxed and this liberalizing and democratizing trend benefited Arab citizens. However, these improvements did not alter the ethnocentric nature of the regime and thus failed to effectively advance Arab-Jewish equality (Ghanem, Rouhana, and Yiftachel, 1998: 265). Haidar argues that some of the economic changes from this period, in fact, had a negative impact on Palestinians in Israel, exposing them to rapid changes and consumption patterns even as they were kept largely at the bottom of the socioeconomic ladder (Haidar, 1997). It is important to note here that Palestinian citizens of Israel fare significantly poorer than their Jewish counterparts on all economic indicators. Using the United Nation's Human Development Index, the Arab minority in Israel ranks sixty-sixth, forty-three slots below the general ranking of Israel (Nahmias, 2007).

The period of liberalization also witnessed the rise in the number of nongovernmental organizations among Palestinians in Israel, yet these organizations faced significant limits on their attempts to transform Israeli society and politics (Jamal, 2008). Similarly, although the Israeli military establishment has undergone recent structural changes, its hegemonic power over political decision-making still stands (Sasson-Levy, 2003). The chapters in this book trace similar fluctuations in the state and analyze the link between various political, economic, and cultural changes.

The geography of Palestinian citizens' identification ebbs and flows depending on the context. It often links Palestinians inside to those outside. However, during the early 1990s Oslo period of optimism about a potential peace agreement between Palestinians in the Territories and Israel, Palestinian citizens were essentially excluded from both sides. The Israeli government tried to distance itself from them as it sought to present a strong Jewish Zionist position to the Israeli public, while the Palestinian "side" shrank to the Territories (or parts thereof) and excluded the Palestinian diaspora and as well "48ers." Some scholars have argued that the negotiations with Palestinian representatives and the growing access to Arab satellite media and to visited Arab countries like Egypt and Jordan, helped expand the public space for Palestinians in Israel (Smooha, 1999; Ghanem, 2000; Ghanem and Ozacky-Lazar, 2003; Jamal, 2008). Palestinian citizens during this period turned to focus on internal issues such as those related to their citizenship, the Jewishness of the state, the right of return for internally displaced refugees, and their own Nakba commemorations.

At other times, Palestinians in Israel contested national politics through the strategy of expanding space—by, for example, reaching beyond Israel's borders to draw on the universalist genre of hip-hop. Groups like DAM have been inspired by 2Pac, Mos Def, and other American artists, and have produced politicized music that has gained popularity among Palestinians inside Israel and in the Occupied Territories, as well as internationally. As Amal Eqeiq explains in chapter 3, though their music was not frequently played on Israeli radio stations, their use of the internet in particular has enabled them to transcend their shrunken space—their song "Min Irhabi?" (Who's the Terrorist?) was released on the net in 2001 and was downloaded by one million people in one month (dampalestine.com).

More traditional forms of protest have abounded, and Palestinians in Israel have organized numerous large-scale demonstrations, many of them in response to Israeli military actions outside of Israel "proper"—for example, in December 2008—January 2009 against the war in Gaza; in July 2006 against the air strike on Qana, Lebanon; and during the First and Second Intifadas in the Occupied Territories. Despite the building of the huge wall around parts of the West Bank and Gaza (starting in 2002) and the network of military checkpoints and closures, the increasing physical separation between Palestinians on both sides of the wall has not necessarily produced increased emotional separation. These protests clearly reflect a refusal of the narrow Israeli boundaries drawn around the "Israeli Arab." They also reflect a strong sense of alienation from Israeli ethno-nationalist policies. This is clearly the case with the beginning of the Second Intifada in October 2000, when Palestinians demonstrated against the killing and oppression of Palestinians in the West Bank and Gaza and also out of frustration over their inferior treatment in the state. During these widespread protests, thirteen Palestinians were killed inside Israel by Israeli police forces.[1] The deaths, together with the Israeli media characterization of the protests as traitorous riots, further fueled the Palestinian sense of outrage. The state defines them legally and in practice as outsiders, and in its various guises, daily reminds them of their fragile second-class status.

During the recent war on Gaza, Palestinians inside Israel widely expressed feelings of intense frustration at their inability to stop the war or alleviate the suffering of Gazans, even though they were citizens of the state launching the attack. Some of our relatives and friends even felt physical illness as a result of their sense of helplessness. At most, they could try to send food and medicines that were unlikely to reach Gaza due to the block-ade. As a collective, they have had limited influence in parliament, despite relatively high rates of participation in elections. Their political isolation is reflected in the fact that 78 percent of Israeli Jews oppose Arab political parties joining the government (ACRI, 2007).

With this sense of intense frustration, Palestinians in Israel showed up to demonstrations in the thousands. An especially large demonstration was held on the annual commemoration of Land Day, the massive strike in 1976 when Palestinians attempted to block government confiscations of Arab land in the Galilee and six Palestinian citizens were killed. The shrinking of space around Palestinians in Israel is literal; government authori-ties seek to maintain a Jewish majority in Israel, settle Jews in areas where Arabs live and transfer Arab-claimed lands to Jewish control (Falah, 1989b; Yiftachel, 1991, 1995; Arab Association for Human Rights, 2004; Adalah, ND; Khamaisi, 2006; ACRI, 2007). So the land available to Palestinians in Israel is increasingly smaller, even as their population grows larger. As the protest against the Gaza War on Land Day in 2009 illustrates, Palestinian link their marginalization inside Israel with the continued brutal occupation of Palestinians in the Occupied Territories.

Other major political mobilizations respond to events outside of Israel and the Occupied Territories, such as during Israel's second War on Lebanon in the summer of 2006. Palestinians in Israel—who make up 20 percent of the population and 50 percent of the northern Galilee region's residents—constituted 50 percent of those killed and injured in Israel during the war (ynetnews, 8/14/2006; Rekhess, 2006). There were no shelters or emergency sirens in Arab communities, yet as Hizbollah's rockets landed on the northern part of the country, the majority of Palestinians in Israel expressed opposition to the war and to the Israeli Air Force's indiscriminate bombing of civilians in Lebanon. From the margins of Israeli society, they broke the national consensus and critiqued the militarized and ethno-nationalist poli-cies of the state. Overall, organizing demonstrations has been an important strategy for many Palestinians to collectively express their politics, but has had less than the desired effect on state policies and parameters.

THE COLLECTION

This volume, the first published in English to focus on Palestinians in Israel, elucidates the ongoing dynamic changes among Palestinians in the state. The scope, diversity, complexity, nuance, and dynamism of the topics discussed and the positionalities of the authors make this collection unique. It offers a rich and multidimensional portrait that eschews some of the limitations of more nationalistically inflected work. On the one hand, scholarship shaped by Zionist priorities tends to exoticize an insular, largely apolitical, traditional Arab culture while masking the influence of the disciplinary state (e.g., Cohen, 1965; Ginat, 1982). Another school treats Palestinians as agentless objects who live in contradiction and suffer from identity crisis (e.g., Smooha, 1989a, 1999; ICG, 2004).

On the other hand, Palestinian nationalism, like many other modern nationalisms, has tended to hide internal differences, sideline gender concerns, and overlook smaller groups within (described in Hasso, 2000; Massad, 1995; Swedenburg, 1995). Palestinians in Israel have been marginalized within the larger Palestinian nationalist discourse and are often dismissed as co-opted by the Israeli state of which they are citizens. This can increase the temptation for those within to offer an overly redemptive nationalist narrative about themselves. Being marginalized and threatened at multiple levels creates a concern for community preservation, making representations of the collective and its traditions in many ways more rigid (Sa'di and Abu-Lughod, 2007). The chapters herein confront these pitfalls by refreshingly attending to differences articulated around gender, clans, sexuality, class, generation, levels of education, urban versus rural backgrounds, internal refugees versus original residents, and "traitors" versus nationalists.

Taghreed Yahia-Younis's analysis of women's voting patterns in local elections in one Palestinian locality not only attends to the conflicting gendered expectations of them, but also to the roles of clan hierarchies, family composition, and residency patterns. The category of "women" is broken down intro several subgroups with a range of voting behaviors within each. She demonstrates how the majority of women are considered to be "strangers within" to different degrees because of their origins from other clans, locales, or countries, and are perceived as posing varying levels of threat to the fluctuating clan, gender, and political orders.

Manal Shalabi's study of sexuality includes women with diverse religious backgrounds (Muslims, Christians, and Druze), levels of religiosity, and education. The experiences and practices of the women in the study were highly varied despite certain "red lines" that they commonly felt they could not cross. One of the study participants, Su'ad, a religious Muslim housewife, apparently displayed the most openness in relation to sexuality, contradicting the common stereotypes about women from different groups. Shalabi argues that factors like education and participation in the workforce are not guarantees of achievement of women's independence.

To date, much of the scholarship on Palestinians in Israel has focused on political elites (Ghanem, 2001) or unnamed masses (Karkabi, 1994), and has produced problematic generalizations and typifications. In contrast, this collection emerges from specific locations and significant well-elaborated contexts often excluded or understudied, such as divided villages, the internal migration of women, Palestinian soldiers, encounters with the military administration, the travel of academics, among others. By situating themselves in diverse locations and intersections, the chapters unsettle common generalizations about Palestinians in Israel and offer a more multivocal view.

Much writing on Palestinians in Israel assumes one of two orientations. The first focuses primarily on the state and its repressive measures (e.g., Jiryis, 1976; Lustick, 1980; Falah, 1996; Sa'di, 2003; Yiftachel and Kedar, 2003). While such measures are certainly vitally important, this exclusive top-down attention to them underplays the agency of Palestinians and unwittingly depicts them as "passive objects of state practices" (Robinson, 2005: 19). The second orientation looks at Palestinian traditions, practices, and culture—with little attention to the powerful structural and political contexts that these are molded by (e.g., Cohen, 2006; Lang, 2005; Ginat, 1982; Stewart, 2007). What distinguishes our collection is the delicate balance the chapters keep between, on the one hand, considering the state and its repressive, coercive, and symbolic aspects, and on the other hand, understanding Palestinians as diverse, active, creative, and strategizing. In some chapters (such as chapters 4 and 6) the state is present but bypassed by border-crossers, or departed from as immigrants (chapter 12), or directly challenged only to have the state shift its tactics (chapter 1).

The chapters address global, national, and local levels—from transnational migrations to local voting patterns and intimate sexual relations—as these intersect and shape the daily lives of Palestinians in Israel. This volume attends to different modes of resistance and attempts to expand their limited space without romanticizing them (Peteet, 2005). From Honaida Ghanim's relatives and neighbors who crossed state-declared borders to visit their families to organizing a political movement, from coping with sexual shaming to taking on new work roles, the agency of Palestinians in the collection ranges from the everyday to the monumental. It also includes morally complex strategies of resistance such as accepting land swaps with the government or serving in the Occupied Territories with the Israeli military.

The spatial practices examined in the book and integrated into the analyses include the segregation of populations (chapter 11), the Judaizing naming of streets and places (chapter 5), the delegalization and demolition of Arab homes in areas to be reterritorialized (chapter 2), and the hiring of Palestinians to farm their former lands by Jewish agricultural settlements that now control them (chapter 7). These sites of authority are also figured here as places of contestation. However, rather than presenting a binary of resistance versus acquiescence, we see diverse Palestinian strategies that fall along a continuum. The Israeli state is not presented as a monolithic entity, but the chapters reflect changes, variation, and openings in its practices that Palestinians use to insert themselves.

THE THEMES

State and Ethnicity

The ethno-national discourse of Israel as a Jewish state has provided the strongest glue for the nation-building project of Zionism (Shafir and Peled, 1999). The state combines both democratic features and nondemocratic components premised on a rigid ethnic hierarchy, the lack of inclusive territorial citizenship, and the power of religious institutions (Ghanem, Rouhana, and Yiftachel, 1998). Such nondemocratic components feed the ongoing conflict between Israel and its minoritized Palestinians and have led to the latter's intensive demands for a comprehensive transformation in the structures and policies of the state (Jamal, 2007; Bishara, 2001). The hegemony of the Jewish majority over state institutions remains a problem that Palestinian citizens seek to overcome (Jamal, 2007b). Issues in the "1948 files" include the question of land ownership, internally displaced refugees, commemorating the Nakba (Rekhess, 2007), and many more. The chapters in this section of the book explore some of these issues directly, but they also underlie much of the volume.

In Amal Eqeiq's chapter (3), Palestinian hip-hop musicians reflect on the marginalization, and in essence, criminalization, of Palestinians as non-Jews in present-day Israel. Rapper Tamer Nafar, for one, chants: "I broke the law? No no, the law broke me." Nafar and other artists rap about how their blue IDs, that is, Israeli citizenships, afford them discrimination ranging from neglect in garbage collection to police brutality.

Palestinians live in three main regions in Israel: the Galilee in the north, the Triangle in the center, and in the Naqab in the south. In addition, some 10 percent of Palestinians in Israel live in so-called mixed cities, mostly in impoverished and overcrowded neighborhoods. Eqeiq argues that while ghettos are usually regarded as urban phenomena, geography works differently in Israel. The Palestinian ghetto in Israel is felt in all of their socially and economically confined communities—in all the Palestinian villages and towns within the State of Israel, including mixed Arab-Jewish areas. These spaces suffer from inadequate or nonexistent public services;

underfunded municipalities, schools, and medical services; and lack, for
example, paved roads and operating sewage systems. This socioeconomic
and political marginalization is reflected in the popular and rich cultural
productions of increasing numbers of hip-hop groups.

Leena Dallasheh's chapter on the history of the al-'Ard movement
(chapter 1) illustrates an early expression of the struggle around the "1948
files." Established in 1959, al-'Ard focused its activities on issues that were
most urgent to Palestinians then, such as the right of return, and on issues
specific to Palestinians within Israel, including the cessation of the military
government and land confiscation, and the extension of social and economic
rights. This history shows that Palestinian citizens resisted Israeli dominance
in innovative ways, some of which have faced profound Israeli repression.

In chapter 3, Kanaaneh describes how the state attempts to confer
"special minority" status on certain groups as part of its explicit policy
to divide and subdivide the Arab population. The Bedouins are one such
group—they are celebrated as special allies of the state and as the Jews'
brothers-in-arms. Generations of them have served as trackers in the military
and hundreds have been killed during service. Despite their preferred status,
the non-Jewishness of these special minorities continues to haunt them and
severely limit their rewards. The state's "divide and rule" policy of fostering
special ties with particular segments of the Palestinian population is not
without contradictions. It is disrupted by the continued importance of the
Jewish/non-Jewish dichotomy at the core of the ideals of a Jewish state. The
major problems facing Palestinians in Israel—including land confiscation,
municipal underfunding, home demolitions, and the refusal to recognize
villages—are also faced by Palestinian soldiers. Crops on Bedouin land the
state claims as its own are burned with toxic chemicals (HRA, 2004), and
Bedouins suffer from the lowest economic status in the country (Jakubowska,
2000). The state thus insists on ethnifying "minorities" and non-Jews despite
individual attempts to bypass these definitions.

Memory and Oral History

The Israeli state is invested in keeping the collective memory of the Holocaust alive, which it uses to legitimize its polices (Lentin, 2000). At the
same time, it is invested in erasing Palestinian collective memories of the
1948 war. A parliamentary bill was introduced in May 2009 to ban Nakba
commemorations; violators of the law, if passed, would face up to three
years in prison (*Haaretz*, May 25, 2009). Memory is thus clearly political
and Palestinian memories are perceived as threatening to Jewish claims of
the state.

History and memory weave their way in and out of the narratives in
this volume. Chapters in this section use a dynamic concept of memory, not
one based on nostalgia and glorification of the past. Oral histories are not

simply a source for bringing silenced voices to light, but have the potential to create counternarratives and histories. The chapters historicize and contextualize the present and explain the effects and consequences of past events as seen from the present. They also examine the gendered nature of memory and the language used to depict it.

For example, Isis Nusair's chapter (4) asks, what does it mean to look at the past from the vantage point of the present? In her generational study, experiences of massive upheaval and dislocation, such as those of the Nakba or the 1967 war and the ongoing occupation of the West Bank and Gaza Strip, have a lasting impact on Palestinian sociopolitical outlooks, often in powerfully gendered ways. The shifting political contexts that three generations of women lived through produce different narratives: of state-detached steadfastness and pain, of state-critiquing restricted educational and marriage choices, and of new mobilizations for private and public change.

Among the various forms of the gendering of history, Nusair notes a striking silence about the 1948 war and the rape of women, despite its implicit presence in nearly everything the women said about the war and its aftermath. The chapters go beyond the victim/survivor narrative and explain the meanings ascribed to events and the effects they had on men and women's lives. The chapters address what it means to have counterdiscourses and examine the possibilities and limits for social change and action.

Fatma Kassem's chapter (5) focuses on the narratives of Palestinian women from so-called mixed cities such as Lydd and Ramleh. These women are some of the most marginalized, as they have been entirely left out of the formation of the collective Palestinian historical-political narrative and deprived of any legitimacy in the public domain of the exclusionary Jewish state. They are engaged in the daily struggle against erasure of their memories and histories both as Palestinians and as women. Kassem analyzes these struggles by attending to their use of particular words to establish the realms of personal and collective memory, and pays close attention to their choice of terms. For example, the use of "when the Jews entered" instead of "the Nakba," or "the English era" or "the days of the Arabs/Palestine" instead of the "British Mandate," creates an alternative vocabulary drawn from the private familial sphere and an alternative sphere of conceptualization.

Honaida Ghanim uses stories from family, neighbors, and friends to explore how the armistice line that partitioned her home village after the war is remembered. Palestinians in Israel developed symbolic and practical actions to cope with the 1948 partition of Palestine, some of them include simple ways of catching a glimpse, however temporary and curtailed, into their lives as they had lived them before that border brutally crossed them. The border came to be a place that the Palestinian ran up against, repeatedly passing and re-passing through it, as when she is expelled or allowed to rejoin her family. In Ghanim's stories, the border becomes, in the end, a place where she resides, almost a home.

Gendering Bodies and Space

An additional contribution of this collection is the infusion of a strong gendered awareness to the field. The existing literature on Palestinians in Israel
either largely ignores gender (e.g., Falah, 1996; Rouhana, 1997; Ghanem,
2001; Firro, 2001; Yiftachel and Kedar, 2003), or focuses exclusively on rei-
fied categories of "Arab women" (e.g., Gorkin and Othman, 1996; Kama,
1984; Halperin-Kaddari, 2004). Several of the chapters in the third section
of this book (along with parts of other chapters) use gender as a key lens:
this includes women's work roles, but also men's military service, women's
sexuality, internal women's migration and voting patterns, emigration patterns among women academics, the styles of male and female rap artists or
generational gendered politics of location. They expose some of the civic
myths that privilege masculinity and sustain unequal forms of inclusion
and exclusion (Joseph, 2000)—along ethnic lines as well as along gendered
ones. These essays enrich the scholarship of the region by insisting on a
contextualization of Palestinians as gendered subjects with personal and
collective histories, opportunities and strategies that are shaped by notions
of femininity and masculinity.

Gender can be traced in male and female bodies, their relative positioning in society, and in the gender ideologies at play—all embedded in
social, economic, and political contexts (Cockburn, 2004: 30). Minutiae
such as a rumor about a girl's reputation, a woman's choice of street names,
another woman finding a job on a Jewish farm, and yet another being
proud of a father's clan—all take on larger social, economic, and political
significance. The collection also challenges binaries of public and private,
coercion and free choice, liberated and oppressed, and stresses a continuum
for understanding the economic and sociopolitical changes in the lives of
Palestinian women in Israel since 1948.

The chapters are informed by the work of the Palestinian feminist
movement in Israel. They are influenced by the publications and activities of
nongovernmental organizations that emerged in the 1990s and have focused
on women's rights (Ghanim, 2005). Particularly important have been the two
nongovernmental organization reports to the United Nations on Israel as a
signatory of the Convention on the Elimination of All Forms of Discrimination Against Women (CEDAW) in 1997 and 2005. These reports have served
as lobbying tools locally and internationally. Palestinian feminists have been
engaged with some Israeli Jewish women's organizations and the resulting
difficulties and limits imposed on Palestinian women in these engagements
have strengthened an analysis that examines the intersections of gender and
ethnic politics. There has also been an expansion in the horizons of these
organizations with meetings of women in the Occupied Territories and in the
Arab world (Salma Network and Aisha), as well as by the establishment of
the Palestinian gay women's group Aswat (meaning voices) (Krahulik, 2005).

They have also been invigorated by the inclusion of women nominees on the list of Palestinian-supported parties. Women worked from inside both the National Democratic Assembly and the Democratic Front for Peace and Equality parties to place a gender quota system that led to the election of Haneen Zu'bi from NDA to Parliament in 2009.

Anxieties of representation emerge among the contributors in this context as gender among Palestinians is haunted by Western rescue narratives and "salvation rhetoric" (Abu-Lughod, 2002: 788). The state frequently deploys a modernizing discourse vis-à-vis Palestinian women that it uses to patronize and control Palestinian citizens (Abdo, 2004; Sa'ar, 2007) and to constitute itself in opposition to this Orientalized image as modern and Western (Eyal, 1996: 420). As Kanaaneh argues elsewhere (2009), gender violence among Palestinians in particular functions as a kind of "colonial scandal" (Dirks, 1997: 209); it is fetishized by the Israeli media and used as proof of Palestinian backwardness—justifying the supposedly liberal state's control and civilizing mission.

Several chapters in this book note that the state in actuality reinforces gender hierarchies (chapters 4, 7, 8, 9, and 11). Lilian Abou-Tabickh's analysis of women's migration upon marriage to their husband's residence not only unmasks a migration that is otherwise made invisible in the literature and unquestioned in social discourse, but notes that "conservative social structures and the racist state . . . collude to imprison Arab women and limit their rights to housing and their choice of living space" (194). That the state shapes these gender inequalities does not lead Abou-Tabickh or the contributors to ignore other factors.

One can read the impact of the militarization of Israel in the formations of gender in these chapters—from women's military administration work permits in the 1950s, to the military empowerment of patriarchal clan authorities, to the ethnic segregation of communities in which women are discouraged from leaving (Enloe, 2000). Israeli Jewish women are of course also marginalized by state policies and by the military nature of the state, albeit differently, and while often simultaneously participating in the ethnonationalist and militarized collective (Jacoby, 1999; Herzog, 2004; Shadmi, 2000; Ferguson, 1995; Sharoni, 1994, 1996; Golan, 1997). The chapters go beyond adding women and stirring—they focus on an understanding of gender as a relation of power in family and state politics.

Migrations

Women and men's movements and migrations are products of sociodemographic, economic, political, and cultural changes (Hawkesworth, 2006). Lilian Abou-Tabickh and Ibtisam Ibrahim's chapters (11 and 12) compel us to examine the operations of capital, class, ethnicity, and gender within state borders but also across them. Ibrahim's chapter shifts the focus to women's agency in the global political economy, and as based on a complex set of patriarchal, racial, and ethnic practices (Naples, 2002). This chapter presents the case of educated Palestinian women from Israel emigrating to Western countries in pursuit of advancing their studies or careers. In addition to a desire to find alternatives to gendered family surveillance and pressure to marry, political and institutionalized discriminatory policies sharpen the desires of these Palestinian women to leave. Lack of opportunities in their home region demonstrated by the minute numbers of Palestinians with tenure-track positions in Israeli universities and the feeling of being strangers in their own land were strong impetuses for these women to seek an alternative country of residence.

Areej Sabbagh-Khoury's chapter (10) raises important questions about how certain migrations are legitimated, forbidden, or shrouded in silence. This chapter, like others before it, addresses the structural confinement of Palestinians in a Jewish state. Sabbagh-Khoury's review of the Arabic press from 1989 to 1991, a period of massive immigration from the former Soviet Union, finds a surprising silence or distortion on the subject. The Palestinian leadership's discourse from this period did not directly oppose Jewish immigration or link it to the absence of Palestinian rights to return, but dealt instead with its effects on the lives of Palestinians on both sides of the Green Line. Underlying this surface silence and self-censoring is a general fear of crossing "red lines" set by the state. There is no longer a central military administration as there was in earlier years that directly harassed, pressured, and imprisoned Palestinian activists and suspects. However, the goals of those who dismantled the military administration—for state authorities to see but not be seen—have to some extent been accomplished (Bauml, 2002).

Abou-Tabickh analyzes women's migration upon marriage in the context of gendered disparities, but also takes into account current events, Palestinian history in Israel, and deep structures of inequality anchored in state practices. She thus links inheritance practices, the biased enforcement of civil family reforms, ethnic limitations on new construction and zoning, and daring visions of love. The chapter astutely describes the social and historical construction of public and private boundaries. She points to women's sense of freedom to choose their spouses coupled simultaneously with a sense that they have no choice in where to live once married as patrilocal residence is so naturalized.

The chapters in this collection directly and indirectly raise a host of questions about language, silence, and representation, for both the people researched and for the scholar herself. In part, these questions emerge in relation to the state and its surveillance. For example, knowing that Palestinian social history, particularly Palestinian women's social history, is voided by official archives, most of the contributors use oral histories and interviews to read against the grain of, or altogether bypass, state documents. Yet issues of representation in relation to the state inevitably raise related questions for collecting oral histories and conducting interviews among Palestinians more generally. What do those whom we interview remember and what do they omit? What words do they use, what subjects do they avoid, and what questions do they redirect? These uncertainties, never fully answered or answerable, of necessity hover over our research.

These same questions can be asked of the authors themselves. Located as we are in particular states (especially Israel and the United States), and in particular academic and research institutions, our scholarly writing is undoubtedly shaped by such contexts. The authors of these chapters are all Palestinian women citizens of Israel. As students of anthropology, comparative literature, history, political theory, sociology, and women's studies, the contributors bring a rich array of perspectives to their analyses of social, cultural, and political dimensions of Palestinian life in Israel. Their scholarship crosses disciplinary boundaries as well as geographic ones, as some are positioned inside Israel and others came to the United States to pursue university degrees. In chapter 12, Ibtisam Ibrahim surveys a related group of Palestinian women academics who have left Israel for various periods of time and their experiences of belonging and displacement.

She asks, and we ask, how does the need to master Hebrew, English, and the terms of colonial modernity—to integrate into Israeli institutions or to succeed in American or Palestinian ones—affect how we speak about and back to the state? How are our choices of terminology, citations, and theoretical frameworks consciously and unconsciously informed by these linguistic and institutional limitations? Many of the contributors in fact raise reflexive methodological questions regarding the role of researchers and authors, issues of audience, sources, visibility, and narrative styles. Readers are invited to revisit these questions while reading the chapters, as we did in editing and re-editing our work.

CONCLUSION

Analyses of the changing political, social, and economic conditions of Palestinians in Israel should not be regarded as merely a discussion of a special minority case. Understanding the workings of nationality, ethnicity, class, and gender is relevant not only for a particular minority group but for the dominant society as well (Berkovitch, 2001). The Israeli state has been described as divided among seven major cultures, challenging one another for control, including Ashkenazi Jews, Mizrahi Jews, religious Orthodox Jews, Russian immigrants, Ethiopian immigrants, noncitizen foreign workers, and Palestinians (Kimmerling, 2004). Though the first five are privileged by being bound together under the umbrella of Jewishness and militarism, the struggles of each are relevant to the whole (Kimmerling, 2004).

This volume raises critical questions regarding the position of Palestinians in Israel. It describes their exclusion from the Israeli polity, collective narrative, and ethos—the shrinking of their space—but also examines their strategies in challenging this marginalization and their attempts to expand space. In 2008, the Israeli state celebrated the sixtieth anniversary of its establishment, and Palestinians commemorated sixty years since their Nakba. Following the creation of the state, "a formidable and exceptional effort was made to construct a new collective identity" that excluded Palestinians (Kimmerling, 2001: 93–94; Segev, 1986). Yet the continued presence of Palestinians inside Israel, despite their sidelining, serves as a constant reminder to the state of the past that it refuses to acknowledge, and the present that it refuses to address. They implicitly and explicitly demand that the constitution currently being drafted by the Israeli parliament address the prospect of full equality for all citizens and not only Jewish ones. They inevitably pose, repose, and reframe the question of "who is a citizen?"

The publication of this volume comes at a critical time for Palestinians in Israel. Palestinian fears regarding their fragile position in Israel have always been present but have intensified in recent years. October 2000 was particularly enraging not only because police and border patrol units killed thirteen Palestinians, twelve of whom were citizens of the state, but because none of those who carried out the killings were held accountable. Palestinian anxiety was also heightened by 2003 and 2007 changes to the immigration and citizenship laws that make them even more discriminatory and prohibit the granting of any residency or citizenship status to Palestinians from the Occupied Territories who are married to Israeli citizens (Adalah, nd).

More recently, the February 2009 parliamentary elections reflect a shift farther to the right among Jewish citizens of Israel. Election campaigns featured open calls for the transfer of Palestinian citizens by the likes of Avigdor Lieberman, whose Yisrael Beitinu Party expanded its parliamentary seats from eleven to fifteen, making it the third-largest party. The electoral platform of Lieberman, now foreign minister, gained much attention for its call to require those who wish to retain Israeli citizenship to declare their loyalty to Israel as a Jewish state. Not to be outdone, the so-called centrist contender for government leadership, Tzipi Livni, said in December 2008 that the establishment of a Palestinian state would enable her to "approach the Palestinian residents of Israel . . . and tell them, 'Your national solution lies elsewhere' " (*Haaretz*, December 11, 2008). Even some Israeli Jews who distance themselves from Lieberman and consider themselves liberals have recently introduced bylaws into their towns that require new residents to pledge support for "Zionism, Jewish heritage and settlement of the land" (Cook, 2009).

Along with the growing fear among Palestinians regarding their tenuous position in Israel, they have simultaneously become increasingly outspoken, or at least more audible to the Jewish majority. This is evident in the recent publication of four important documents that represent a collective voice for Palestinians in Israel. The first is a 2006 document published by the National Committee for the Heads of Arab Local Authorities in Israel titled *The Future Vision of the Palestinian Arabs in Israel*. It makes clear that "[d]efining the Israeli state as a Jewish state and exploiting democracy in the service of its Jewishness is exclusionary and creates tension between us and the nature and essence of the state. Therefore, we call for a consensual democratic system that enables us to be fully active in the decision making process and guarantee[s] our individual and collective civil, historic, and national rights" (NCHALAI, 2006). Three additional documents, *An Equal Constitution for All?* drafted by Mossawa Center: The Advocacy Center for Arab Citizens in Israel; *The Democratic Constitution* drafted by Adalah: The Legal Center for Arab Minority Rights in Israel; and the Haifa Declaration by Mada al-Carmel: Arab Center for Applied Social Research were released in 2007.

The drafting of all four documents started soon after the October 2000 events and involved collaborations between political figures, nongovernmental organizations, and intellectuals. The documents are significant in that, unlike earlier Palestinian statements in Israel, they do not focus only on the Palestinian cause and its relationship to the state. Rather they offer an internal examination of the political, social, and economic development of Palestinians in Israel as a national minority and articulate new priorities in relation to the limits on their citizenship there. The documents reflect the more general growth in Palestinian non-governmental organizations and actions.

The state is now pushing Palestinian citizens to perform "civil service." Since unlike Jewish citizens, they are not conscripted and the majority of them do not serve in the Israeli military, they cannot be part of the "security complex," which plays a central role in the Israeli economy (Sa'di, Shalev, and Schnell, 2000: 48),[2] and in creating a sense of belonging to the polity as a "community of warriors" (Helman, 1999: 211). The demand that Palestinian citizens perform an alternative service that is inferior—both economically and by Israeli measures, culturally—amounts to a request that they justify their presence in the state as outsiders and prove their loyalty to the Jewish and militarized state by which they have been colonized and of which they are subordinate members. In voicing its opposition to "civil service," the Haifa Declaration states that "steps that could lead to our involvement in Israeli militarism and the distribution of the spoils of wars are incompatible in our case with the principal of equality because they disfigure our identity and disregard historical injustices" (Mada al-Carmel, 2007: 14). This illustrates Palestinian resistance to repeated Israeli attempts to normalize their inferiority and to silence their historical memories. This volume helps readers understand how Palestinians navigate this terrain and pose new challenges to the practices and conceptualization of democracy in Israel.

NOTES

1. Though one of the thirteen killed was from Gaza and the rest were citizens of Israel, the protests did not make this distinction.

2. The following benefits apply only to the Jewish sector: a) a large share of the labor force works for the armed forces; b) many others are employed in government-operated military industries, military and civilian firms working under contract to the army, or in other jobs that for justified or unjustified reasons require a security clearance; c) the army and the military industries also make indispensable contributions to the development of high-tech industry, by training computer engineers and programmers at no cost to the individuals that get the training or the civilian firms that later benefit from it (Sa'di, Shalev, and Schnell 2000: 48).

I

STATE AND ETHNICITY

Figure 2. The unrecognized village of Arab al-Na'im with the city of Karmi'el in the background. Courtesy of Nadera Abu Dubey-Saadi from al-Tufula Center in Nazareth.

ONE

POLITICAL MOBILIZATION OF

PALESTINIANS IN ISRAEL

The al-'Ard Movement

Leena Dallasheh

In this chapter, I explore the history of al-'Ard (The Land, hereafter referred to as al-'Ard or the movement), a political movement established in 1959 by a group of young nationalist/pan-Arab Palestinian citizens of Israel. Al-'Ard remained active from 1959 until 1965, when it was banned by the Israeli government and many of its activists were imprisoned or exiled. I explore the history of al-'Ard, the challenges it faced, and the way it was perceived during its years of activism. I focus on the legal battles that al-'Ard waged in order to gain recognition within the Israeli system, which constituted most of its activities during its six years of existence. I argue that although al-'Ard was part of a wider ideological movement in the Arab world, it also had a unique character that combined pan-Arab ideology with local concerns.

Al-'Ard is significant in that it presents one example of the ways in which Palestinians within Israel sought to maintain their identity and rights within the newly established state and in the repressive framework of the military government. Ultimately, however, the movement faced fierce opposition to its political ideology, which was perceived as incompatible with Israeli state ideology, and it was suppressed as a security threat to the Israeli state project. Thus, the history of al-'Ard is also exemplary of the limitations of Israeli democracy and citizenship: although Palestinians are allowed to participate in the system, they are forbidden from challenging its fundamentals (Sa'adi, 1996: 395–396). In addition, by presenting the history

of al-'Ard, I critique the scholarship on the Palestinian citizens of Israel that
has tended to focus on Israeli state control while Palestinians, including the
al-'Ard movement, are presented as passive recipients of history.[1] While
little has been written on the movement itself, the literature on Palestinian
citizens often briefly mentions al-'Ard, focusing on its repression (Stendel,
1992: 234–240, Benziman and Mansour, 1992: 137–138).

In order to understand the history and importance of al-'Ard, I draw
on the following main sources. First, I use the newspaper al-'Ard that was
published in late 1959 and early 1960. Second, I use court decisions and
police files related to al-'Ard in the Israel State Archive (ISA). Third, I
utilize files from the office of the Prime Minister's Advisor for Arab Affairs.[2]
I have also made use of mainstream Israeli newspaper articles about the
movement[3] as well as articles from the Israeli Communist Party's Arabic
newspaper al-Ittihad. I also examine books and articles written by members
of the movement after its dissolution that illustrate how they perceived the
movement and their experiences in it. Finally, I interviewed several surviving
members of the movement. This range of sources enables a development of
a more complete and nuanced understanding of the history of al-'Ard and
of its significance.

THE STORY OF AL-'ARD

After the Nakba, the Palestinians who stayed within Israel became a leaderless
minority, as the greatest part of the "political class," comprised of Palestinian
leaders, intellectuals, and the urban population, had become refugees (Sayigh,
1997: 38). Under the military administration that was imposed on almost 75
percent of the Palestinian population in Israel, in the Galilee, the Triangle,
and the Naqab, Palestinian political and economic life in Israel were greatly
restricted (Jiryis, 1976: 13–55). In these years, the political activism of the
Arab community in Israel was centered on three main parties: the government
party MAPAI (Mifleget Po'ale Erets Yisrael [Land of Israel Worker's Party]),
MAPAM (Mifleget ha-Po'alim ha-Me'uhedet [United Workers' Party]), and
MAKI (ha-Miflagah ha-Qomonistit ha-Yisraelit [the Communist Party of
Israel, hereafter referred to as the CPI]) (Harris, 2001: 112). The CPI was
the only non-Zionist political party to represent the Palestinians and advocate
for their rights during the decade after 1948, and by 1955 had become the
preeminent force in the Arab community (Beinin, 1990: 141).

In the mid-1950s, after the coup d'état in Egypt led by Nasser that was
widely viewed as spearheading Arab nationalism and pan-Arabism, especially
following the 1956 Suez War, there was a rise in nationalist mobilization
among the Palestinians in Israel. Support for Nasserist pan-Arab nationalism
was widespread, including among leaders and members of the CPI, leading
it to adopt the rhetorical framework of Arab anti-imperialism employed by
Nasser and to publicly support the United Arab Republic (Beinin, 1990:

195 and 201).[4] In this atmosphere of growing nationalist mobilization, a new political group, the Popular Front (hereafter referred to as the Front), was established in 1958. This group was established by Arab CPI leaders and national non-party personalities. It was based on the widest common platform that could have been agreed upon: the group demanded the abolition of military rule and all forms of discrimination, the right of return, the end of land confiscation, and the use of Arabic in all governmental departments (Jiryis, 1976: 186). It was politically active until the beginning of 1959, when tensions caused it to break into two parts: one continued to function under the banner of the Front and agreed to maintain cooperation with the CPI, while the other, the pan-Arab nationalist faction, broke with the Front and eventually decided to establish al-'Ard. Tensions in the Front began when relations between Nasser and the Communists in the Arab world fell apart. While the pan-Arab nationalists in the Front supported Nasser's positions and actions, the Communists attacked him and supported Abd al-Karim Qasim, the president of Iraq, who was backed by the Iraqi Communists.

ESTABLISHING AL-'ARD

The founding meeting of al-'Ard was held in April 1959 in Nazareth. It was initiated by Mansur Kardosh and Habib Qahwaji, who were members of the nationalist faction of the Front. They decided at this meeting to establish a newspaper in order to spread the opinions of the movement (Qahwaji, 1978: 20). The name that was chosen for the newspaper was *al-'Ard*, to symbolize the attachment of Arabs to their land (Baransi, 1981b: 19). In their eyes, 'Usrat al-'Ard (the al-'Ard family, the name by which the movement was often referred to in Arabic) was a group of young Palestinians, mostly men, who were brought up under the shock of the Nakba and who were part of the "political awakening" of the Arab world under the banner of Arab national-ism and Arab unity (*Hadhih al-'Ard*, October 5, 1959). On this basis, al-'Ard perceived itself as a nationalist movement that believed in Nasserist ideology and "Arab socialism" (Qahwaji, 1978: 56 and 64), and saw Arab unity as the way to liberate Palestine (*Hadhih al-'Ard*, October 5, 1959). Al-'Ard had no connections with any political party in the Arab world, but it did have intel-lectual and ideological bonds with pan-Arab movements there. Its members saw themselves as part of the revolutionary pan-Arab movement, led by Nasser, although they focused on the internal situation of the Arabs in Israel.

The objectives of al-'Ard fell into two categories: international and regional. The movement called for change in Israel's policies in a way that would allow it to become a genuine part of the Middle East and to fit within the Arab world. Al-'Ard called on the Israeli government to change its policies by acknowledging the Arab nationalist movement as the "decisive power" in the region (*Hadhih al-'Ard*, October 5, 1959). It further called on the government to disconnect itself from Zionism and colonialism, to adopt a policy of "positive neutralism" and to acknowledge the right of return of the Palestinian refugees (Qahwaji, 1978: 21). In the local Israeli context, the movement demanded full equality between Arabs and Jews and the cancellation of military rule and all discriminatory laws and policies as well as the return of confiscated lands to their lawful owners and the improvement of the educational and economic situation of the Arabs in Israel (*Hadhih al-'Ard*, October 5,1959). These demands were made in the framework of demanding full citizenship (*Ghayth al-'Ard*, January 4, 1960). In its statements, al-'Ard also referenced the Israeli public, asserting its desire to work for the good of all people (*Hadhih al-'Ard*, October 5, 1959). Although the political framework of al-'Ard and the CPI were different, al-'Ard's specific objectives in the local context were similar to the demands advanced by the latter, but the pan-Arab rhetoric of the former distinguished it from other existing Palestinian political groups.

At the center of the disputes about al-'Ard was the question of whether it recognized (from *hakarah* in Hebrew) the state of Israel. In his book *The Full Story of the Movement al-'Ard*, Habib Qahwaji, one of the movement's founding members, asserts that its goals did not include recognition of Israel and were aimed in fact at emptying Israel of its Zionist political, economic, and ideological content so that Israel could be assimilated in the Arab world. He insisted that the founders of al-'Ard had made a strategic decision to present their demands this way because they could not have stated openly that they did not recognize Israel; they would have faced persecution and imprisonment (Qahwaji, 1978: 22 and 66).

It is understandable that the leaders of the movement would make such a strategic decision to allow them this space of activity that would be denied if they openly stated that they refused to recognize the state. However, while rejecting the Zionist nature of the state, the activists of al-'Ard clearly made a conscious decision to act within the framework of the Israeli system, concentrating on a legal struggle to gain legitimacy. This can be seen from the repeated recourse to Israeli courts, appealing to the Supreme Court six times within six years, and the repeated calls for struggle for reform within the Israeli system, such as demanding an official commission of inquiry (*Sir al-'Ard*, October 30, 1959). Al-'Ard chose this strategy as a form of resistance, which allowed them some achievements and granted them more time and space for their activities (interview, Me'ari, 2005). Adopting this strategy, the same strategy that was adopted in the civil rights struggle in the United States, implied recognition of the basic principles of the state (Harris, 2001: 135–137).

EXPANSION AND ACTIVITIES

The legal efforts of al-'Ard to gain status that would allow it to operate legally occupied most of its energy (interview, Jiryis, 2005). In addition to these legal efforts, the movement tried to expand its activities and base of supporters. It founded chapters, held meetings, and generated support for the group, which was reflected by the purchase of shares of the company it established (Harris, 2001: 114). Among the strongholds of the movement was Jerusalem, where the chapter was supported by the Arab Students' Committee, which included most of the Arab students of the Hebrew University in Jerusalem (Sigaut, 2001: 59). In addition, there were chapters in Lydd, Shafa-'Amir, Kufur Kanna, 'Arrabeh, al-Taybeh, and al-Tireh (interview, Me'ari, 2005). After encountering various official restrictions on its activities, including repeated harassment from security forces, al-'Ard used sports clubs in an effort to expand while avoiding state control and limitations, as the authorities had few legal means of preventing the establishment of sports clubs.[5] Yet, when state authorities realized the clubs' connections to al-'Ard, many of them were closed (Qahwaji, 1978: 31–32; Sorek, 2003: 427).

During al-'Ard's years of activity, it developed and expanded, although there is no record of the number of activists that were in the movement. It was socially diverse though predominantly male; its activists were mostly academics, however there were also workers and farmers from all Palestinian areas in Israel (Qahwaji, 1978: 46). There was a small hardcore group of men that gathered scores of supporters around itself (Sigaut, 2001: 63). One indicator of the movement's reach was the distribution of the newspaper al-'Ard, which was printed in 3,000 copies (Qahwaji, 1978: 25) that the movement claimed were all sold. This is a significant number compared to al-Yawm, MAPAI's newspaper, which sold 5,000 copies (that included 1,800 copies for teachers, whose subscriptions were deducted automatically from their salaries [Jiryis, 1976: 170]), and to al-Ittihad, which sold between 2,000 and 3,000 copies of every issue at the same time (Beinin, 1990: 229).

Another indication can be found in the number of people who signed the official support papers to allow the movement to run for elections in 1965. The movement submitted 1,500 signatures, and claimed to have had 1,000 more (Qahwaji, 1972: 470). Qahwaji claims that some 150 of its activists were arrested, detained, or tried because of their support for the movement (1972: 475). Such numbers, especially after the movement was outlawed, imply that the movement had reached a significant core of activists and a high level of commitment among its members. Within the Israeli mainstream press, some estimated that although al-'Ard began as a small intellectual group, it became influential in Arab society within Israel (Yedi'ot Ahronot, July 27, 1964 and November 24, 1965). Other sources argued that al-'Ard was only a minor marginal group (Jerusalem Post and Haaretz, November 25, 1964). Notwithstanding the assessment of these newspapers about the number of the movement's activists, both the frequency and tone of the articles published in the Israeli press show that the movement was perceived as a significant factor in the political reality in Israel at the time.

The Israeli government was wary of al-'Ard from the outset. As early as September 1959, the advisor for Arab affairs wrote that the government should seek to stop the activities of the al-'Ard movement before it became "a natural home for most of the Arab citizens in the country."[6] The primary concern was that al-'Ard would raise the demands of the Arab minority in Israel and if represented in the Israeli parliament, would cause hardship to the government. The government did in fact move against al-'Ard beginning in early 1960 when it banned al-'Ard from publishing a newspaper and prosecuted its members for doing so.

PUBLISHING THE NEWSPAPER

Soon after its founding, the movement applied for a license to publish a newspaper, in accordance with Clause 22 in the Press Ordinance, but the district commissioner stalled for five months without responding to its application.[7] As a result, the leaders of al-'Ard chose to use a lacuna in the Press Ordinance, a mandate-era law regulating the publication of periodicals, which allowed for the publication of a single issue without a license. They decided to publish every issue under a different name, although each name included the word "al-'Ard" and the name of a different editor. With this maneuver, the movement's leaders manifested a solid knowledge of Israeli law and tactical flexibility. The production of the first issue of the newspaper was arduous, since the movement faced difficulties finding a publishing house willing to publish the newspaper and members of the movement were concerned about the danger they could face for publishing it. Financing the newspaper was an additional concern as it had to rely on the personal resources of members and repeated appeals to supporters (e.g., in *Akhbar al-'Ard*, October 17, 1965).

The editors of the newspaper were among the founding members of the movement and the major contributors were some of its most active members, including Habib Qahwaji, Mansur Kardosh, Sabri Jiryis, Saleh Baransi, and Mahmoud Srouji. In addition, there were a few nonaffiliated nationalist leaders who also wrote for some issues of the newspaper, such as Shukri al-Khazen, the principal of the Orthodox High School in Haifa (*Hadhih al-'Ard*, October 5, 1959) and Jabur Jabur, then mayor of Shafa 'Amir (*Shadha al-'Ard*, November 28, 1959). In its content and language, the newspaper expressed the nationalist ideology of al-'Ard. It sympathetically reported news about Nasser and pan-Arab projects, presented Nasserist-inspired analysis of the international cold war context, and criticized Israeli policies, focusing on the status and rights of Palestinians within Israel.

After a few issues of the newspaper were published, the authorities started pressuring members to leave al-'Ard. They were offered money and jobs, and when they declined, they were threatened with having their belongings confiscated (Qahwaji, 1978: 24). The newspaper described other forms of harassment against its leading members, including depriving them of permits to travel, investigations, and threats of arrest and of jeopardizing livelihoods. In one case, Habib Qahwaji was prevented from spending the holiday with his family in his village of Fasutta, as he was not given a permit to stay in the village (*Ghayth al-'Ard*, January 4, 1960).[8] The *al-'Ard* newspaper contended that, at first, the government believed that the movement would weaken the CPI, but once it realized that it did not challenge and compete with the CPI and was "raising Arab national awareness," the government increased its harassment of the movement (*Wihdat al-'Ard*, January 16, 1960).

After publishing thirteen issues of the newspaper, members of the movement were arrested and their houses were searched. Using Clause 22 of the Press Ordinance, six of them, each from a different area, were put on trial for publishing a newspaper without a license. This was the first time in the history of the State of Israel that anyone was charged with this felony.[9] The district attorney stated that the charges were brought because of the content of the newspapers, which he claimed were inflammatory against the Israeli government. The activists of al-'Ard were tried and sentenced to a fine of 1,000 Israeli liras (about $550, a significant amount at the time) and to three months probation each. They appealed their convictions to the district court, which reduced the sentences of two defendants but rejected the others' claims. In deciding their punishment, the court accepted that the content of the newspapers constituted incitement against Israel and the Jewish people.[10] The activists of al-'Ard then appealed to the Supreme Court, which ruled that although the criminal charges about the content had been dropped, the charges against the group should not be seen as merely technical, as they had manipulated the law in order to publish the newspaper. The court nonetheless reduced the sentence since the incitement charges had not been proven.[11]

The different court decisions in this case are an indication of the repression the movement faced and the legal space it utilized to fight against this repression, which allowed it narrow successes in challenging the government. However, the movement's political message was still scrutinized and censored by the government and, to a lesser extent, by the court, in which the protection of the law was narrowed. Although by 1960 the Supreme Court had established high standards of protecting the freedom of speech, these standards were lessened when judging al-'Ard.

REGISTERING AS A COMPANY

After failing to obtain a license to publish the newspaper, the movement decided to register as a company in order to publish a newspaper and to raise the required funds for doing so. In April 1960, they filed to register as a company with the Israeli Companies Registrar. Their request was rejected by the registrar, who claimed that the applicants would use the company to spread opinions that might endanger the state. In his decision, the registrar relied on the documents that were submitted to the court in the criminal case regarding the newspaper.

The movement appealed this decision in court, thus attempting to utilize the law again in order to create a space for its struggle and to promote its political program. In this case, the Supreme Court affirmed the right of al-'Ard to establish a company, despite the state's appeal, in a decision that limited the government's authority in order to protect human rights.[12] However, this decision did not guarantee that the company could publish a newspaper. In fact, at the end of the majority decision, Justice Sussman stated that allowing the company to register did not necessarily give the company a license to print a newspaper, and that the government had other legal tools for preventing the printing of a newspaper, including criminal procedures.[13] In the end, the company was established and its shares were sold to political activists who were willing to act on behalf of the movement in their areas, and to disseminate its ideas and materials (Qahwaji, 1978: 28). However, after a legal process that lasted from April 1960 until June 1962, the company could not publish a newspaper, as will be discussed herein.

LICENSE TO PUBLISH A NEWSPAPER

In late 1963, al-'Ard Company applied for a license to publish a newspaper. Their request was declined on the pretext that the editor, Saleh Baransi, did not hold an Israeli matriculation certificate. The company then appointed Sabri Jiryis as the editor. The district commissioner then rejected the request again, this time relying on the Emergency Regulations.[14] The company appealed to the Supreme Court against this decision,[15] again demonstrating the movement's desire to utilize the spaces that could be created by the law. The Supreme Court rejected the appeal in a short and formalistic decision. This decision was in striking contrast to the court's previous decision that highlighted the vitality of protecting the freedom of speech by ruling that the state had to prove an immediate and clear jeopardy to public security in order to limit the freedom of speech.[16]

After al-'Ard renewed its activity at the end of 1963, the government made a political decision to stop the movement that it viewed as "the Israeli Nasserist organization" (Bauml, 2001: 255). A document distributed to senior officials during this period proclaimed that the government had already tried to locate and neutralize the members of the movement who were a small minority that the Arab population did not dare support. However, the document asserted that, due to the renewed wave of activism, any tolerance toward the movement might be interpreted as weakness, and that the Emergency Regulations should be used in "decontaminating the disease."[17]

Another report from June 1964 entitled "The Minorities in Israel: The Positions of al-'Ard about Israel and the Jewish People" asserted that "members of al-'Ard have expressed extreme opinions about the state [of Israel] and the Jews." In order to prove these claims, the report relied on al-'Ard's newspaper, public meetings, and intelligence reports.[18] An examination of the report indicates that its authors viewed calls for Arab unity, struggle against Israel's oppressive measures, and protests against injustices inflicted on Arabs as inherently illegitimate. Relying on information from the public meetings of the movement, the report asserted that al-'Ard's main goals were implementing the right of return of Palestinian refugees, forcing Israel to accept the 1947 UN partition plan, and organizing refugees to act to assert their rights. Based on these statements, the report insisted that the movement did not in fact recognize the State of Israel. The report also claimed that members of the movement called for the use of violence in order to return to Palestine, without relying on the Arab world to achieve this end. Using statements from private conversations as reproduced by informants, the report also ascribed further extreme elements to the movement including some clear anti-Semitic statements and calls for the extermination of Israel and the use of force.[19]

Some of the ideas attributed to al-'Ard and rejected by the report were accepted by Jewish anti-Zionist groups at that time, such as Matzpen, including the demand for the right of return. In fact many of the ideas were also within the policies of the Israeli Communist Party, including, in the early years, the acceptance of the Partition Plan. While these claims were tolerated when coming from these latter groups, they were strictly rejected when expressed by al-'Ard. Hence, this report presents the limits of the tolerated discourse for Palestinian citizens: the rejection of any challenge to the Zionist character of the state.

LETTER TO THE UN

In June 1964, as a reaction to the decision to forbid it from publishing a newspaper, the movement decided to send a letter, signed by the Board of Directors of al-'Ard Co. Ltd. to the Secretary-General of the United Nations about the situation of the Arabs in Israel. The letter was framed in legal terms referring frequently to Israeli laws and court decisions in order to prove its claims of injustice. It protested the laws and legal tools that Israel was using to confiscate Arab lands and the restriction of the rights and freedoms of Arabs under military rule. It claimed that Israel treated its Arab citizens as second-class citizens and asserted that there was discrimination in public employment, health and public services, allocation of funds to local authorities and political rights. The letter also described the al-'Ard movement and the mistreatment it had encountered from the Israeli authorities as an example of this discrimination. It claimed that the state's repressive policies were designed "to extinguish Arab national feelings and to completely liquidate the Arab national entity in Israel" in order to fulfill the Zionist plan to establish a solely Jewish state.[20] The letter concluded by requesting that the United Nations intervene to protect the rights of Arab citizens of Israel, as the movement declared that it no longer had any confidence in the Israeli Supreme Court. Finally, the letter stated that the "peace and stability of the region, as well as the enigmatic future of Israel, depend on the behavior of the Israeli leaders alone."[21] This letter represents another attempt of the movement to break the silence enforced on it within the Israeli state and to resist its marginalization, in this case by turning to international institutions.

The letter received much attention in Israel. Mainstream Israeli newspapers reported that the government was aware of the letter and was collecting materials about the activities of al-'Ard (*Yedi'ot Ahronot*, July 12, 1964). They further reported that the government was considering undertaking "strict measures" against the movement to prevent subversive activities against the state (*Davar* and *ha-Boker*, July 13, 1964).

THE ASSOCIATION

After registering as a company and communicating with the UN, in mid-1964 al-'Ard registered as an association.[22] The goals of the new association were advancing the conditions of its members, promoting equality and social justice for all people in Israel, supporting Arab socialist unity in all legitimate ways, promoting peace in the Middle East, and supporting all progressive anticolonial movements in the world (Qahwaji, 1972: 458). The most controversial clause in the statement of goals was the third clause:

> To find a just solution for the Palestinian question, considering it a whole and indivisible unit, in accordance with the wishes of the Palestinian Arab people; . . . restores it to its political existence, ensures its full legal rights, and regards it as the first possessor of the right to decide its own fate for itself, within the framework of the supreme wishes of the Arab nation. (Jiryis, 1976: 190)

Different interpretations of the goals of the movement were offered, especially the third clause. Jiryis and Kardosh, among the leading members of al-'Ard, stated in interviews with the Israeli media after submitting the registration papers that although the movement recognized the State of Israel, it did not recognize its current borders and wanted to determine them through negotiations with the Palestinians (*Ma'ariv*, July 23, 1964). Qahwaji, also a leading member of the movement, explained these goals as combining Palestinian nationalism with pan-Arab nationalism (Qahwaji, 1978: 34). As will be shown further on, the court interpreted these goals as a complete negation of Israel's existence in general, and its existence within its current borders in particular.[23]

After submitting this request, the government held a special meeting to discuss the dangers posed by this political movement and how to respond to it (*Haaretz*, July 24, 1964). The ministers in the government were united in the belief in the "subversive nature and the poisonous nationalist character" of the movement (*Yedi'ot Ahronot*, July 27, 1964), and were determined to stop its activities using all possible legal means (*ha-Boker*, July 24, 1964). Although technically not authorized to do so, the district commissioner declined al-'Ard's request to register as an association, asserting that the association was established with the purpose of jeopardizing Israel's existence and its territorial integrity.

The movement appealed the commissioner's decision to the Supreme Court.[24] Rather than offer a technical decision to accept the appeal,[25] the court decided not to discuss the technical aspects of the case and stated instead that this appeal was an opportunity for the movement "to have their goals judicially examined, and that it was just that they know where they stand."[26] The court examined the goals of the association and concluded that they included the complete negation of Israel's existence, which it did not believe could be achieved in peaceful ways. It contended that al-'Ard's demands to treat Palestine as one geographical unit and to see the Palestinians as the only people to decide their own destiny was a negation of Israel's existence and of the rights of the Jewish people.

The court was cynical in understanding the petitioners; it interpreted their words but rejected their explanations. The court decided that although the movement's registration documents did not openly negate Israel's existence, it could be clearly understood from them. The court stated that it was acting within a defensive democracy: it had to protect itself from those who would subvert its own existence. With this decision, the court sent a clear message to the government: it saw the movement as an illegal organization, a danger to be stopped. This message was fully understood by government authorities. On November 11, 1964, the day the Supreme Court decision was published, a meeting that included the legal advisor, the chief military attorney, and others was held to discuss further steps to eliminate al-'Ard. The security minister subsequently declared the movement and any related body illegal. This decision allowed wide limitations on the movement's members and facilitated the campaign of arrests and searches that followed.[27] In addition to outlawing al-'Ard, propaganda activities were launched to win support for the campaign against it within Arab, Jewish, and international public opinion.[28]

On November 19, 1964, Kardosh, Jiryis, Qahwaji, and Baransi—the leading activists of the movement—were arrested and charged with contacting hostile Arab countries and the PLO, endangering state security, and establishing an illegal organization. Jiryis and Qahwaji were released on December 1, 1964, while Kardosh and Baransi were released on December 4, 1964 (ha-Boker, December 1, 1964 and Haaretz, December 4, 1964). Their release was conditional, with personal bail and severe restrictions imposed on their movement (Qahwaji, 1978: 37). After these arrests, police conducted a well-planned campaign of house searches, interrogations, and arrests against a large number of al-'Ard's members (Yedi'ot Ahronot, November 24, 1964). The extensive and well-planned campaign conducted against such a large group of the movement's supporters, the fact that they were compelled to cease participation in the movement, and the clear statements by the police about the decision to abolish the movement all confirm the idea that there was a decision by the government to eliminate al-'Ard and to reject its political ideology.

ESTABLISHING A POLITICAL PARTY

After the court decision, the movements of the leaders of al-'Ard were restricted for almost a year. During this period, they decided to establish a political party, the Socialist Party, and participate in the Israeli parliament elections. They hoped that they could elect several members to the Knesset who would then enjoy parliamentary immunity, which would allow the movement to reorganize and to continue to defend the rights of the Arab minority (Qahwaji, 1972: 467). On the other hand, if they were prevented from participating in the elections, they would at least have exposed what they saw as the real face of Israeli democracy (Qahwaji, 1978: 38). Immediately after submitting the registration documents, the leaders of the movement were arrested and expelled to distant Jewish cities, including Tiberias, Bet Shan, and 'Arad (Qahwaji, 1978: 39).

In September 1965, the Central Elections Committee rejected the party's request to run for elections. The committee claimed that the party was an illegal organization as its members "denied Israel's territorial integrity and its very existence."[29] Although the committee was aware that according to the Israeli Elections Law it had no authority to disqualify a party other than for technical reasons, it decided to interpret the law in a manner that allowed it to prevent a party from subverting the state by democratic means, which it claimed al-'Ard was attempting to do.

The movement appealed this decision to the Supreme Court, which delivered its decision in October 1965.[30] The majority discussion and decision were highly political in character. The court agreed that under normal circumstances the Elections Committee had no authority to examine the political positions of candidates, but it argued that this was a special case, as the committee knew that the Supreme Court had already decided that al-'Ard was an illegal group that aimed to negate Israel's existence. The court stated that any group that subverted the existence of the state could not take part in elections. Justice Sussman, who gave the second majority opinion in the appeal, relied on the term "defensive democracy" (*dimukraṭia mitgonenet*), equating this situation to the Weimar Republic and declaring that a state must protect itself from groups that try to use democracy to subvert its basic structure (*Yardor* case, 1965: 390). Justice Cohen, who gave a dissenting opinion in the appeal, argued that the legislature would first have to change the law in order to allow such a grave offense to human rights (*Yardor* case, 1965: 384).

The discussion in this case, similar to the earlier appeals discussed previously, was entirely focused on the Jewishness of the state and was situated within a completely Jewish-Zionist discourse. It ignored the Palestinian minority as part of the state to the extent that it automatically assumed the illegality of al-'Ard without examining it. In so doing, the Israeli Supreme Court was acting in accordance with official (and widespread Israeli-Jewish popular) hostility toward the movement. In this context, Justice Agranat, who delivered the majority decision, later stated "I did what the people wanted" (Lahav, 1999: 399). After the Supreme Court's decision that prevented the movement from participating in the elections, and although al-'Ard had officially ceased to exist, its members were still persecuted, and eventually some of them were forced to pay a great personal price for their political activism, including severe restrictions on their freedom of movement, imprisonment, and even being forced into exile.[31]

According to my analysis of the police files on the movement, which mostly referred to the years 1964–1965, the police and secret services were highly preoccupied with al-'Ard and made great efforts to monitor and eventually crush it. The police files include surveillance reports on some of the members, reports from informants about movement activities and meetings, and inquiries about some of al-'Ard's members.

This preoccupation of security authorities with al-'Ard can be viewed as a political as well as a security concern. The nature of the security hazard posed by the movement is questionable. It seems unlikely that the government believed that al-'Ard was significant enough to reach public opinion to the extent that it could achieve its political agenda in a manner that could jeopardize the state's existence or geographical integrity. The number of members in the movement, and the maximum potential number given a full expansion among the Palestinian community within Israel—which was less than 20 percent of the population at the time—meant that there was no chance that al-'Ard would win the necessary majority to bring about a change in the Jewish nature of the state or its borders. It is also clear that there was no conceivable danger of the movement committing any acts of violence to change the political reality in the state. There was no reference to any attempts to overthrow the government or jeopardize the state through use of force. There are no known instances of al-'Ard advocating the use of violence. It is plausible that had al-'Ard harbored any intentions to jeopardize Israel's security by means of violence it would have contacted and cooperated with outside organizations and states. Yet al-'Ard never established any connections with the surrounding Arab countries that Israel perceived as hostile and as security threats (interviews, Me'ari and Jiryis, 2005), nor did it make any significant military or political contacts with Fatah (*Harakat al-Tahrir al-Watani al-Falastini* [Palestine National Liberation Movement]) or the PLO, which were undertaking armed attacks on Israel (Harris, 2001: 131).

Al-'Ard acted in all possible legal and legitimate ways and within the framework of democracy to change Israeli policies, which it viewed as oppressive, and concentrated on receiving legitimacy for political actions. The security files indicate that the authorities' interest was focused on political considerations, since they examined and censored the content of the movement's ideology. In the context of the Supreme Court discussions about the movement, Harris agrees that the question in debate was not about security but rather "the question of the *ideological inconsistency* of the goals of al-'Ard with the basic moral values of the state [of Israel]" (Harris, 2001: 153, emphasis added). This ideological inconsistency is the result of the movement's rejection of the Zionist nature of the state. Hence, al-'Ard crossed the limits of the tolerated political mobilization of Palestinians in Israel by aspiring to change the character of the state. In doing so, it was viewed and treated as a security threat that needed to be eliminated.

CONCLUSION

During the rise in Arab nationalist mobilization in the 1950s throughout the Arab world, al-'Ard was established in Israel parallel to these movements but with a unique combination of nationalist pan-Arab ideology tailored to the special situation of Palestinians in Israel. While its ideology was pan-Arab, its activities and demands focused on issues that were most urgent to Palestinians, such as the right of return, and on issues specific to Palestinians within Israel, including the cessation of the military government and of land confiscation, and the extension of social and economic rights.

In my discussion of al-'Ard, I attend to the agency of Palestinian citizens who resisted Israeli dominance in various and innovative ways; they presented a challenge to Israeli claims of democracy by asserting their rights to negotiate their status as part of the new state and as part of their history. These attempts faced profound Israeli repression and an extensive system that the Israeli government utilized to maintain its control over the Palestinians. This repression and control were part of the Israeli rejection of Palestinian political rights as a national minority and as citizens of the state. It is also an expression of the Israeli policy that clearly viewed Palestinian rights as limited by the existing definition of the state as Jewish. Any attempt to challenge this definition led the state to combat it, asserting that it was acting as a "defensive democracy" in repressing Palestinian political mobilization.

When al-'Ard started as a political movement, the Israeli government was still in the zenith of its use of military repression against the Arab minority that stayed within the state in order to assure they would remain a marginalized minority that would not interfere with the Zionist program to build the "Jewish state" in Palestine. The international situation, the tension with Egypt and the Arab world, and the fresh memories of the 1948 and 1956 wars did not allow any space for Palestinian discourse within Israeli society to be voiced. The Israeli-Jewish public, told that its very existence was still endangered, was all too ready to accept governmental policies toward and representations of the Palestinian minority, including the claim that al-'Ard was an agent of the Arab world set to destroy the state.

In this tense context, al-'Ard's leaders expressed their ideas in a direct, uncompromising manner and were influenced by statements of Nasser and the nationalist discourse in the Arab world that they often repeated. This contributed to alienating the movement from the Israeli public, which viewed it as a threat. It also isolated al-'Ard from big segments of the Palestinian community who lived under the repressive mechanisms of military rule and witnessed the suppressive measures used against the movement. This isolation aided the government in its determination to break it. Al-'Ard members were harassed and the movement was restricted and eventually banned. It was not allowed to practice political freedom in a democratic way and could not compete to win the support of public opinion for the ideas it represented. Although many of the positions and struggles that al-'Ard assumed at the time already existed within the Israeli Communist Party, the latter was tolerated more due to the CPI's joint Arab-Jewish nature, and to the greater caution that its activists exercised in expressing their positions.

By 1965, al-'Ard was banned and all its activities were terminated. Edward Said asserts that it was the first resurgence of Palestinian national consciousness after 1948 (Said and Barsamian, 1994: 24). Its members maintain that the movement's political impact and inspiration remained (Qahwaji, 1978: 66). They claim that they raised and strengthened national awareness, organized national activism, exposed oppressive Israeli policies, and led to a greater involvement of Communist activists in the nationalist movement (Qahwaji, 1972: 474). They also maintain that they developed a young leadership who were pioneers in the struggle for Arabs' rights in Israel thereafter (Amun et al. 1981: 27). They contend that the founding of al-'Ard led to an ideological continuation in nationalist Palestinian groups and parties that developed later, including Abna' al-Balad (Sons of the Village) and al-Tajamu' al-Watani al-Dimuqrati (National Democratic Assembly) (interviews, Me'ari and Jiryis, 2005). However, although both of these movements espoused an ideology similar to al-'Ard, they developed in different historical contexts and played different roles, especially after the 1967 occupation of the West Bank and the Gaza Strip.

At the same time, it could be argued that the oppressive measures that were taken against al-'Ard deterred others from trying to establish other political parties and from being active within the Palestinian community in Israel. It took almost twenty years until another independent party, the Socialist List led by Muhammad Me'ari, was established. However, during that time, there was no lack of Palestinian community activities, as the CPI gained strength as the main oppositional voice of the community.

It is hard to determine, after the fact, what the long-term impact of al-'Ard was. In particular, it is difficult to assess the extent of the support it achieved; furthermore, the support it could have achieved had it not been suppressed is hard to verify. The openly pan-Arab nationalist discourse it used helped make it part of the wider Palestinian discourse outside Israel. Yet, even members of the movement itself were obliged to take further precautions in their future political activities or leave the country altogether. What is clear from exploring the history of al-'Ard is that Palestinians within Israel found various ways and utilized different spaces in order to resist Israeli hegemonic and exclusionary policies and assert their identity.

NOTES

This chapter is based on my thesis for the master's degree in Middle Eastern Studies at New York University, 2007. I'm grateful to my adviser, Zachary Lockman, and to Shareah Taleghani for their valuable comments.

1. Such is the case of Israeli literature on the subject; see Harris (2001). One example of the claim that Palestinians in Israel were quiescent, lacked political awareness, and failed to resist Israeli oppression can be found in Lustick (1980).

2. Most of the files related to the movement remain classified or inaccessible to the public.

3. I only use articles that were included in one of the files of the Prime Minister's Advisor for Arab Affairs that was entitled "Clips from newspapers—Al-'Ard" ISA GL 17032/14, which included newspaper clips about al-'Ard from the years 1964–1965.

4. However, the Communists' support for Nasserist policies was limited and the alliance with pro-Nasserist activists eventually broke after the breakup of the Nasserist-communist alliance in the Arab world (Beinin, 1990: 203).

5. ISA GL 17018/1. The document has no title but states that it is "taken from a summary of discussion of the North Region Committee from June 14, 1964."

6. ISA 2-926-1958-18, "Recommendations for handling the Arab minority in Israel," September 1959, 9. As brought forth in Bauml (2001: 245).

7. The movement applied for a license on July 10, 1959, and had not received an answer by October 1959, when it began publishing the newspaper (Sir al-'Ard, November 28, 1959). They finally received an answer in January 1960 in which the request for a license to publish a newspaper was rejected (Nada al-'Ard, January 25, 1960).

8. According to military government regulations, Palestinians needed a permit to leave their place of residence.

9. Supreme Court File number 288/60. The criminal appeal submitted by al-'Ard activists in Criminal Appeal 288/60.

10. Discussion and decision of the district court in Haifa. In Supreme Court File number 288/60.

11. Criminal Appeal 228/60, *Qahwaji and others v. The Legal Adviser*, PD 14, 1929 (hereafter, *Qahwaji* case).

12. High Court of Justice (HCJ) 241/60 *Kardosh v. The Companies Registrar*, PD 15, 1151 (hereafter, *Kardosh* case) and HCJ 16/61 *The Companies Registrar v. Kardosh*, PD 16, 1209.

13. Ibid., 1220.

14. The Emergency Regulations are a set of draconian measures adopted by Israel from the British mandate (see B'Tselem, nd)

15. HCJ 39/64 *al-'Ard Company Ltd. v. The District Commissioner of the Northern Region*, PD 18(2), 340 (hereafter, *al-'Ard Ltd.* case).

16. HCJ 73/53 *Kul ha-'Am Ltd. and al-Ittihad v. The Minister of Interior*, PD 7, 817.

17. ISA G 6337/1653/3, "Draft of the Tzofin Telegram," undated. As brought forth in Bauml (2001: 255).

18. ISA L 255/17, "The Minorities in Israel: The Positions of al-'Ard about Israel and the Jewish People," June 9, 1964, 1–2.

19. Ibid., 3–4.

20. ISA 4326/10 HTS, Letter to the UN, 1.

21. Ibid., 12.

22. Clause 6 in the Ottoman Law of Associations of 1909, which was adopted into Israeli law, declares that an association must register with the district commissioner immediately upon establishment. Al-'Ard as a political group fell within the definition of an association, hence it was compelled to register.

23. HCJ 253/64 *Jiryis v. The Commissioner of Haifa Region*, PD 18(4), 673, (hereafter, *Jiryis* appeal).

24. Jiryis appeal.

25. This could have been done by examining only the movement's claim that according to the Ottoman Law of Associations, the district commissioner was not authorized to decline the registration notice of any association.

26. Jiryis appeal, 676.

27. Defense Regulations (Emergency), 1945, Announcement of an Illegal Association, The Official Announcement Gazette no. 1134, 638. By Israeli law, the order is enacted from the day of its publication.

28. ISA L 255/17, entitled "Al-'Ard movement" which includes the summary of a meeting including the legal advisor, chief military attorney, and others on November 11, 1964.

29. Elections Appeal 1/65 *Yardor v. Chairman of the Elections Committee*, PD 19(3), 365, 369 (hereafter, Yardor Case) quoting the response that the Elections Committee sent to the Socialist Party rejecting its request to run for election.

30. Yardor Case.

31. Some of its former members were arrested in 1967 and accused of having contact with hostile foreign agents. However, none of the claims were directly related

to their membership in al-'Ard. Among those arrested was Habib Qahwaji, who after being held under administrative detention for a year was forced to leave the country together with his wife (Qahwaji, 1978: 41). Saleh Baransi was arrested in 1969 and accused of belonging to a hostile Palestinian organization and sentenced to ten years imprisonment (Baransi, 1981b: 3). Mansur Kardosh was kept under house arrest and restrictive conditions for the following ten years (Sigaut, 2001: 75).

TWO

A GOOD ARAB IN A BAD HOUSE?

Unrecognized Villagers in the Israeli Military

Rhoda Ann Kanaaneh

Ishmael served in the Israeli border patrol, in the police force, as a political analyst for the military and as a foreign service trainee at the Israeli Embassy in the United States. He regularly tours university campuses in the United States. to lecture about his love of Israel. When I heard him speak at American University in Washington, D.C., he boasted of his frontline service and his grandmother's command of Yiddish.[1] Ishmael Khaldi,[2] however, is not Jewish. He is the Israeli government's model for a category of identity it has long worked to create. Ishmael, "Ish" for short, is a "Good Arab" (Firro, 2001: 40).

"When you say Israel, the first thing that comes to mind is Jews fighting Arabs. It's unfortunately mostly true. But I'm not Jewish . . . ," Khaldi began. "I'm of the third generation of Bedouins whose fate is tied to the community who came to establish Israel." He described a history of Bedouin loyalty to the state and assistance to it from its very beginnings. His grandmother learned Yiddish from early Jewish settlers. He claimed that 60 percent of Bedouins in the north volunteer to serve in the Israeli military and many make "the ultimate sacrifice." In 2002 alone, nine Bedouin soldiers were killed in service with the Israeli military. Khaldi was particularly proud of his efforts to be even more loyal to the state than many Jews. When a group of Jewish pilots became refuseniks and would not serve in the occupied territories, Mr. Khaldi, together with a few other Bedouin reservists, volunteered to serve extra weeks of reserve duty to compensate. At one key point in his lecture, Ishmael intoned, "Israel's fate is our fate, Israel's fate is our fate, Israel's fate is our fate."

The sympathetic audience of mostly Zionist students did not seem entirely convinced. They demanded answers to essential questions of identity they presumed Mr. Khaldi had glossed over. "How do you self-identify? Are you Bedouin first or Israeli?" "Does it bother you that your passport says 'Arab'?" and "Do you identify with the Palestinian cause or state?" Like many other demonstrations of Palestinian citizens' loyalty to the Jewish state, Khaldi's performance that day, as eager as it was, remained vexed by its underlying contradiction. How can a Muslim Arab be loyal to a state that defines itself as being of and for the Jewish people? Arab citizens in Israel are asked to be loyal not to a neutral state, but to another people, the Jewish collective (Jabareen, 1999: 27). The students prodded Ishmael to repeat his allegiance to the Jewish state again and again. In the end, they did not seem to buy it.

Khaldi belongs to one of the groups accorded special status in Israel as almost other than Arab or, as one Israeli journalist put it, "Arab lite" (*Haaretz*, February 15, 2005). This includes to varying degrees Druze, Bedouins, Christian Arabs, and residents of certain preferred villages. Some members of these groups, Khaldi included, go to great lengths to conform to the state's expectations of its special minorities. As non-Jews, however, they are structurally haunted by their Arabness, "lite" as it may be. This chapter looks at how the Israeli state uses military service to divide its Palestinian population into separate ethnicities with varying shades of acceptance of and by the state and the severe limits and contradictions built into these attempts (Enloe, 1980).

THE RULES OF DIVIDE AND RULE

Ian Lustick argues: "There is a highly effective system of control which since 1948 has operated over Israeli Arabs" that is based on policies "specifically designed to preserve and strengthen . . . the segmentation of the Arab community, both internally and in its relations with the Jewish sector" (Lustick, 1980: 25 and 122). This policy of divide, subdivide, and rule was explicitly aimed to "prevent the Arab minorities from coalescing into one group" (Firro, 2001: 41), whereby Israeli authorities attempted to consolidate their power by "feeding and reinforcing confessional loyalties until they eclipsed national feelings" (Jiryis, 1976: 197) and exacerbating intergroup tensions, disputes, and rivalries (Cohen, 2006: 43).

One group within the Arab community that has been targeted as a special minority is the Bedouins. The state has tried to emphasize divisions between Bedouins and other Palestinians (Jakubowska, 1992: 85), exploiting and recreating differences between this most disadvantaged group and the larger Arab community. The state required Bedouins, for example, to register their nationality on their ID cards as Bedouin rather than Arab. Stereotyped as "non-political" and "disinclined to follow political ideas or groups that might commit them to action not conducive to their tenuous existence" (*Haaretz*, February 24, 2002), Bedouins were figured as "rootless," "movable objects" (Shamir, 1996: 231, 237) that "could be easily evacuated from any given piece of land when it was needed" by the state (Hajj, Lavie, and Rouse, 1993: 375). Certain Bedouin leaders were cultivated during the pre-state period to secure their collaboration during the 1948 war. While the Bedouin population of the southern Naqab region was reduced to roughly one-fifth of its original size and in the Galilee to one-third by the end of 1948, some cooperating families were spared expulsion outside the emerging borders of the state (though not relocation or land confiscation) (Falah, 1985: 37–38).

Military service is key to the attempted production of good Arabs in Israel. Bedouins, particularly those from "friendly" tribes, are encouraged to volunteer to serve in the Israeli armed forces and are celebrated as warriors and friends of the Jews in both popular and official discourse. The recruitment of Arabs in the military is not simply to add their strength to the ranks of the "Israeli Defense Forces." From early on, supporters of "the Minorities' Unit"[3] argued that, "the unit served an important social goal that transcended its military utility" (Peled, 1998: 147), or in other words, a political propaganda goal (Parsons, 2001: 63). As a sign on the door of the Bedouin recruitment center in Bir al-Sabiʿ states, their recruitment is supposed to "strengthen the identification between the Bedouin sector and the state/IDF."

I draw here on ten months of fieldwork conducted between 2000 and 2005 and interviews with over twenty self-identified Bedouin men (as well as over fifty interviews with other Palestinian soldiers) serving in various branches of the Israeli security apparatus for periods ranging from several months to twenty-three years. These were strained and difficult interviews because of the highly sensitive nature of the subject matter. On the one hand, soldiers were wary of discussing their politics because of the risk that this might expose them to in relation to the state. On several occasions they expressed concern that their words could be used to label them as disloyal to the suspecting authorities. On the other hand, there was an opposite source of mistrust—resulting from a wide Palestinian consensus that serving in the Israeli military is fundamentally wrong and the soldiers' fear that I might expose them in the Arabic media. Unlike the traditional anthropological expectation of "empathetic rapport" with informants (Ballinger, 2002: 10), all parties to these ethnographic encounters probably recognized an element of mistrust in them (Robben, 1995: 96). The soldiers' complex positionalities lend themselves to the textured and multilayered analysis I attempt here.

From the soldiers' perspective, military service offers the incentive of becoming *mesudar*,[4] a Hebrew term for being "organized," or less literally, being "made"—regular paychecks, tax breaks, better loan terms, educational grants, and early and comfortable pensions (for career soldiers). In some Bedouin communities with high rates of military service and poverty, the term for military service is *mitwazzif*—simply meaning "employed." Beyond soldiering itself being a key form of employment for an underprivileged population, it also potentially presents further work opportunities after completion of service. As Said, a former soldier, explained to me:

> If a man[5] wants to get a good job here, military service is very important. Look at the job listings in the [Hebrew] newspapers. . . . I dare you to find a good job that doesn't require completion of military service. I got into the business of heavy equipment. Most of my contracts are in restricted areas, areas other Arabs are not even allowed to enter, not to mention to work in. I was able to raise my family from the lowest economic levels to a comfortable situation.

Another major incentive the military offers is the opportunity to lease residential land (available in certain locations) from the state at discounted prices. In essence, the state seizes indigenous lands then induces some members of the dispossessed groups to serve in the military by holding out the promise of leasing land—sometimes the same land they originally owned—back to them.

In addition to the portfolio of official benefits, a system of clientelism encourages soldiers to build personal connections with state officials to accrue individual favors and facilitate "key transactions with the state" (Gill, 1997: 537). These favors include escaping some of the limitations and punishments of being an Arab citizen of the state. A retired soldier told me:

> In eleven years I did many things for the family: licenses, buildings, telephone lines, electricity, water. I started going to government offices and finding someone who'd listen. At first, my extended family objected to me joining the military, but when they understood that I was doing it for a purpose, to advance the family, they accepted. My uncles had tried to get a water pipe to our neighborhood for so long—they knew how important this was.

This notion that "made" soldiers receive potentially less-negligent treatment by state authorities was repeated to me by another former soldier:

> I needed to license my house and to get rid of the tax debt I owed. When I wanted to close my tax file, they [tax officials] advised me to go to the army. After I enlisted I went to the tax office—I told the man, "Tomorrow I am going to Lebanon [with the army], and

I don't know if I will come back or not." He signed away the debt on the spot. Out of over 100,000 shekels I ended up paying 2,000. I showed them my army card and they immediately said, "Sa'" [Hebrew for "drive away" or "go"]. This state is a Mafia.

This situation was summarized to me by Ali, a former soldier, as follows: "We are, like the rest of the Arabs in Israel, mitkhuzqīn (screwed). But they provide this door for us. If you 'get employed' [join the military], the door will open. So you have no choice if you want to make that door open. But it doesn't open all the way." The opportunities presented by military service should be understood as resulting from particular state policies. The confiscation of Arab lands and interior ministry planning that seeks to Judaize them (Falah, 1989b; Yiftachel, 1995), discriminatory employment policies (Lewin-Epstein and Semyonov, 1993), a segregated and hierarchical education system (HRW, 2001), differential treatment by welfare agencies (Rosenhek, 1999), together with the linking of citizenship rights to military service (Helman, 2001: 303) all contribute to positioning soldiering as an economic and political opportunity for Bedouin soldiers.

EVEN GOOD ARABS ARE NOT JEWS

The state often describes Bedouins as special allies of the state and as the Jews' brothers-in-arms. Generations of them have served as trackers in the military and dozens have been killed during service, as the monument to the fallen Bedouin in the Batuf Valley commemorates. Yet crops on Bedouin land the state claims as its own are burned with toxic chemicals, Bedouin fertility rates loom exceptionally large in the Israeli fears of the Arab demographic time bomb (see Kanaaneh, 2002), their economic status is the lowest, and their unemployment rates the highest in the country (Jakubowska, 2000). Khaldi's certainty that Bedouins and Israeli Jews share the same destiny aside, state officials voice their fears of a "Bedouin intifada," and view Bedouins as lawless trespassers, criminal "foreigners" invading state land (for example, Guardian Oct 4, 2000, HRA, 2005a: 16) to be subjected to the "removal of intruders" law.

Despite their preferred status, the non-Jewishness of these special minorities continues to haunt them and severely limit their rewards. The hopes of these soldiers for fuller citizenship as a reward for their service founders, again and again, on the Jewish/non-Jewish dichotomy at the core of the ideals of the Jewish state. That Bedouins and other "good Arabs" remain "non-Jews" in a state that continues to prioritize its Jewish character puts a significant damper on the elevation of their status as "special minorities." As one Naqab soldier told Jansson, a Swedish researcher: "We wanted to become equal. He is doing the army so I will do the army. He fights for the country so I will fight for the country, he will get chocolate, I will get chocolate. You understand? Now he goes to the army, I go to the army, he gets chocolate, I get a slap" (Jansson, 2004: 45).

The Jewish/non-Jewish binary places limitations on Bedouins even within the military. Israeli governments historically exempted most Arab citizens from military service because their recruitment would "breach security" (Peled, 1998: 147). Senior military and Ministry of Defense officials argued that allowing Muslims and Christians in the military would amount to "assisting a fifth column to penetrate its ranks" (Peled, 1998: 137–138). As a preferred minority, Bedouins have been constructed as more trustworthy than other Arabs. The history of their recruitment in the military, however, shows that their acceptance has been gradual and incomplete. There has always been a strong trope of distrust and concern that these special minorities could become an Arab "Trojan Horse" (Peled, 1998) in the Israeli military. Until the 1970s, all Arabs were placed in segregated units under Jewish officer command, denied participation in Israeli-Arab combat, and limited in rank (ibid.). "Minority" soldiers have since been allowed positions outside the segregated brigade and although all units were declared open in 1991, the air force and intelligence remain inaccessible. Moreover, the largely segregated units continue to exist and "minority" soldiers continue to be directed primarily to them (Kanaaneh, 2009: chap. 5).

For example, roughly 80 percent of Bedouins in the Naqab who join serve in one of the two Bedouin units, the so-called Trackers or the Desert Patrol (Jansson, 2004: 31). According to Colonel Ganon, a commander of the tracker unit, "They are more successful there . . . it is easier for them" (Jansson, 2004: 31). The continued predominance of minority units highlights that such soldiers are not just Israeli soldiers, but "minority" Israeli soldiers, since "Israeli" on its own is used to mean Jewish. A Ministry of Defense official history of Bedouins in the military recognizes that the minorities units are perceived to be less prestigious (Havakook, 1998: 205). Many soldiers I interviewed emphasized that such units, unlike the Ashkenazi-dominated combat units, offer limited opportunities for advancement.

In addition to ethnically specific units, the so-called military melting pot segments soldiers with ethnically specific memorials (such as the memorial to the fallen Bedouin near the Batuf Valley in the Galilee), benefits (such as the Bedouin military educational track whereby Bedouins receive subsidized teacher training after basic training), commands (particular positions are designated for Bedouins), and celebrations (graduations, for example, are held at the homes of key Bedouin sheikhs). Thus within the military, as within the state at large, Arabs are distinctly marked as such.

The recruitment of Bedouins into the military is often advocated by state officials in the hopes that this will "discourage them from turning into Islamic radicals" (*Haaretz*, June 14, 2001). Similar statements to the effect that drafting Arabs can counter their otherwise sure path to political radicalization are commonplace in Israel. It may be argued that Jewish security requires and depends on the embodiment of Arabs as a source of insecurity in order to justify the continued centrality of the security apparatus (Kimmerling, 2005). If Arab ethnicity functions as a signifier of insecurity, and membership in the military as a signifier of security, then the Arab soldier in the military is a security enforcer who must fight against the very insecurity he embodies and of which he cannot entirely rid himself.

"GOOD FOR WAR, BUT NOT FOR LIVING WITH"

Despite their efforts to conform to the state's requirements, "good Arabs" continue to be defined in terms of their non-Jewishness. The state's "divide and rule" policy of awarding certain privileges and fostering special ties with particular segments of the Palestinian population, such as Bedouins, is not without contradictions. In principle, it is disrupted by the continued importance of the Jewish/non-Jewish dichotomy at the core of the ideals of a Jewish state. The major problems facing Palestinians in Israel—including land confiscation, municipal underfunding, home demolitions, and the refusal to recognize villages—are also faced by Palestinian soldiers.

Although some Bedouins have historically collaborated with state forces as informants and soldiers, many were victims of the ethnic cleansing of the land during the 1948 war. In 1951, Israeli authorities physically evicted two-thirds of the remaining Bedouins in the Naqab and transferred them to a newly designated closed area (Falah, 1989a: 78). Having confiscated most of their lands and prevented their flocks from grazing, a policy of "concentration by choice" forced Bedouins to settle in townships. To date, seven such townships have been established, designed with an economic infrastructure that can only support landless migrant laborers (Falah, 1989a: 86). Three more townships are planned to absorb the remaining Naqab Bedouins, a population of 70,000, who have refused to move. This latter group of residents lives in villages unrecognized by the government without basic services such as water, electricity, permanent housing, health care, schools, and roads. They do not have the right to elect and to be elected to local government (El-Okbi, 2004: 100). The same holds true for the unrecognized villages of Galilee Bedouins, who are also pressured to give up their land and relocate to designated townships.

The question then is: are Bedouin soldiers spared the confiscation of Arab land for the common (read: Jewish) good? One activist on behalf of unrecognized villages described to me how he felt his service in the border guard allowed him to speak assertively (he used the Hebrew term *'im peh maleh*, literally meaning "with a full mouth"), and helped him win the ear of state officials in fighting for his village's recognition. The sought-after symbolic rewards in this case—the potential for gaining legitimacy and voice among the "community of warriors" (Helman, 1999: 194)—could produce material ones. This man hoped that his ability to declare, "I am a veteran and my brother gave his life in Lebanon," will result in the "listening ear" of state officials. This could potentially mean running water, electricity, health care, and schools for his village. But he believes his success has been limited: "So far I think my military service helped me to a certain degree. I can clearly see the change in the behavior of officials as soon as I say 'I just came back from reserve duty [used Hebrew *milu'im*].' One official heard this and immediately gave me an invitation to a very important meeting. But I can't say for sure, since they haven't recognized our village yet!"

In an Israeli documentary, former soldier Bassam complains about the demolition of his family's home in Shafa 'Amir, while emphasizing that he is a disabled veteran from the war in Lebanon (Tuba and Migdal, 1998). He pleads: "I don't want the regime to forget me. Suddenly I find myself not belonging and that is painful. And I ask, 'Why me?' I was [worth something], and now I am not worth anything, why?" At a memorial for fallen soldiers, Bassam confronts a state official who was one of the signatories on the demolition orders. The official responds: "I am for protecting the law. If I don't enforce the law, then I would be neglecting my job" (Tuba and Migdal, 1998).[6]

In this case, Judaizing goals of the state trump its attempts at co-opting non-Jews through military service and ethnic fragmentation. This order of priorities is clearly crystallized in the attempt (though unsuccessful) by then Agriculture Minister Rafael Eitan who intensified the policy of Bedouin displacement in the Naqab, and began advocating the "disbandment of the army's Bedouin unit, so as to disarm its soldiers lest they raise their weapons in anticipated defense" (*Haaretz*, February 24, 2002).

A retired soldier whose building was demolished in the Naqab region told me:

> There was a big officer who was about to step on a mine, and I stopped him. He thanked me. But he didn't teach his daughter and son that it is because of me (used Hebrew *bizkhuti*) that he is alive. I personally have saved maybe 200 Jews from being blown up. . . . In Za'nun, the people who had their home demolished, their father served for nine years and used to be a recruiter for them. It didn't help. We served more than the north, but no one cares.

Homes slated for demolition are not only in unrecognized villages, but also within recognized villages and state-planned townships—provocatively referred to by one soldier as an extermination camp (used Hebrew *mahane hashmada*). Another soldier's family land lay on the outskirts of a state planned Bedouin township in the north.

> We are fifty meters from the village [official zoning] plan and we've tried to get electricity with much difficulty, running illegal lines to

borrow electrical power from others. The cow stables near us have electricity. Consider us cows! . . . My father served eighteen years in the military and he lives in a shack and can't build a home. They demolished his home while he was at work. When they came to demolish the house, people in the village came out to plead with them and told them that he was away serving with the army. They [the authorities] said: 'How is that relevant [used Hebrew *ma ze kashur*]?' You know in our area—there is one woman whose brother died in the military, and another one whose brother also died in the military, and the third whose brother's son died in the military. The three of them are living in an area that is unrecognized. And the government doesn't care.

A Hebrew newspaper covering a demonstration protesting demolition orders for "razing homes built illegally by former IDF soldiers" interviewed one of the organizers, Salem al-Atrash, then aged twenty-five, who had been discharged from the military five months earlier and was now living in a tiny shanty he built. Al-Atrash said that several months ago, he received a demolition order on his home: "This was my discharge present. After discovering seven booby traps and sacrificing my spirit for the state, the state is destroying my home . . . when it became clear to me that at least fifty discharged soldiers faced the same situation as I . . . we decided to act" (*Haaretz*, January 18, 2002). And the strategy that they pursued was to try to emphasize their service to the state in the hopes of protecting their homes. However, it appears that both military service and collaborating family leaders are commonly overridden, as the following interviewee argues: "My friend put two flags on his house and held up his military ID, but what did they care? The sheikh in the village had a good past [used Hebrew *'avar tov*] with the state, but they didn't take that into consideration at all." Another soldier decided to quit the military when the authorities "rejected his request to lease and work the plot of land his family had been cultivating for generations." He explained: "I can't take government officials treating me like an enemy. I risk my life for the state and don't deserve this disdain" (*Haaretz*, February 24. 2002).

Another case that received some media attention in Israel involved a Bedouin, Khalid Sawa'id, who had served seven years in the military, and lived on his ancestral land in Kammaneh in the Galilee, but was now engulfed by the Jewish settlement of Makhmunim that was trying to evict him and demolish his home. In 1988, Sawa'id applied to be admitted as a member of the settlement, promising to then sell them his land "so as not to harm the development of the lookout (settlement)" (Farah, 1993: 16). He was rejected. The head of the committee of Makhmunim asserted that "with all the friendship with Khalid, it would not be a natural situation if he lives with us" (Farah, 1993: 16). The Jewish residents of the settlement expressed fear that the Sawa'id family would reproduce more rapidly,

become a larger minority, and take control of the settlement (Farah, 1993:
16). Sawaʻid even "agreed to accept land in [the nearby partly recognized
Arab village of] Kammaneh, where my extended family lives, but this too
they rejected" (Farah, 1993: 17).

When asked about his military service, he said: "I was stupid. I thought
that if I serve I will receive my rights. I said, 'I will fight beside them and
receive what I deserve, just like Jews receive.' But this is not the reality. I
am good for war, but not for living with" (Farah, 1993: 17). When I visited
the Sawaʻid family in 2004, the entrance to the gated, barbwire-encircled
settlement read in Hebrew "Makhmunim: Dreams That Come True." The
sign would be more accurate if it stated "Makhmunim: Zionist Dreams That
Come True."

Still, some soldiers feel they have had better luck and others continue
to try to use their military service to hold on to their lands. In an unrecognized village in the Naqab, twenty homes have been issued demolition
orders. I was told that one resident who retired after twenty years of military
service asked that his case be separated from the other nineteen, and the
Israeli authorities "agreed on the condition that he won't publicize it." The
case was reportedly still pending at the time of writing, but such rumors of
patronage likely feed some soldiers' hopes for special treatment. In a separate
case, one of my interviewees told me that his military service "personally
helped me, they didn't demolish my home. They closed their eyes to the
violation. But other people, it didn't work for them. One day the man is a
president of the state, the next day they are demolishing his home."

Criticism of this contradiction in policy comes from across the spectrum,
and not only from embittered former soldiers who have been personally
victimized or from nationalistically inclined Arabs. Salame Abu-Ghanim is
a "veteran enlistment activist" in the Naqab, who served as an adviser on
Bedouin affairs to extreme rightist Infrastructure Minister Avigdor Lieberman
and "founded the Organization of Negev Bedouin Heroes of Israel." "It's
hard to argue with the youth who don't want to sign up," he told *Haaretz*.
"The youth sees that the state doesn't help the veterans. They die for the
Jewish state, for the Jews, and the Jews treat them like lepers" (*Haaretz*,
January 10, 2002). Ibrahim al-Hzayyil from Rahat, who recently volunteered
his fifth son to the military, told *Haaretz*: "Today's Bedouin youth knows
that after he takes off his uniform, he'll go back to the world of discrimination from which the entire Bedouin community suffers. . . . It shouldn't
be this way. . . . These kids should be given something, so they don't feel
like suckers" (*Haaretz*, January 10, 2002). The Israeli military itself blames
recent declines in the number of Bedouin recruits on insufficient rewards
(Arabs48, April 5, 2007).

In general, it appears that the waving of Israeli flags above homes slotted
for demolition in unrecognized villages and the tens of years of service of

family members are not significant enough to prevent their demolition. The goals of the Jewish state call for the removal of all Arabs living in unrecognized villages, soldiers or not. Judaization policies target all Arabs—whatever their loyalties, military service, or political affiliations—and largely override any attempts to "co-opt," "Israelize," or "integrate" groups within the Arab population. The occasional Israeli media outrage that Arab soldiers, loyal friends of Israel, are not being rewarded, conveniently elides this basic contradiction by characterizing such cases as matters of bureaucratic oversight, lack of agency coordination, or as Moshe Arens (former foreign minister and three times former defense minister) puts it, a "non-policy" on the part of the state (*Jerusalem Post*, April 10, 1998). Yet, these cases are results of the supremacy of one set of goals: that of creating a homogenous nation-state of and for Jews and promoting their particular demographic, economic, linguistic, cultural, and political interests (Smooha, 1997: 199–200). The individual non-Jewish soldier may be able to achieve certain material and symbolic gains as long as they do not conflict with the ethnic goals of the state. In the end, the military is a tool, like other state institutions such as interior planning committees and schools, that the dominant majority uses to preserve Jewish privilege (Jamal, 2003: 4).

CONCLUSION

Palestinians in Israel employ a wide spectrum of strategies in their struggles with the state. While the majority strongly identify as Palestinian and struggle for equal rights, others, like Ishmael Khaldi, try a different route. If Khaldi's mantras of a "shared destiny" seem particularly eager and subservient, this is certainly not true of all Bedouins or all "special minorities." While the state's segmentation policy and its partial attempts to de-Arabize particular Arabs have succeeded in producing performances of acquiescence to the state, they certainly are not the exclusive forms of identity presented. Service in the military is widely questioned, contested, and criticized within Bedouin as well as other Arab communities and even among Arab soldiers who serve in the military. In addition, as good an Arab as Khaldi might try to be, he still hails from an unrecognized village—the very existence of which automatically places him in conflict with the state.

The state's insistence on the prioritization of Jews has directly backfired in some cases. The Council of Unrecognized Villages has started calling its constituents in the south "Naqab Arabs" rather than "Bedouin," reflecting in part, according to council chairman Hassan al-Rafiah, "feelings of frustration and despair over the state's treatment of the Bedouin" and in rejection of state attempts to distance them from the rest of the Arab population (*Haaretz*, January 25, 2006). According to Parliament member Talab al-Sani' (from the Naqab):

The new terminology also reflects disappointment with Bedouin efforts to integrate into Israeli society. "They believed that if they were more Bedouin and less Arab, this would help them enter Israeli society; it would give them more rights," he said. But this failed. The policy is the same policy, the demolition of houses continues, the lack of recognition continues, and Shimon Peres [formerly Prime Minister and current Deputy PM and Minister for the Development of the Negev, Galilee, and Regional Economy and current President of Israel] continues to talk about Judaizing the Negev. (*Haaretz*, January 25, 2006)

That one person sometimes calls himself Bedouin while another prefers, in certain contexts, Naqab Arab, does not delegitimize their identities as exceptionally fragmented or not "real." These contradictions should be understood neither as exceptional nor as ubiquitous and thus neutral or apolitical. Rather, they reflect the constructed nature of identities in general and are best positioned in relation to the state and its power of setting and changing structural parameters. One young soldier from an unrecognized village often calls himself Bedouin rather than Arab because he argued that "when Jews hear the word Arab they are startled; the word Bedouin relaxes them more." One policeman, who belongs to another so-called special minority, the Druze, told me, "The word Arab in this country is like a curse. So if they are going to throw that word at me, 'Arab,' that way, then no, I'm not an Arab." Other soldiers in different contexts emphasize Arabness and Palestinianness: "I know eight ancestors back," a soldier from the partly recognized village of Kammaneh told me, "even more than the *fallah* (farmer or peasant) knows about his ancestors. How can I deny that I am Palestinian and Arab?" A Druze translator for the military courts in the Occupied Territories explained: "When I am in Tel Aviv I am a Jew. When I am in Rame (an Arab town in northern Israel) I am an Arab. When I am in Julis (a Druze village) I am a Druze" (quoted in Hajjar, 2005: 152).

Given the relatively limited range of strategies available to them, the circumscribed structural incentives offered for serving, as well as the context of martial citizenship (D'Amico, 2000:105) in Israel, it is not surprising that some Palestinians volunteer to serve in the Israeli military. Seen from a wider geographic and historical perspective, such behavior is not rare or isolated. African Americans served in the U.S. army during the height of segregation, Japanese Americans interred in camps served during World War II, South Asians made up the British Indian army under British colonial rule, Irish Catholics joined the British army in Northern Ireland, and Algerians fought with the French army against Algerian independence. Rather than quaint anomalies, such examples suggest the complexity of the relationships subalterns have to the military powers that subjugate them.

When Sawa'id expresses his disappointment with the rewards for his military service by saying, "I was stupid. I thought that if I serve I will receive my rights . . . ," he of course is not stupid. All the soldiers in this study make choices, try strategies, and take chances—in limited contexts. Rather than seeing these soldiers as naïve dupes, or eager victims of the state, their choices should be understood within the powerful structural constraints imposed upon them. While one may attribute to individual soldiers certain personal backgrounds, motivations, intentions, and resistances in joining the military, they are not the focus of this chapter because overriding structural limitations remain paramount. As one career soldier told me: "We don't trick ourselves; we all know the game. But sometimes one has no choice but to play it." I take this not as a comment on the soldiers' weak moral fiber, but rather as an indication of the absurd and contradictory situation that Arabs in Israel are placed in. This condition of having to play a game with unfair rules holds true more generally for all Palestinians in Israel. They find themselves continuing to largely play by the state's rules, in the state's high-stake games, despite—or perhaps also because of—decades of losing at those games.

Moreover, the bitterness that soldiers sometimes articulate, that despite their loyalty and sacrifices "no one cares," seems to express their frustration at the broken promises that the state, presenting itself as a military democracy, after all, explicitly made to them. Like for all Palestinians in the state, the Israeli story holds the promise—as fleeting, misleading, and unactualized as it is—of inclusion that they have little choice but to try to hold on to.

These dynamics are highly visible in the example of Arabs in the military, but they are in no way exceptional. The military, like other state institutions, produces subjects it assumes are destined to be the source of threat and insecurity, who are then asked to fight these "inherent" characteristics. What the state considers to be "good Arabs" and "bad Arabs" are perhaps better understood not as two separate categories, but as state-imputed qualities coexisting in every Arab in Israel. State disciplines—whether carried out by educational, court, or health-delivery systems—attempt to produce subjects who are self-alarmed by their own existence: students reading about Arab enemies of the state in their history textbooks, court petitioners using state laws that exclude them by definition, and patients using contraceptives that will lower their demographic threat to the state.

Sa'id Ighbariyyi, who helped mediate contacts with several soldiers, told me: "If the state really intended to Israelize us, two-thirds of us would have already been lost among them by now, dissolved into their society. But the state has never been interested in really Israelizing Arabs. It is not possible. It would mean the failure of the principle of a Jewish state." Arabs utilize myriad strategies, some of them creative and unexpected, in their attempts to cope with their marginality in Israel. However, the structural constraints imposed by the state powerfully limit the results of these attempts. The experiences of the Arab soldiers in my study illustrate the ultimate impossibility of ever being a "good Arab" in Israel and offer a particularly compelling critique, perhaps from an unexpected group, of the ethnic logic of the state.

NOTES

Portions of this chapter are from *Surrounded: Palestinian Soldiers in the Israeli Military*, by Rhoda Ann Kanaaneh, © 2008 by the Board of Trustees of the Leland Stanford Jr. University, all rights reserved, by permission of the publisher, www.sup.org, and from "Blood in the Same Mud? Palestinian Veterans of the Israeli Military," *Anthropology News* 50, 5 (May 2009): 5–6, with the permission of the American Anthropological Association. Research and writing were supported by a Richard Carley Hunt Writing Fellowship from the Wenner Gren Foundation for Anthropological Research, a Palestinian American Research Center fellowship, an American University Faculty Research Award, a Faculty Fellowship at New York University's Center for the Study of Gender and Sexuality, a Jean Monnet Fellowship at the Robert Schuman Center for Advanced Studies of the European University Institute, and visiting scholar apppointments at Columbia University's departments of Anthropology and Middle East Languages and Civilizations, and NYU's Department of Social and Cultural Analysis and the Department of Middle Eastern and Islamic Studies.

1. Lecture by Ishmael Khaldi, "An Arab Muslim in an Israeli World," March 16, 2004, American University, Ward Room 104, Washington, D.C.

2. Ismael wrote his name in English in its Hebrew version, "Ishmael," and preferred the more Israeli-sounding, shortened "Ish."

3. Note the plural "minorities" in the preferred Israeli term Bnei mi'utim—rather than a single Arab minority (Cohen, 2006: 204).

4. Note that although my interviews were conducted in Arabic, most interviewees sprinkled Hebrew terms throughout their discourse. When quoting them I point to such language switches whenever they occur—they often suggest certain political genealogies of power.

5. The masculine form here suggests this discourse of economic opportunity is strongly gendered. See Kanaaneh (2005) for more on this aspect.

6. In the Naqab alone, some 113 Arabs homes were demolished in 2002, 132 in 2003, and 150 demolitions in 2004 (HRA, 2005a: 27–28).

THREE

LOUDER THAN THE BLUE ID

Palestinian Hip-Hop in Israel

Amal Eqeiq

Palestinian hip-hop in Israel is on the rise and is talking back to the state. Its critique is powerfully articulated around the question of Palestinian citizenship in a Jewish national state. Since the emergence of Palestinian hip-hop less than a decade ago, it has alluded to the problematics of defining the current status of the Palestinian subject in Israel in terms of citizenship in both its themes and form. This study offers a historical, anthropological, and cultural exploration of how Palestinian hip-hop represents, contests, and reproduces the notion of Israeli citizenship.[1]

From a historical perspective, the dramatic emergence of Palestinian hip-hop coincides with a moment of crisis in the history of Palestinians in Israel and their relationship to the state. Though there is sufficient evidence to argue that the history of Palestinians in Israel since 1948 has been a continuous "crisis," I use the term here to refer specifically to the post-October 2000 period. Palestinian hip-hop first appeared after the unraveling of the Oslo Accords and shortly before the outbreak of the al-Aqsa Intifada in late September 2000. However, it became widely circulated after October 2000 when Israeli police and military forces shot and killed thirteen Palestinians, twelve of them citizens of Israel. The fallen young men were shot during protests against the killing and oppression of fellow Palestinians in the West Bank and the Gaza Strip. But these were spontaneous protests by Palestinians in Israel already aggrieved by their treatment as inferior citizens of the state. Palestinian hip-hop in Israel emerged in this environment and spoke the language of these protests.

I was first introduced to Palestinian hip-hop in late 2001 through my students at al-Taybeh High School. Two young male students, one an activist in the Communist Party, and the other, a member of the local Muslim Youth Group, handed me a copy of a CD that had the letters TN written on it and said, "You have to listen to this." I learned later that TN were the initials of Tamer Nafar, the first and perhaps best-known artist in this emerging form, a name already well known among nationalist and Islamist youth alike. In October 2006, Nafar (twenty-seven years old at the time) told me in a phone interview that he began experimenting with rap in English in 1998. In 2001, shortly after the outbreak of the al-Aqsa Intifada, when he had "to put [himself] under the microscope and reexamine [his] identity," he decided to do rap in Arabic because he wanted his message to be understood by all Palestinian youth. Currently he is a full-time rapper as a member of DAM (Arabic for "to remain," "to last"), together with Suhell Nafar and Mahmood Jrere, the first Palestinian hip-hop group. In November 2006, DAM's first CD *Ihdaa* (Dedication) (Red Circle Music) was released and sold out online in less than two weeks. In January 2007, it was selected as CD of the month by the online magazine *This Week in Palestine* (thisweekinpalestine.com).

In this chapter, I focus on the work of DAM because of their position as pioneers of Palestinian hip-hop as well as their increasing popularity and prominence in the local and international hip-hop scene. Prior to *Ihdaa*, Tamer Nafar produced the album *Stop Selling Drugs*, released locally in 1998. Three years later, Mahmood Jreri joined the two brothers and together they produced the single "Min Irhabi" (Who's the Terrorist?) in 2001. Despite its recent inception, DAM has been performing widely both locally and in Europe and North America, including a show at the renowned Trans Musicales De Rennes Festival in France in December 2006. DAM is featured in *Slingshot Hip Hop*, a documentary on the contemporary Palestinian rap scene by Jackie Salloum that premiered at the 2008 Sundance Film Festival.[2] The group continues to participate in films, events, and collaborative efforts worldwide.

Palestinian hip-hop is an anthropologically rich site. Demographically speaking, it is everywhere; listeners can be found wherever Palestinians live in Israel and the young artists, whose number is estimated at sixty, come from different cities, small towns, and villages (Haifa, Acre, Lydd, Shafa 'Amir, Nazareth, Umm al-Fahim, Baqah al-Gharbiyyah, Jatt, Qalansawah, and 'Iksal). This demographic diversity, especially the emergence of artists from small villages, demands a rethinking of the notion of the ghetto and its location in the history of hip-hop. Scholars usually see the phenomenon as essentially urban, since it is inspired by the general marginalization and disenfranchisement experienced by those who live in urban slums (Saxton, 1995). In Palestinian hip-hop, however, geographical spaces work differently. The experience of the slum is conveyed in angry words performed by artists who live in forsaken Arab neighborhoods in large mixed Arab and Jewish cities, as DAM does in Lydd, as well as by those who live in small villages, like Muhammad Yahya, who is from 'Iksal in the Galilee. For these artists, the Palestinian ghetto in Israel is felt everywhere in their socially and economically confined communities.

I consider these young artists ghetto intellectuals. While in general terms, the word "ghetto" is used to describe marginalized urban spaces, I am using it here to refer to all the Palestinian villages and towns within the State of Israel, including mixed Arab-Jewish areas. These spaces suffer from significant overcrowding as well as inadequate or nonexistent public services, lacking, for example, paved roads and operating sewage systems. A recent report highlights the ghettoization of the Arab Palestinian communities in Israel through the restrictions that the state has placed on urban planning and development in Arab areas, including urban spaces in mixed cities, small villages and towns, and unrecognized villages (Groag and Hartman, nd; Sikkuy, 2003). According to the report, although the Arab Palestinian population is 18.9 percent of the general population, recognized Arab localities are still only 9 percent of all Israeli localities (Groag and Hartman, nd: 2). And within these localities, population density is nearly four times greater than in Jewish localities (Groag and Hartman, nd: 3). Despite the fact that numerous requests to enlarge municipal boundaries have been submitted by the Palestinian Arab communities since the 1950s, only a few have had any response, "and even in those cases, the additional territory allocated has been very limited" (Groag and Hartman, nd: 2). With the ethnic hierarchy of spaces imposed by the state, Arab spaces are ghettos whether they are urban neighborhoods or remote unrecognized villages.

I use the term "intellectuals" to denote the educational backgrounds of these artists. Their songs deal with topics ranging from opposing Zionism, protesting racism and occupation, to songs that speak for and about freedom, gender equality, Arab nationalism, love, and motherhood. This diversity in subject matter demonstrates an intellectual maturity that transcends the limits of poor education characteristic of the ghetto. Many Palestinian hip-hop artists are actually enrolled in hip-hop classes. DJ-Yo, for example, produced his first CD, *Magic Sound*, after graduating from the music institute DJ School in Nazareth. Loop School, also in Nazareth, and many after-school clubs in the Galilee and the Triangle are now offering hip-hop writing and dancing workshops as part of their curricula. Others engage in vibrant discussions, analyses, and critical reviews of local and international hip-hop online (e.g., arabrappers.net).[3] These artists did not drop out of school. Some of them are college students or graduates. For example, Yehya Natour (nineteen years old), from Abnaa Al Ghadab (Anger Boys), another emerging group with four releases and a forthcoming first CD, is currently studying at the Hebrew University in Jerusalem. Lastly, unlike many others in their peer group, some of these artists demonstrate a relatively strong grasp of English, the third language for Palestinians in Israel after Arabic and Hebrew. This level of multilingualism seems to facilitate the success of these artists abroad, especially in Europe and the United States, as the growing number of performances and tours outside the region of both DAM and Arapeyat (the first group of Palestinian women rappers) suggests.

Palestinian hip-hop provides insight into how Palestinian national and cultural identities intersect. Through performance of rap in the national language of Arabic and usage of Palestinian iconography in graffiti, Palestinian hip-hop culture affirms its Palestinianness. Apart from some songs that include direct quotes from poems and speeches in classical Arabic—including a poem by the Palestinian poet Tawfiq Zayyad and part of a speech delivered by former Egyptian leader Gamal Abdel Nasser that both appeared in DAM's *Ihdaa*—all lyrics are in colloquial Palestinian dialect. Adhering to the local spoken dialect, Palestinian rappers embrace linguistic aesthetics common to earlier forms of Palestinian oral narrative. In the long tradition of Palestinian folktales, for example, stories "are told in the Palestinian dialect, with its two major divisions of *fallāḥī* (village speak) and *madanī* (city speech)" (Muhawi and Kanaana, 1989: 7). Due to the demographic diversity of Palestinian rappers, the lyrics are in both *fallāḥī* and *madanī*.

One of the most notable motifs in rap-related graffiti has been Handhala, Naji al-'Ali's famous cartoon character symbolizing Palestinian identity and defiance. Handhala, "bitterness" in Arabic, is a cartoon of a ten-year-old boy that first appeared in *al-Siyasa* newspaper in Kuwait in 1969. The figure turned his back to readers in 1973, and clasped his hands behind him. Describing the meaning of Handhala's pose, Naji al-'Ali says: "He is an icon that stands to watch me from slipping. And his hands behind his back are a symbol of rejection of all the present negative tides in our regions" (quoted in *Colors from Palestine*, 2008).[4] Not only is the image of Handhala painted on walls (both random walls as well as the Separation Wall),[5] it also appears on necklaces, shirts, buttons, and CD covers and tattooed on the bodies of both the artists and their fans.

In the years after the Nakba, Israeli citizenship was imposed on native Palestinians who remained on their lands, and they were eventually given blue Israeli ID documents. This document was supposed to distinguish its holders from other Palestinians, creating the category of the so-called Arab citizens of Israel. A system of military government was established by the new state to handle its relations with this distinct group of citizens and remained in effect until 1966. Using "emergency regulations," this system restricted the movement of the Arab population, isolated them from Jewish Israeli society, limited their employment, and denied them their freedom of expression (Jiryis, 1976: 16). According to Shira Robinson (2003), the nascent state attempted to erase the collective memory, "independent expression—and even public visibility—of its Arab residents" (Robinson, 2003: 394). That Arab Palestinians' path to Israeli citizenship was historically mediated through a military apparatus suggests the limits of Palestinian citizenship in Israel.

The challenges of being a Palestinian citizen in Israel form a recurring theme in Palestinian hip-hop. In the lyrics of numerous songs, the acclaimed Israeli citizenship of Palestinians is portrayed as superficial, merely a blue document that does not translate into actual citizenship. Thematically, this trend is treated through three main channels: a celebration of Palestinian indigeneity, a critique of state laws that discriminate against Palestinians, as well as a critique of the brutal practices of the Israeli police against the Palestinian community.

DELETING THE VIRTUAL GREEN LINE

Prominent examples of the celebration of Palestinian indigeneity appear in DAM's singles "Min Irhabi?" (Who's the Terrorist?) and "Mali Huriye" (I Don't Have Freedom). "Min Irhabi?"[6] was released on the net in 2001 and downloaded more than a million times in less than a month from the website www.arabrap.net.[7] It was distributed for free with *Rolling Stone* magazine in France in 2003 and became a "street" anthem. It was also featured in a compilation in France with Manu Chao, Zebda, Noir Desir, and many other French protest singers (dampalestine.com). At the beginning of this song, DAM insists that Palestinians in Israel are not immigrants, transit passersby, or "present absentees," as the liberal Zionist discourse describes them.[8] Rather, they are natives of the land, and thus their continuous struggle to liberate it from occupation cannot be labeled terrorism:

> Who's the terrorist?
> I'm the terrorist?!
> How am I the terrorist when you've taken my land?
> Who's the terrorist?
> You're the terrorist!
> You've taken everything I own while I'm living in my homeland
> You're killing us like you've killed our ancestors[9]

DAM asserts that Palestinians are deeply attached to their land. In "Holding My Head for My Homeland," DAM suggests that the fact that Palestinians in Israel have become a homeland minority after the depopulation of the land of its native Palestinian majority during the Nakba does not undermine their indigeneity or their connection to the land. These sentiments are conveyed in the image of "boiling blood," which can be read as an expression of deep passion. Framing the question "Why terrorist?!" as rhetorical, the speaker explains that "boiling blood" is an emotional and physical reaction to a foreign attack on one's land:

Why terrorist?! Because my blood is not calm
It's boiling!
Because I hold my head for my homeland
You've killed my loved ones
Now I'm all alone
My parents driven out
But I will remain to shout out
I'm not against peace
Peace is against me

Through the employment of the first-person pronouns "my" and "us" in "my land," "my homeland," and "my loved ones," DAM suggests that the borders and the different documents that separate Palestinians from their land and from each other remain virtual. For these rappers, the occupation of the land is not confined to the territories of the West Bank and Gaza only, but also includes the territories within the Green Line. In light of this, using the first-person pronoun becomes a linguistic tool to symbolically reappropriate Palestinian ownership of the land.

The celebration of Palestinian indigeneity continues in one of DAM's latest releases, "Mali Huriye" (I Have No Freedom, 2006). Here, the rappers of DAM assert that their national identity as Palestinians emerges from their deep physical connection to the land they live on rather than the state they live in:

You won't limit my hope by a
Wall of separation
and if this barrier comes
between me and my land
I'll still be connected to
Palestine
like an embryo to the
umbilical cord
my feet are the roots of the
olive tree
keep on prospering, fathering
and renewing branches

Using the pronoun "you," the rappers in these lines address the state directly with a dismissive tone. The term "my land" affirms Palestinian indigeneity linguistically and "the olive tree" does the same figuratively.

Describing their feet as "roots of the olive tree" that "keep on prospering, fathering and renewing branches," DAM alludes to the fact that the physical existence of Palestinians within the State of Israel is nothing but natural historical continuity. DAM's use of the olive tree as a symbolic expression of

Palestinianness is a continuation of a long tradition. In modern Palestinian poetry, rocks, mountains, and the roots of olive, fig, and palm trees have been significant sources of inspiration for poets, used to affirm their deep-rooted and unbreakable relationship with the soil (Altoma, 1972). This is evident in the works of Fadwa Tuqan, Tawfiq Zayyad, and Samih al-Qasim, to name a few. It is also particularly prominent in the poetry of Mahmoud Darwish, who declares that for him as a poet, the tree stands as a symbol of life's continuity, hope, endurance, and nativeness (Abu Murad, 2004).

Against this image of the firm roots of the ever-growing olive tree, the fragility and temporality of the racist Wall of Separation emerges. By asserting that this wall "won't limit my hope" or cut the "umbilical cord" to Palestine, DAM limits the wall's restrictions to the purely physical realm. The description of the rapper's connection to the land as that of a child to his mother via the "umbilical cord" depicts a natural and spiritual connection that cannot be severed by the erection of a wall. The potential of the wall as a physical form of separation is thus challenged.

Allegorically, one way to read the juxtaposition of the wall versus the olive tree and embryo is in comparison with the juxtaposition of the state to the nation. On the one hand, the wall is a material manifestation of Israeli state regulations, economic policies, and other political machinations. The umbilical cord and the olive tree, on the other hand, are from the realm of nature and convey sustainability, growth, and physical connection. The roots of the olive tree can continue to grow despite the state and the wall, which it can cross under. Thus, if the olive tree, the symbol of Palestinian nationhood, is able to cross the wall, then we can conclude that for DAM, nationhood overpowers the state.

THE ILLEGALITY OF THE LAW

DAM's earlier single "Nwaladit Hon" (Born Here, 2003) and their most recent single "Matlub 'Arabi faqad al-dhakira"[10] (Wanted: An Arab Who Lost His Memory, 2007) also center on the criticism of state practices. Both songs call for the reassessment of Palestinian citizenship within Israel and focus on the racism, oppression, and discrimination faced by Palestinians in their daily lives in the state. They explicitly deal with two of the most prominent frontiers in the struggle for Palestinian civil rights in Israel: land rights and civil rights.

In "Born Here," DAM describes the harsh reality that is everyday life in the Arab neighborhoods of their city, Lydd. The lyrics demonstrate that in these neighborhoods, Israeli citizenship entails garbage accumulating in every street, open sewage, home demolitions, police and army barriers, separation walls and hazardous railroad tracks that constrict Arab residents. It is noteworthy that there are two different versions of this song, one in Arabic and another in Hebrew. The demolition of Palestinian homes within

Israel is a theme that appears in both versions but is treated differently. When I asked Nafar about the difference between the two, he replied: "To describe the problem, I write in Hebrew to inform those in power, so they could hear me. But to solve it, I write in Arabic" (phone interview, October 26, 2006). The Arabic version begins with a call to Palestinian youth. In the first couplet, the rappers of DAM, who admit that these lines echo a preaching tone, invite them to take action against the conflict:

> The first thing we must possess is the initiative
> listen, understand, conclude, you could call it a lecture
> we're in a conflict that we've been stuck in for so long
> they call it conspiracy and lack of awareness is what allows it to remain

The Hebrew version, on the other hand, begins with a call directed at the state. While Lydd, the hometown of DAM, is known to suffer from problems of drug trafficking, the group asserts that the police come to the Arab part of Lydd not to protect the locals, but rather to supervise the demolition of their homes. These demolitions are the product of the state's attempt to place as much land as possible under Jewish control and to limit the expansion of Palestinian communities. Authorities withhold permits to build and repair Arabs homes, thus making many of them illegal and subject to demolition.

Referring to the heavy presence of the police in their neighborhood as a quotidian morning scene, DAM highlights not only the commonality of home demolitions in their area, but also the strict disciplinary and policing attitude of the state:

> Of a dove trying to survive under the hawk's regime
> [sound of page ripped] let's try something more optimistic:
> each day I wake up and see like 1000 cops
> maybe they came to arrest a dealer . . . (he's over here, over here, oh no they came to destroy his neighbor's home)

The video clip for "Born Here" visually depicts the sentiments conveyed in both versions of the song. Under the sponsorship of Shatil's Mixed Cities Project,[11] the Hebrew version of the song was produced as a video clip by director Juliano Mer-Khamis. The clip begins with a close-up of two Israeli policemen questioning the members of DAM while getting out of a car. Later when the cops realize that a camera is videotaping the scene, they ask the person behind the camera to stop shooting. The rest of the clip, which was filmed in Lydd, includes images of checkpoints patrolled by Israeli soldiers, a bulldozer demolishing a house, and local youth protesting in the street while being videotaped by military surveillance cameras.

Currently, home demolition is one of the most visible and harsh violations of the civil rights of Palestinians in Israel. While home demolitions in
unrecognized villages have received relatively more attention, DAM's work
highlights their occurrence in mixed Arab-Jewish cities. The lyrics of the
Hebrew version of DAM's song question the legality of state actions and
criticize the institutionalized discrimination against its Palestinian "virtual"
citizens, while the Arabic version reminds Palestinian youth of their agency
and asks them to work actively against the problems they face:

Hebrew Version

> Here I build my home and here you have destroyed my home
> And if this is not legal what about yours, my cousin?! . . .
> I'm trying to build a home and what is built for me is found
> In do re mi or will be found in a place with lots
> Of people with promises that will be the light at the end of the
>   tunnel
> but that is just a bulldozer or another train running over

Arabic Version

> Oh man! One hundred people were in a demonstration against home
>   demolition
> the other day, ninety of them were Jewish!
> If you stand today to watch how they are transferring your neighbor,
> Tomorrow they [state authorities] will approach your house,
> and your neighbor will stand in your place.
> The chain is long, but has an end.
> Failure to the impotent power that sees but fears
> If terror lives in us, our children will not live
> so, what do we say to the weak circle?? Farewell

In rapping about the demolition of Palestinian homes in Israel, both songs
question the legality of the Jewish state in the first place. For example, in the
lines "Here I build my home and here you have destroyed my home / And
if this is not legal what about yours, my cousin?!" DAM calls for rethinking
the creation of Jewish homes on lands wrenched from Palestinians as being
at the expense of Palestinians and their homes destroyed during the Nakba.
By addressing these lines to "my cousin" of the Abrahamic story, that is, the
Jew, DAM mocks the un-cousinly behavior of Jews in the Zionist movement
and their colonization of Palestine.

    DAM continues to question the rationale behind home demolitions
in another section of the Arabic version of the song. In the lines "Within
here are those who kill without paying the price and those who destroy /

The people who make the mistake of building on their land," the construction of Palestinian homes is seen as a natural given right of the natives,
and thus any punishment for it is invalid. As these lines criticize basic
assumptions of the legal system in Israel, they question the legitimacy of
state laws and regulations.

In response to a proposal to draft Palestinians into national civil service,
the chairman of Baladna: The Association for Arab Youth, Nadim Nashef,
contacted DAM and asked them to compose a song for the campaign.[12]
A month later, on November 8, 2007, DAM released the single "Wanted:
An Arab Who Lost His Memory." The single was aired on Arabic-speaking
radio stations in Israel, such as al-Shams in Nazareth, as part of a campaign
against the proposal, and received wide coverage in both the Arabic and
Hebrew media. When asked about his choice to commission this particular
art form, Nashef said: "[DAM] is a very famous group" and "We chose this
time to express our protests through art, to reach the youth through their own
language and not by giving speeches" (ynetnews, November 7, 2007).

The lyrics of this song adopt an ironic tone to the state's call for civil
service for Palestinians in Israel. The song opens with a mocking call for
an Arab who lost his memory, articulated in heavily accented Arabic such
as that spoken by an Ashkenazi Hebrew speaker. The commanding tone,
the mispronounced formal Arabic of the speaker, and the background sound
of a military march give the impression that the speaker is a high military
official. The song mocks the state for not giving Palestinians their rights
and yet making demands of them. For DAM, the absence of Palestinian
rights in Israel is evident even in the most basic services, such as garbage
collection, where Palestinians are virtually invisible:

Are we really citizens? Will the civil service lead us anywhere?
Even from the map of the municipal waste collectors, our neighborhoods
    are deleted

Other lines highlight the deficiency of enlisting in civil service:

What do you want me to do in the civil service in schools?
Shall I teach them how we live?
Or from the beginning to teach them how to say ahlan,[13] hummus,
    chips, by heart?
Or do you want me to work in a hospital? What will I do there?
Open a tourism office, and for every Arab that is born, I will import
    a Jew from overseas,
or maybe I will serve in one of these retirement homes . . . As if we
    ever get to live to this age?
If yes, then it must be an Israeli structural error

These lyrics emphasize that Palestinians will not improve their status or gain rights by engaging in civil service in Israel. On the contrary, such service will lead to further marginalization and disenfranchisement of their communities. For DAM, civil service might mean teaching Israeli school children how to say "*ahlan, hummus, chips*, by heart." This line ridicules the superficial and Orientalizing culture of dialogue with Arabs that Israeli Jews practice. The lines about working in Israeli hospitals, but only to "import a Jew from overseas" for every newborn Arab baby, frame civil service as ridiculous, but also self-destructive because it promotes Zionist ideology.

Although the scene of a Palestinian youth working in an Israeli hospital to import Jews and monitor the number of Arab children born is a parody of civil service, it is a critical allusion to real citizenship laws in Israel. According to Elia Zureik (1979), Israel has been waging a "demographic battle" since its inception to maintain a Jewish majority in the state. The 1950 Law of Return and the 1952 Israeli Nationality Act make "any Jew anywhere in the world . . . entitled to Israeli citizenship. Palestinian Arabs, on the other hand, who had been residing in the country for generations and whose ancestors had been there for centuries, were denied this automatic right of citizenship which was granted to Jewish settlers" (Zureik, 1979: 106). The 1953 National Insurance Law was meant to encourage Jews to have larger families through financial benefits, but was repealed when it became apparent that Arabs were disproportionately benefiting from it because of the large size of their families (ibid.). In its place, the government passed the Discharged Soldiers Law to guarantee that primarily Jewish families, whose parents are conscripted into the military, would benefit from this family allowance "since most Arabs (except for the Druze) do not serve in the armed forces" (ibid.).[14] By contextualizing their call against civil service within a critical evocation of these laws and policies, DAM disputes the logic of defining citizenship within the ethnic hierarchy of the Jewish state.

The last three lines in the lyrics question the very possibility of Palestinians growing to an old age in Israel. DAM deploys human rights rhetoric, but also evokes the fragility of Palestinian existence in Israel. By asking the rhetorical question, "As if we ever get to live to this age?" DAM implies that the right to live is not to be taken for granted. By characterizing Palestinians who survive to old age as an "Israeli structural error," DAM highlights the state's direct control over Palestinian life expectancy. In the shadow of the killing of Palestinian youths in October 2000, DAM's question becomes an allusion to the threat of death at the hands of the Israeli police.

Though some Palestinians might consider these lyrics too subversive, they do express an overall sentiment of existential fear that came to the surface among the young generation of Palestinians in Israel after October 2000. This existential concern is articulated explicitly and dramatically in the work of other young Palestinian artists as well. This is the case, for example, with a painting titled *Happy New Nakba*, by Salam Diab, a Palestinian artist from Tamra. The painting features a procession of fourteen martyrs and was painted in 2001 in memoriam of the thirteen Palestinians killed during the demonstrations of October 2000. Diab explained that the identity of the fourteenth martyr in the painting represents the victim of the next demonstration, and no one knows yet who this will be; it could be the artist himself or any other Palestinian who lives in Israel and tries to protest (personal interview, August 2002 at 13 Live Bullets exhibit in Tel Aviv).

BLUE ANGELS OF DEATH

Police brutality is another recurrent theme in Palestinian hip-hop. Its most dramatic expression appears in DAM's 2003 Hebrew single "Innocent Criminals." The song is a duet with the Israeli singer Aviv Gefen, produced as a video clip by Gefen. The clip features a scene of Tamer Nafar bleeding after being physically attacked by a young woman wearing an Israeli military uniform. This scene is a fictional reproduction of a very possible encounter between the police and Palestinians in Israel. The realism of this scene is echoed in the lyrics where DAM alludes to the October 2000 deaths: "Jews protest, the police take out hickory sticks / Arabs protest, the police take souls." After this criticism of the unequal treatment of the police, the song proceeds to assert that "there is no value for Arab souls," and when an Arab soul rises up, "it is faced by rubber bullets." When the clip first appeared, it faced severe criticism from Israeli media outlets and despite the popularity of Gefen, the song won limited broadcast on Hebrew radio channels due to its political content.[15]

MWR is another hip-hop group that protests Israeli police brutality against Palestinians in Israel. The group, whose initials stand for the names of its three members, Mahmoud Shalaby, Waseem Aker, and Richard Shaby, began to rap about the epidemic of unemployment and drug abuse among the youth in the Arab neighborhoods of their hometown Acre in 2001. MWR is best known for its 2001 hit single "Ashanak Arabi" (Because You're an Arab). In it, the group complains about beatings and harassment from Israeli police, who stop them to check their ID cards that list a nationality (Muslim, Christian, or Druze in the case of most Arabs). The group shouts, "A policeman sees me, immediately arrests me, asks me some racist questions, and why? Because I'm an Arab. Let me live. I'm just trying to live." The lyrics state

> Wherever you go they want you to show your ID—
> Without cause Why can't we be equal?
> Why are we not treated as humans?

Instead of setting free the most beautiful doves of peace
They invented effective devices to kill

MWR presents police harassment as the norm. They thus challenge the official narrative of the State, such as that offered by the Or Commission that investigated the October 2000 killings, that reduces police brutality against its Palestinian residents to isolated exceptions and the fault of individual officers.[16]

TOWARD A PALESTINIAN HIP-HOP MANIFESTO OF CITIZENSHIP

With their celebratory lyrics for Palestinian nationhood and defiant songs against home demolition, civil service, and police brutality, DAM enhances the existing discourse among Palestinians regarding Palestinian citizenship in Israel. Although not formally elected officials, DAM members offer a political manifesto of citizenship based simultaneously on Palestinian nationalism, and civil and human rights. This manifesto echoes similar sentiments expressed by other Palestinian political scholars, NGO activists, and intellectuals who are currently working on the formulation of a collective vision of Palestinians in Israel.

DAM's lyrics mirror to some extent three recent documents the Haifa Declaration, the *Democratic Constitution, and the Future Vision of the Palestinian Arabs in Israel*. But unlike the printed documents, DAM relies on the performed spoken word and uses the stage to vocally articulate its manifesto. As a hip-hop group engaged in direct and face-to-face interaction with the audience, DAM creates an open dialogue on the subject. George Lipsitz argues that:

> Popular music is nothing if not dialogic, the product of an ongoing historical conversation in which no one has the first or last word. The traces of the past that pervade the popular music of the present amount to more than mere chance: they are not simply juxtaposition of incompatible realities. They reflect a dialogic process, one embedded in collective history and nurtured by the ingenuity of artists interested in fashioning icons of opposition. (Lipsitz, 1990: 99)

Keeping in mind that the question of Palestinian citizenship in Israel has been a subject of internal dialogue among Palestinians themselves since 1948, DAM's use of the stage as an open platform to rap about that question expands the circle of those involved and the vocabulary used in the ongoing historical conversation.

An example for this discursive expansion is evident in DAM's collaboration with the female rappers of Arapeyat.[17] The duet "al-Huriye Unt'a" (which literarily translates as Freedom is Female, but has been translated by DAM as Freedom for My Sisters) features a debate in rap about sexism and women's rights between Tamer Nafar from DAM and female rapper Safa' Hathoot from Arapeyat. The title draws a direct connection between women's liberation and freedom, and the lyrics engage a larger social discourse on the location of Arab women's bodies in relation to cultural practices and social and political struggles.

The song begins with lines that echo the title where the speaker equates the oppression of Palestinian women with the discriminatory practices of U.S. imperialism and Zionist colonialism. Addressing Arab men in particular, the speaker calls on them to rethink their attitude toward Palestinian women:

> Discrimination, we all suffer from it
> Americans discriminate against the Arabs
> Zionists discriminate against the Arabs
> you know what, Arabs, if we discriminate against each other
> then others will discriminate against us too
> These words go out to all our mothers and sisters
> who got lost in our customs, primitive and stupid customs

In the second part of the song, Hathoot proceeds to demand women's liberation from the injustice of sexism. In a monologue, she recounts how sexism controls the bodies of women through subjugation to physical and emotional abuse and exclusion from the public sphere. Hathoot draws a direct link between the fate of the future generations of the Arab nation to the liberation of her own body. With an assertive voice, Hathoot reminds Nafar that because women give birth to men, any project of national liberation, struggle for equality, or definition of citizenship is inherently a project that is inclusive of women:

> The Arabic woman's life is written
> what should she do, where should she go, it's all written
> She's like a wounded bird in the sky
> scared to land because of the hunters
> imprisoned in her own house, thirsty for freedom
> And can drink nothing but her own tears
> then they dare ask me: why do I cry?
> Because I'm a body without a spirit
> you abuse it and then I'm wrong while u are right?
> Who the hell are you to tell me how to behave?
> Asking me "where r u going?"
> What? You forgot where u came from? You came from me
> but from now on I'm going to be independent

and the new generation will follow suit
We should fight for our rights, let men ask questions
but let our sisters answer

Echoing Hathoot's tone of independence, Nafar recognizes his role as an agent who contributes to the oppression of women in his own society. Thus, he offers the song as a formal apology to all women:

This is for you, the woman, the mother of the house
This is from me, the man,
The one who builds walls of limitation around you

In this artistic dialogue, both Hathoot and Nafar emphasize the link between national liberation and women's liberation and present this relationship as one of mutual interest. Demonstrating that both are equally invested in nationalism and feminism, their collaboration breaks the stereotypes about women rappers as feminist voices using rap to combat male rappers' sexism (Rose, 1994). In this collaborative work, Hathoot is not positioned as an opponent to Nafar, as much as the latter is portrayed as a feminist. In addition to this single, Hathoot, together with the second member of Arapeyat, Nahwa Abdel-Al, have independently produced several singles that deal with a variety of topics ranging from women's rights to the racism of the Israeli state.

For over sixty years the state of Israel has been struggling with how to treat the Palestinians within its borders. This dilemma intensified after October 2000. Alarmed by October's posttraumatic reaction and the sociopolitical volatility of the Palestinian community at that time, rushed attempts were made to find an immediate solution for the question of citizenship. These attempts produced two contradictory documents in late 2000.

One document was an unsolicited report presented to then prime minister Ehud Barak by twenty-six researchers that has been described as a "radical, post-Zionist departure from the accepted dogmas of Israel" (Rabinowitz and Abu-Baker, 2005: 13–14). The second document, known as the Herzeliyya Report, "frames the relationship between the Palestinian minority and the Jewish majority primarily as a demographic struggle, then goes on to detail the means by which hegemony can be perpetuated. Explicitly seeking to reduce the role of Palestinian citizens in shaping the character of the state, it calls for limiting the rights of Palestinian individuals and communities" (ibid.).

While both documents contemplated whether to include or control Palestinians in Israel, DAM protests against the very category of "Palestinian citizens of Israel" created by the state and embraced by the Jewish majority. The group's celebration of Palestinian indigeneity and nationhood in "Born Here" and "I Have No Freedom" contends that Palestinians cannot be viewed as disempowered citizens if they are not recognized as natives of the land in the first place. Hence, for DAM, Palestinian citizenship in Israel should be reconsidered in terms of rights rather than grace.

DAM also challenges the state's dominant discourse about military service as a condition for full citizenship. By condemning discriminatory laws and police brutality and refuting the concept of civil service as an alternative to military service, the lyrics of "Born Here," "Innocent Criminals," and "Wanted: An Arab Who Lost His Memory" question the logic of citizenship in Israel. To date, Palestinian citizenship has been framed in Israeli governmental and juridical circles by linking rights to duties. In the popular political discourse, Palestinians are told that they do not have their full rights as citizens because they do not serve in the Israeli army or, in other words, that they did not fulfill their duties to the state (Rouhana and Sultany, 2003). However, Laurence Louër argues that while the Israeli state adopted the Greek city-state system, which views the ability to bear arms as "the criterion which fundamentally defines citizenship," it exempted most Arabs from enlisting in the Israeli military (Louër, 2007: 13).[18] The Israeli state thus inserted questions of loyalty into the equation. Apart from the Druze and some Bedouins who were recruited into special units to act as trackers, frontier guards, scouts, or workers behind enemy lines, military officials "had no wish to risk the recruitment of soldiers stigmatized by the permanent suspicion of treachery" (Louër, 2001: 11–13). Rhoda Kanaaneh notes that ID-less Bedouins in the Naqab who have served in the military have not been recognized as citizens by the state. This suggests that even military service does not garner citizenship for Palestinians (Kanaaneh, 2009: 28). Making civil service, regarded as inferior to military service, a condition to full citizenship is thus problematic. As DAM's "Wanted: An Arab Who Lost His Memory" demonstrates, apart from perpetuating their own marginality, civil service does no service for the Palestinians in Israel.

Because DAM uses the relatively new form of hip-hop to articulate a vision of Palestinian citizenship different from that currently promoted by the state, their political potential cannot be disregarded. Since DAM is able to reach a young, dynamic audience who could generate new discourses, it could potentially create a new public sphere. Because hip-hop performances are a direct form of communication where the audience uses the microphone to respond to the calls of the MC, there is fertile ground for a collective communicative collaboration (Perry, 2004). If DAM can make the audience participate on the dance floor, it is possible that this could translate into wider public participation.

The phenomenon of spoken-word-based political participation has something of a historical precedence in the widespread and populist poetry festivals of the 1950s. Organized like village weddings to which everyone is invited, these poetry festivals were open to the public and offered traditional lyrical poetry to the large audience. However, these festivals were short-lived since Palestinian towns and villages were under Israeli military rule; and as literary-political and populist occasions, the festivals were often replete with danger for those who attended them (Furani, 2004). Palestinian hip-hop, with its public performance, is in some ways a cultural revival of these Palestinian poetry festivals. However, Palestinian hip-hop seems to have a potential to last longer and leave its mark in history. Technological advancements in the dissemination of mass popular culture via the internet allow hip-hop wider exposure to an international audience and transcendence beyond many forms of state restriction and censorship.

CONCLUSION

The increasing popularity of Palestinian hip-hop and the emergence of several rappers in Israel as well as in the Palestinian Occupied Territories and the Diaspora call special attention to this form of lyrical movement. Khaled Furani (2004) notes that in the years following the Nakba, poets were widely heard. A sense of urgency prevailed in their poetry, and their need to write for the "masses" pushed them to keep with modern social realism then prevalent in other Arab countries and to use the *'amūdi* (pillar-based) form. The question becomes: is rap the new *'amūdi* form that allows Palestinian youth to express their concerns using social realism? DAM's rapping about citizenship suggests that the answer is yes.

The emergence of the Palestinian rapper as a historical figure, both pan-Arab and transnational, is a trend that needs to be addressed in future research. DAM has collaborated with the Algerian French group MBS since 2005 and Nafar comments that: "As an Arab minority living in the ghetto, our immigrant Algerian brothers and sisters in France have a similar experience to ours here" (phone interview, October 20, 2007). In addition to the global context of this phenomenon, its local historical roots must be investigated. Maha Nassar observes that despite the political and geographical isolation from the rest of the Arab world, Palestinians in Israel during the 1950s "expressed their concern with their status as Arabs in Israel, but they were increasingly aware of their place as Arabs in the Middle East and closely followed events in the region" (Nassar, 2006: 116). This trend was manifested in editorials in the daily newspapers, such as *al-Ittihad*, and in poetry that expressed pan-Arab sentiments. Future research should explore the similarities and differences between the roles of Palestinian journalists and poets of the 1950s and those of the rappers of the late 1990s and early 2000s.

Future studies of Palestinian hip-hop must examine its relationship to other forms of Palestinian cultural production. Much as the question of citizenship played a role in the production of different forms of Palestinian cinema (al-Qattan, 2006), Palestinian hip-hop varies according to where it is produced. These differences are related to economic resources, publicity, restricted mobility and access to a transnational audience. Unlike Palestinian rappers in the United States, such as Iron Sheik, Free the P Project, and Patriarch, Palestinian hip-hop groups in Israel and the Occupied Palestinian territories, including DAM and Ramallah Underground, grew through personal and communal efforts. They mostly relied on private financial resources and ran their shows single-handedly. They produced their music with limited resources, or as Nafar puts it: "There are no platforms for us in the first place. And sometimes we have to physically build them ourselves in order to stand and do our thing" (phone interview, October 20, 2007).

NOTES

Since my interview with Tamer Nafar, DAM's work has developed extensively. In addition to a busy schedule of international touring with the film *Slingshot Hip-Hop*, DAM started their own production company, Shamatan Production, in November 2009. Group member Suhell Nafar released his first Arabic reggae single titled "Oh Gaza" in January 2009. Mahmood Jrere also released his own single, "Letters," in April 2009. Throughout 2009, DAM collaborated with other Palestinian and Arab rappers in the Diaspora including in duets with Shadia Mansour in London, Ragtop in L.A, and The Narcicyst in Canada.

1. Other recent analyses of Palestinian rap include writings by David McDonald (2006) and Sunaina Maira (2008).

2. Since the writing of this chapter, the film *Slingshot Hip Hop* has been released—it offers much material for future analysis, particularly its international reception and its focus on the collaborations of artists across borders.

3. On November 15, 2006, I accessed the site www.arabrappers.net. At the time, many of the artists were active on the site that was described as "the biggest Arabic hip-hop society in the world." Today, the site is no longer functioning, but the artists are active through their own websites, MySpace, YouTube, and Facebook pages.

4. For more about the cartoons of Naji al-'Ali, see www.resistanceart.com.

5. The Wall of Separation refers to the barrier built around and through parts of the West Bank. See the introduction to this volume for more details.

6. The transliteration of the song titles is as it appears on the CD or as circulated by DAM on their website www.dampalestine.com, unless otherwise indicated.

7. This website is no longer active.

8. This term is part of the Absentee's Property Laws (first version in 1950), which declare that anyone who left the country in 1948 is an absentee, and that his/her property comes under the control of the state. This law was used only against Arabs, even in reference to people who remained in the country but were compelled to leave their land. These individuals are called "present absentees." This is also the Hebrew title of David Grossman's book, *Sleeping on a Wire* (Tel Aviv: Nokhehim Nifkadim, 1992).

9. The translations of lyrics are the author's unless otherwise noted.

10. The transliteration of the titles of these singles is by the author.

11. Shatil is a branch of the New Israel Fund that aims at promoting democracy, tolerance, and social justice in Israel. See www.shatil.org.il/site/static. asp?apd=27&scd=98.

12. Baladna ("Our Land" in Arabic) was established in 2000 and officially given NGO status in 2001. Since then they have set up thirteen youth groups across Israel, established an international network of youth exchanges, seminars and workshops, and a leadership training program. For more information, see http://www.momken.org/.

13. "Hello" or "welcome" in Arabic.

14. Family benefits were equalized for Arabs and Jews by the Rabin government in 1997, but subsequent governments have attempted to reintroduce disparities through emergency budgets (Kanaaneh, 2009: 147).

15. Gaya is another Israeli group that had a duet in Arabic and Hebrew with DAM titled "This Land." They argue that Hebrew-speaking radio stations boycotted their single as well as this song for political reasons. See http://www.ynet.co.il/articles/0,7340,L-2800702,00.html.

16. For more on the Or Commission, see http://www.adalah.org/eng/commission.php.

17. The name Arapeyat is a play on the Arabic term 'Arabiyyat, meaning Arab females, and rap.

18. Formally, Arabs are not exempt from military service. Yet, it is up to the Ministry of Defense to choose to enforce the law of compulsory service.

II

MEMORY AND ORAL HISTORY

Figure 3. A girls' choir with an accordionist at the celebrations of the tenth anniversary of the State of Israel, organized by the military government in Umm al-Fahim, 1958. Photograph courtesy of Moshe Pridan, Government Press Office.

FOUR

GENDERING THE NARRATIVES OF
THREE GENERATIONS OF
PALESTINIAN WOMEN IN ISRAEL

Isis Nusair

January 1, 2004 was supposed to be my third day of research at the Israel
State Archives in Jerusalem. I arrived at the archives early in the morning
and left my identity card at the front desk. On my way to the reading room,
I was stopped by the guard who asked for my passport. I told him that I
left it at a friend's house where I was staying and suggested I could go get
it. I showed him my U.S. faculty and social security cards but he suspected
that I had a fake Israeli identity card and decided to call the police. Within
less than ten minutes, I found myself escorted for the first time in my life
to the police station. After a brief interrogation by the head of the fraud
department, I was cleared and walked back to the archives to continue my
work. The head of the fraud department told me after clearing my record
with the Ministry of Interior that the security guards in the Jerusalem area
are extremely sensitive to national security issues.

I started my research on the gendered politics of location of three
generations of Palestinian women in Israel as Israel celebrated fifty years of
independence and Palestinians commemorated fifty years since the Nakba. My
grandmother, Rahija Farah, was the third person I interviewed. Unfortunately,
she suffered a heart attack a few hours after the interview and died at her
home at the age of seventy-six. My grandmother's death—together with the
questioning of my identity at the archives—hover over this research and
raise questions about the personal and collective consequences of remembering and narrating the past, and about who is "entitled" to access historical

75

documents and write history (Ueno, 2004). The absence of Palestinian women in both Israeli and Palestinian official history and the majority of academic writing is troubling since it renders them invisible and makes gender-neutral assumptions about them (Fleischmann, 2003). My analysis offers a continuum for tracing major events in their lives and the meanings they attach to these events. I focus on their politics of location, which are the historical, geographic, cultural, psychic, and imaginative boundaries that provide the ground for political self-definition (Mohanty, 2003).

I conducted seventy open-ended interviews via a snowball approach with Palestinian women in the Galilee and Triangle regions.[1] Generational units in this context bring themselves into being through an active identification with particular shared historical events whereby each generation bears the imprint of those events (Collins, 2004; Mannheim, 1952). It also provides a critical examination of private and public discourses for these constitute the universe of meaning within which generational identities are negotiated (Collins, 2004). I argue that women from all three generations were marked, albeit differently, by particular sociopolitical events that affected how they looked at themselves, and how they defined their generational experience and relation to the State of Israel. The experiences of each generation of women during their adolescences and early twenties in particular seem to make a lasting impact on their outlooks in their later years.

LIVING AND NOT LIVING IN THE STATE OF ISRAEL

First-generation women were born in the 1920s and 1930s during the British Mandate of Palestine and came of age with the creation of the Israeli state. The majority of their narratives centered on two themes: how difficult life was before 1948, especially for women who worked the land (Nashat and Tucker, 1999; Sayigh, 1979), and how "life was turned upside down" during and in the aftermath of the 1948 war. They started their narratives from their location as mothers—their marriages often at an early age, and their multiple pregnancies and births.[2] The women, especially those who worked the land and who became internally displaced in the aftermath of the 1948 war, emphasized their loss of both home and land.[3] Samira from Ma'lul, born in 1928 and currently living in Jaffa (adjacent to Nazareth), said, "We departed for Nazareth with nearly nothing. The Jews entered and occupied. . . . We used to go back to Ma'lul and pick carob and sell to those who had pigs. We used to infiltrate and steal the food that we left behind. . . . People are allowed to go there today only on [Israel's] Independence Day."[4] She described how she lived with her family in a rented room in Nazareth for eight years and how she had hopes to return. Hasna, born in 1928 in Kufur Manda, mentioned how she became internally displaced and lived in zinc houses in Nazareth in the aftermath of the war. "I used to breastfeed with bitterness. We left the way God created us. We were unable to take anything with us. We fled to Lebanon and stayed at a camp in B'albak for one year and two months. There were people [refugees] as much as there is hair on your head."

For women who did not become internally displaced and who did not work the land, the emphasis was on the dispersal of their families and the hardships they had to endure as the economic situation deteriorated during and in the aftermath of the war. Rasmiyya, born in 1921 in Nazareth, described how her husband, a policeman with the British, lost his job in 1947. "For five years he was without a job. It was an extremely difficult period and I had to sell my gold . . . Refugees came [to our neighborhood] from Ma'lul and al-Mjaidil, and they had nothing.[5] We had some stored food and I used to help out. We needed someone to help us, though!" She emphasized how shy and humiliated she felt when seeking aid. "During the first four to five years we had a very hard time. . . . In 1952, I worked in the cigarette factory. My youngest [and fifth] child was two years old. I was supposed to be a teacher. After a few months the cigarette factory closed, and I was without a job. I hated the Jews because everything in our lives was turned upside down."

The majority of first-generation women worked inside their homes, had minimal education, did not speak Hebrew, and their narratives emphasized their alienation from the public sphere and from Israeli state politics more generally. Rasmiyya said, "Israel is better for us, we have rights and they help us. If only the politics were different and they would love the Arabs. They are good if you do not get close to them. We did not see much in Nazareth, especially us, the women. No Jew lived in Nazareth. . . . I did not interfere in their business; I did not have any interaction with them." Myassar, born in 1933 in Nazareth, added, "Although I live in Israel, I do not define myself as Israeli. There is discrimination and we do not live like they do. It is as if I live and do not live in this state and this bothers me. . . . The army was here from 1948 until 1966. They harassed the population and we were not allowed to leave without permits." The past and the present intertwined in Myassar's narrative as she made direct links between her living under Israeli military rule and Israel's continued occupation of the West Bank and Gaza. "Today, we understand the state. We do not interfere in their affairs but I hear that the situation in the West Bank and Gaza is not any better. The oppression continues. . . . If there is peace, the doors will open and we could come and go. It is really disturbing that the situation is like this, oppressive. Democracy, where is democracy?"

Ghanem (2001: 9) argues that Israel relies in its dealing with Palestinians on two policy elements: "a maximum ethnic component and a limited democratic one, where the ethnic component emphasizes the superiority of the Jews in all spheres" (see Dowty, 1991; Peretz, 1991; Rekhess, 1991; Meyer, 1982). Robinson (2005) adds that the democratic and egalitarian policy is no more than a verbal ethos as the Israeli regime did not want nor did it strive to achieve integration or absorption of the Arab population into the Jewish community; the overriding objective was to control that population. With Jewish interests embedded in the concept of security, the state simultaneously reinforces its Jewish identity and emphasizes the separateness from non-Jews in the country (Rouhana, 1997). These exclusionary ideologies and practices are framed and legitimized by patterns of national and gender inequality (Sasson-Levy, 2003; Kimmerling, 2001; Helman, 1999; Herzog, 2004b, 1998; Yuval-Davis, 1987).

Many women described how they "have seen a lot" and the effect that had on their health and well-being (see Sered, 1999). Some women even wondered how they were still sane. Rasmiyya mentioned how she had a stroke at age fifty-one, and has had high blood pressure since the age of thirty-six. "There was too much fear, tension, and worries. I was sick from what we went through and from the changes that took place." The narratives of first-generation women reflected their politicized consciousness. They produced the past from the vantage point of their particular gendered location and generational experience. In addition, they anchored their location in their communities and used the personal as a site of resistance and empowerment. This gave many of them considerable satisfaction in the improvements they witnessed in their lives, especially in regard to the education of their children. It also gave them pride in the dignity they maintained during turbulent times, particularly in the early years following the creation of the State of Israel.

MILITARY RULE AND THE POLITICS OF EDUCATION AND MARRAIGE

Second-generation women were born in the 1940s and 1950s as the Israeli state was being created, and came of age under Israeli military rule. The majority followed a similar pattern of defining their identity and location, and going back in time to describe major political events that shaped their lives. Although the women's narratives intertwined the political with the personal, the descriptions and analyses of their private lives always came at the end of the interview. It was at this point in their narratives that they chose to analyze the causal relations between non-state familial and state-created political limitations and the impact of both sets of limitations on their lives.

Many second-generation women focused on the story of their parents in order to set the analytical ground for their own experiences. They started with their early childhood memories and traced the effects of certain sociopolitical events on their lives, especially their opportunities during girlhood and early womanhood. Many used the words "under siege" and "crushed" to describe their feelings while growing up. Their narratives reflected their awareness and engagement with national politics even though they were only girls when the Israeli state was created and were often kept physically close to their homes by their families. As young girls, they witnessed the effect of the military administration rule on the ability of their families to work, travel, or engage in politics freely. Many considered the state as constituting an imposed presence in their lives, and as defining them as alien. Some went as far as describing it as occupation.

Schooling was another area where they experienced control and oppression, and understood what it means to speak up or keep silent. Israeli state control of the elementary and high school system was designed by the officials of the Department of Education to create a new ethnic identity, that of the "de-Palestinized" Israeli Arabs where their culture was presented as consonant with the history of the State of Israel (Kimmerling, 2001). Nahida, born in 1947 in Nazareth, looked back and recounted her experiences in the state-run public school in the mid-1950s. "They used to stress the story of Israel and the importance of Independence Day. There were celebrations and flags. I remember how a girl in my class was asked to sing Hatikva for a delegation from the Ministry of Education (see Robinson, 2003).[6] She stood and sang [in Hebrew] and she had a beautiful voice." Nahida stressed the silencing impact of this event, "We knew we could not say anything, and that we were forbidden from expressing our views because our parents could get in trouble."

The narratives of second-generation women reflected their exclusion from the new Israeli collective identity. Baruch Kimmerling (2001) argues that during the first decade of the formation of the state, a huge effort was made to create a new collective identity and Israeli nationalism. A new state civil religion was created with its own cults, ceremonies, calendar, holidays, and commemorations that were constructed, first around the military, and later around the Holocaust (Kimmerling 2001; Aronoff, 1991; Liebman and Don-Yihya, 1983), and fixed the Yishuv culture as the only source of political and cultural capital (Kimmerling, 2001). This so-called melting pot was supposed to incorporate most of the newly immigrated (de-Arabized) Jews, but not the Palestinians, who were excluded from the new Israeliness, through mechanisms of geographical segregation, separation, and confinement (Kimmerling, 2001; Torstrick 2000; Lustick 1980).

Sumayya, born in 1944 in Nazareth, recounted how she grew up under Israeli military rule. "During the military administration period, people were without jobs. They needed permission from the military governor to work. They [Israeli Jews] took the land from Nazareth to build Nazareth Elite and people started to demonstrate against land confiscation . . . My father was fired from his job because he was a Communist. We were young and my mother had to sell her gold and the house furniture." Sumayya added, "People did not know what was about to happen, and they were afraid for their daughters. . . . Fear and poverty is what I remember about this period. I remember how my father used to cry." Sumayya made clear that the aftermath of the 1948 war, compounded with the imposition of Israeli military rule, brought fear, uncertainty, and poverty into her life. This resulted, in her estimation, in her inability to continue her high school education and her early marriage at the age of sixteen-and-a-half (see Hart, 2008). Sumayya's narrative, as well as the narratives of many women from her generation, reflected the sense of siege that she lived through during that period. She added, "The refugees who came from Ma'lul lived opposite our house. People received them well. Their kids went to school and people thought that it was a short and passing period. People were confined. They were afraid that new people were coming to our neighborhood. They accepted the refugees but did not know what would happen next. . . . We were living as if in a ghetto without openness to the outside world."

Soon after the establishment of the state, a military bureaucratic mechanism infiltrated and extended tight control over Palestinians in Israel from 1948–1966 (Cohen, 2006; Sa'di, 2003; Kimmerling, 2001; Segev, 1986; Jiryis, 1976). Yussur, born in Tarshiha in 1940, described the changing political reality during and in the aftermath of the 1948 war, and the effect it had on her family and life. She said, "After two to three months following the fall of the city, and as my brother and I were still outside [in Lebanon], the [Israeli] army came and took my father. . . . got my mother out of our house and occupied it." Yussur goes on to describe the pressure exerted on her father by the Israeli military authorities to cooperate with them (see Cohen, 2006). She said, "There were always confrontations with the [Israeli] military governor because my father was active. . . . During the elections, they [the Israeli authorities] needed the votes of the Arabs and my father was with MAPAI. This is not because he supported the occupation, the party or its policy, but because he wanted authority (she used the Hebrew term *samkhut*) so that he could have influence." As Yussur described her father's cooperation with the Israeli authorities, she separated her political position from his. She added, "My hand would be cut and I would not vote for MAPAI. The Jewish National Fund would substitute every ten dunums of land confiscated for only two. My father used to pay from his pocket to help people, and the [Israeli] authorities bought out some of the people he helped and they later worked against him." Yusssur continued to describe how in the late 1950s the Israeli authorities came and told her father that his name is very clean and that his family outside is large and should work for them. "They told him that in return, they would give money to his son, and appoint his daughter to a job with a very good salary. He was told to go home and consult with his wife and come back with an answer after three days. . . . The answer was negative, and they said, 'If something happens to you, we are not responsible.' "

Yussur's memories of that period focused on mistrust, scarcity, and displacement. She emphasized how "there were lots of informants and the walls had eyes and ears," and that "it was a state of war and there was not much of anything." She continued to describe the personal impact that displacement and dispossession had on her childhood and adult life, and how her mother was pregnant nine times and only three children survived. "There was no childhood. It was gone. . . . My mother's brothers were out of the country [they fled during the 1948 war], and she was in mourning. Instead of learning [happy] songs, I learned mourning songs. I do not feel anything and there is no anger. I still feel that we did everything we could for our cause and this is my consolation." This sentiment was echoed by Farha, born in 'Ilabun in 1963, who described how throughout her child-hood, her mother never put on lipstick in mourning for her two uncles killed during the 1948 war.

Yussur ended the interview by talking about her personal life and pursuit of higher education at the Teachers College in Jaffa. She said, "I had a traditional upbringing and there was a hidden message that I accepted without it being imposed on me. . . . I missed out on lots of opportunities to enjoy my youth. I did not want my father to be angry and I wanted to be a good girl." She described how as a girl she was brought up to sacrifice without limits and how her work as a teacher kept her alive. She ended by saying, "I would have preferred to be more daring and active. Sometimes your fear of something prevents you from approaching it." Nuhaila, born in Nazareth in 1953, reiterated Yussur's analysis of gender roles. She said, "You work, have kids, and life passes you by. . . . I didn't want to take things by force. My demands were limited [unlike her sister Zada]. I did what my husband wanted reasonably and logically."

Another woman from Nazareth, 'Abla, who was born in 1948, added, "I vividly remember the first years. . . . We were told not to play outside. . . . It is as if this was a warning about a strange body coming into town. . . . They [the Israeli authorities] got a widow to work for them. They terrified the people with the Shabak [General Security Service] and with the idea that you cannot hide anything from them." Throughout the interview, 'Abla, like many women from her generation, juxtaposed the repression of the Israeli military regime with her resistance and love for Gamal Abdel Nasser. 'Abla became a teacher, a government employee, in 1971. She was well aware of the limits of Israeli democracy and how the school principal where she taught told her that although there is democracy, she should not incite the students (see Cohen, 2006). Decades after the abolishment of the military administration rule, many second-generation women still referred to the impact it had on their lives. Nahida made similar connections to those of 'Abla and Yussur. She recounted, "We used to run to the radio and listen to Nasser's speeches because he was against the colonialism that we suffered from. We were colonized as well. We were not happy and until today we have no presence. This is not our state while the country is our country. We used to take a lot into account and silence ourselves."

Many second-generation women analyzed the connection between the Israeli military system of control and the increased surveillance of their families over their bodies. Sumayya recounted, "I did everything for my family and nothing for myself. I am trying to change but I do not know how. . . . I am not satisfied because I can do more. . . . My husband was strict and I believe that I gave up. Our generation gave to the younger generation what we could not get." She added, "The occupation affected us. We could not finish our education. People were afraid of something; they did not know what it was." Sumayya continued to describe the reasons behind her early marriage, "The Jews were modern, and people [Palestinians in Israel] were afraid that their daughters would become loose. The main reason for my early marriage was fear and poverty. I do not believe that I have a healthy marriage despite my being satisfied with it. I believe that I was deprived of my childhood and adulthood, and I blame the occupation for that." Sumayya analyzed how the lack of jobs caused violence in the family, and how her father was short tempered. "He was violent with my mother and older brother. He was not too violent though. He stayed at home without a job and without authority. People were neither happy nor relaxed. I should have finished my education. Opportunity came and my husband did not want to wait. . . . I found it a way to escape from this life into a better one. I was a coward." Sumayya took full responsibility for her actions, and her narrative echoed that of her mother, Rasmiyya, who said when describing the limitations in her life, "I was not daring, and I had pride. Now I regret it."

Another woman from Nazareth, Rihab, who was born in 1948, described the circumstances that led to her marriage. She recounted, "I was crushed and I am still crushed until today. I wanted one thing and something else was imposed on me. In 1947 my father left Haifa. . . . We lived under siege, and we had to accept the situation. We could not come and go. . . . At the time, the father's authority and the authority of life's circumstances were very bad." Rihab described how her father was degraded by their neighbors because he was internally displaced. "It was a state of siege!" Rihab, like Sumayya, made direct links between the limitations imposed on her life by her family and the Israeli authorities. She described at the end of the interview her gradual resistance to various public and private forms of control. As the majority of second-generation women analyzed the national and gendered limitations imposed on their lives in the aftermath of the 1948 war and the imposition of Israeli military rule from 1948–1966, a few of them, especially those who worked outside the home, stressed their gradual resistance to these varying systems of control.

GENDERING THE BODY

Although first-generation women were born before the State of Israel was created, many came of age during and in the aftermath of the 1948 war. This, combined with the imposition of Israeli military administration rule over Palestinians in Israel from 1948–1966, marked their personal and political experiences and shaped their relation to the State of Israel. They simultaneously treated the state as present and absent in their lives while emphasizing the traumas they had to endure in the aftermath of the war, and the steadfastness they had to employ in order to sustain their dignity and survive.

The narratives of first- and second-generation women reflected the gendered nature of memory, and the language used to depict it. I interviewed twenty women from the first generation, four of whom related directly to the events of Deir Yassin when describing the fear and terror that accompanied the 1948 war, and the reasons that prompted many families to flee for Lebanon. Jamileh, born in Nazareth in 1932 said, "When the war broke out, there was fear from what happened in other villages. . . . in Deir Yassin, where they killed and raped. People did not flee because they were afraid of just the Israeli occupation." Husniyya, born in 'Ayn Mahil in 1918, recounted, "During the Deir Yassin [massacre], honor was violated.[7] When Nazareth and Saffuryeh fell, people were scared that the honor of their women would be violated." She described how the rich people of Nazareth ran away in an attempt to protect their money and lives. "The common people stayed behind and we made it to Sakhnin. No one remained in 'Ayn Mahil. . . . The Jews attacked us from Masha. People started to run, sometimes without shoes. May God protect you from the horrors of war!" Zahra, born in Nazareth in 1925, added, "In Deir Yassin, the pregnant women were cut. . . . this is what got us to run. . . . many people brought ladders and jumped into the monastery [in Nazareth]. . . . we ran into the fields. . . . my family did not leave [and was able to return home]. Rahmeh, born in Jerusalem in 1925, shared her memories of the war, "We tried to leave [Nazareth], we tried to leave. Do you remember Deir Yassin?. . . . There were attacks on women and one woman's belly was cut open. . . . I was pregnant with my first child at the time. . . . I told my husband, 'What do you want? Do you want them to come and open my belly?'. . . . I was quite pregnant then." She described the number of people who died as they were trying to flee. "Our relatives could not come back. . . . this affected me a lot. . . . I do not like to talk about this in front of my kids. . . . Sometimes I wake up at night and wonder why they left. . . . We stayed and nothing happened to us. . . . We are not happy with Israel but we are still here. . . . yet, despite me staying [she is the only one from her family who stayed], I feel displaced and like a refugee." She concluded the interview by saying, "I am not optimistic that the situation will change. We take our rights and we get social security but that is not enough. . . . There is still discrimination. . . . [there needs to be] equality and a state for all its citizens."

Although the majority of first- and second-generation women chose to be silent or speak indirectly about the rape of Palestinian women during the 1948 war, the gendered impact of these events was present in nearly everything the women said. Silence for many women was about fear and uncertainty especially that they lived under Israeli military rule immediately after the war. Salma, born in Nazareth in 1926, said, "We were obliged to be silent in order to see what they were about to do to us." Fadila from Umm al-Fahim who was born in 1923, reiterated, "It was a killer when they first came, there was no freedom and women were not free." Silence about the gendered impact of the war on women's bodies is not necessarily about denial or forgetting but about the moments in which memory does not speak and what that speaks for (Hodgkin and Radstone, 2003; Eber and Neal, 2001). Memory in this context is not pure and unmediated; it is political and reflective of the context and lager cultural narratives in which it operates (Abu-Lughod and Sa'di, 2007; Peteet 2005; McClintock, 1995).

Rape of women in wartime is employed strategically as a booty and ethnic marker, to humiliate men as unable to protect their women, and to promote solidarity and bonding among soldiers (Mazurana et al., 2005). In the case of Palestine, rape was used during the 1948 war to terrorize the population, and ethnically cleanse certain areas in order to mark the new territories.[8] Second-generation women were born as the Israeli state was created and came of age under its military regime. Their narratives reflected the combined effect of these structural systems of control and the increased surveillance by their families over their bodies and lives (al-Ali, 2007; Cockburn, 2004; Kelly 2000). As the narratives of second-generation women zigzagged between the personal and the political, they depicted the Israeli state as an omnipresent body infiltrating nearly every aspect of their lives, crushing childhood dreams, and imposing siege. They viewed this siege as gendered, nationalized, and militarized (Enloe, 2000; Shadmi, 2000; Ferguson, 1995; Sharoni, 1994; Mazali, 1998), leaving them with limited space to publicly resist and organize for change.

Second-generation women developed a gendered understanding of these changes, and their narratives referred indirectly to the rape of Palestinian women during the 1948 war. They recalled how their families were afraid of "something they did not know what it was," and how the abrupt economic, social, and political changes following the 1948 war increased this fear and control. Some also referred to the perceived modernity and difference of the Jews (Katz, 2003, 1996; Hasso, 2000), and the fear that Palestinian girls and women might become loose. This control was part of a larger continuum that ran through the social, economic, and political with gender relations embedded in these dynamics in both the private and public spheres and in pre, during and post-conflict situations (Cockburn, 2004; Kelly 2000). This continuum extended throughout the Israeli military administration period and had a negative impact on the lives and opportunities of second-generation women.

A few second-generation women, especially those who worked outside the home, spoke about how hard they had to work to break away from these restrictions. Both the 1967 war and the 1976 Land Day were turning points for Palestinians in Israel. Many second-generation women used the words defeat or *khabta* (blow) to describe what took place in 1967. For many this was a moment of disillusionment with the idea that the solution could come from the outside, from Nasser or the Arab countries. According to Summaya, "After 1967, there was work and people with their own initiative improved their situation. . . . They also lifted the Israeli military rule and we had a chance to go out and see the world." In addition, Land Day in 1976 was a turning point in the political organizing of Palestinians in Israel, and was followed by significant changes in the structure of the community's local and national leadership (Cohen, 2006). It is within this context that a number of second-generation women started to contest in public in the 1980s the personal and political limitations in their lives. Rihab started writing books and had a weekly column in a local newspaper while Yussur began giving public lectures on education. Nada, born in Nazareth in 1954, whose father did not allow her to go to the university but only to the Teachers College, managed to go to university after her children grew up to pursue her graduate degree.[9]

BELONGING TO THE LOCAL

The perception among all women interviewed is that third-generation women made headway in gaining education and access to the workplace, and in forging new grounds in collective and public organizing. Third-generation women were mostly born after the 1966 dismantling of the Israeli military rule, and the 1967 Israeli occupation of the West Bank, Gaza, the Sinai Peninsula, and the Golan Heights. During the 1970–1990s, a period when many third-generation women were coming of age, the State of Israel was going through major social and political transformations following the 1973 war and the 1982 Israeli invasion of Lebanon (Rekhess, 2007). This was manifested in a slight decline in the hegemonic power of the state over its citizens, which allowed many third-generation women to challenge and transform gender roles as well as expand the personal and public space available for social action and change.

The narratives of third-generation women resounded with explicit gender and national contestations (see Garcia, 2004). Many started their narratives by defining themselves, and describing what they study and their plans for the future. They critiqued the Israeli educational system and the lack of cultural opportunities in their communities. Maha, a woman from 'Ayn Mahil who was born in 1979, said, "I study special education and define myself as Arab Palestinian living in the State of Israel. . . . On a national level, they [the Israeli authorities] took the land. You can feel it today when your sisters and brothers are getting married and there is no land for them to live on." These were the exact words that Maha's grandmother, Husniyya, used to protest land confiscation in their village. Maha continued, "I would have liked to attend a better school. There are no budgets and no cultural centers in our town." Haneen, a woman from Nazareth who was born in 1976, echoed Maha's concerns and said, "Everything around, whether it is the school, street, television, or newspaper, differentiates between Palestinians and Jews. . . . I do not see things as if they [Israeli Jews] are part of the progressive West and we are part of the backward East."

The narratives of many third-generation women intertwined and zigzagged between the personal and the political and what it means to be a young woman and Palestinian in Israel at the end of the 1990s. Their narratives also emphasized the changing nature of their relation to the state. On the one hand, unlike women from the first and second generations, they felt that they knew the Hebrew language and were therefore better equipped to interact with Israeli state institutions. Yet, they too defined their relation to the state as that of alienation and subordination. Nuhad, a woman from Nazareth who was born in 1974, added, "There are people who prefer to say they are Palestinians but we have an Israeli identity card, and even if I were to say that I am not Israeli, I still have to go to the bank and deal with state institutions." Nuhad, a young mother at the time, wondered, "When I look deep into this situation, I feel that I want to explode. . . . I would like to remain a citizen but do not want to serve in the military. The flag has religious symbols. . . . I take what I like from Jewish society . . . Yet, my interaction with them remains limited and isolated." Nuhad was well aware of her alienation from the state and Israeli society, and like the majority of women from all three generations she defined her local town as her milieu.

Lama, born in 1977 in Nazareth, elaborated on Nuhad's views, "I live in the State of Israel. I only live in this state . . . We do not have full rights in society. We are always discriminated against." Lama placed conditions on her Israeli citizenship, "First, there needs to be peace and equality in rights between Jews and Arabs. . . . There needs to be a Palestinian state in the West Bank and Gaza. . . . Everyone has a role in change and it is not only in the hands of the authorities." Despite feeling limited in her ability to influence the political situation, Lama still believed in collective action and change.

As many third-generation women were making sense of their lives, they seemed to have developed gender awareness in describing and explaining the forces that shaped their experiences. The majority of the interviewees opened with a problematization of the discrimination they faced both as women and as Palestinians. Ruwaida, a woman from Umm al-Fahim who was born in 1968, said, "There is everything in the State of Israel, but for the Arabs lots of things are still lacking. . . . When I travel to Haifa, I feel that people make fun of me [because she wears a headscarf]. I belong more to Umm al-Fahim." She ended the interview by emphasizing that there is nothing called freedom for women, and that men are still in control.

Haneen echoed some of the themes that came up in Ruwaida's narrative. She added, "I have zero belonging to the state.... Even if they give us our rights, I do not know if I could belong. The crack is deep and who knows if it will ever heal.... There are two nationalisms under one roof here. How can I belong more? I cannot imagine that happening unless there is real equality where people could live in peace and dignity, or if things were not as bad in the West Bank and Gaza." She continued, "Many times I wonder whether there will ever be a day when I would say that I am Israeli without feeling that I am lying to myself. I will say it, I want to say it, but only after there is no humiliation. [Israel as] a Jewish state! What are we then, fools (ṭaraṭīr)? What are we?" According to Haneen, "lack of respect starts with these little things, and if the state does not want to recognize us, then why should we recognize it?" Haneen's narrative reflected her continued attempt to expand the private and public space in her life. She added, "We have the basic things but we are still stuck.... Public space is minimized and suppression increases as you grow up.... Now that I am married I have to get pregnant. This [pressure] is more on me than on my husband. Although we share our lives and decisions, the assumption is that I should not say no because he is the head of the family." Haneen was not shy about criticizing her society, "It allowed me to wear pants and the superficial things do change.... but my role as a woman did not change and society's expectations of my mother and I are still the same." She ended the interview by acknowledging that, politically, her mother is more aware and more of an activist than she is.[10]

As the narratives emphasized state discrimination and the limitations imposed on the meaning and practice of full citizenship, they also problematized the relation between nationalism and feminism (Humphries and Khalili, 2007; Najjar, 2003; Gocek, 2002; Joseph, 2000; Hasso, 1998; Abdo, 1994; Moghadam, 1994; Kuttab, 1993; Jayawardena, 1986). Women's agency and coping mechanisms were present in the narratives of women from all three generations, yet were more explicit in the narratives of women from the third generation. Some of the women elaborated on the development of their feminist consciousness. Manal, a woman from Nazareth who was born in 1978, said, "I was born in Israel and it is important that they acknowledge my existence.... There is discrimination and I feel angry but I do not feel powerless.... There is no flag and no symbols that tie me to the state except the fact that I was born here, and the history of my family.... I will struggle against those who deprive me of the right to live in dignity." Manal continued to describe the difference between her and her mother: "My mother's views are more conservative.... I believe that a woman should be in control of her life and body and my mother thinks that a girl has to protect herself and her body. There is definitely a difference between us but we are the same politically." She emphasized how empowered she feels because there are institutions that address women's rights, and concluded the interview by saying, "My belonging is to my family and to my city. Politics are important and my definition of myself is first of all political. Israel is a state that I deal with but do not feel connected to. My belonging is more to the local."

Fida's narrative is similar to that of Manal, as it illustrated the development and intersection between her national, class, and feminist identities. Fida, born in 1964, stressed how when she went to the university, the bubble was gone. "I started to interact with Israeli institutions which allowed me to see things differently and to be more realistic. The feeling of anger does not go away and you start to deal with it differently." Fida described how she started to question why male students who supported her in private would stand up in public meetings and say that a woman cannot be the head of the Arab Student Committee. Like many women from her generation, she acknowledged that although her social, economic, and political awareness developed in her late girlhood and early adulthood, her understanding of gender issues lagged behind. It was not until she started working with women in Acre in 1987 that her feminist consciousness developed. "We came into close contact with people from the lower classes, and started to see things that shook us from the inside. This in turn contributed to more focus on women and feminist issues."

Whereas the majority of first-generation women related to the Israeli state as present/absent in their lives, and the narratives of second-generation women focused on their limited ability to implement change on the institutional and personal levels, the narratives of the majority of third-generation women reflected their determination to address inequalities in their lives as women and Palestinians. Fida described the frameworks that helped her develop her feminist consciousness, including her interaction with Jewish feminists and the ability to attend regional and international gatherings in the early 1990s (Basu, 1995). She continued to problematize the link between gender and nationalism and what it means for Palestinian women to have a feminist agenda in an ethnonationalist and militarized state like Israel. "We are going through changes. . . . Consumerism is creeping on us. . . . Today, I benefit from many laws and the situation is complex and not black and white." She acknowledged that the Israeli system was not created for Palestinians but they benefited from it.

Reem, born in Nazareth in 1966, also maintained a pragmatic approach to dealing with Israeli state institutions. She said, "I need the Ministry of Education to implement change, and in order to do so I need to behave like a 'good girl.' That is when the fig leaf thing comes in and where they [the Israeli authorities] present themselves as generous because they grant budgets to the Arab community. . . . After they gave me the recognition to open an alternative school, I told one of them that I got what I wanted because I deserved it." She added, "I sit in my chair comfortably but I am weak from the inside and I do not say what I really want. It is hypocritical. . . . They would say: 'She is the first [Arab] woman to enter the Ministry of Education.' . . . This is based on their feeling of superiority as if they are the 'thing' and we are the phenomenon." She compared the ways in which the ministries treat the Arabs to that of occupation, "I take it personally when they tell me [she said the phrase in Hebrew]: 'You do look Israeli; you do not look like an Arab,' as if we are categories: a, b, c. This is not about the clothes I wear. . . . It is important that he does not tell me, 'You do not look like an Arab.' Why should he decide?" Many third-generation women interviewed wanted to move beyond token democracy. Nabila, born in Rameh in 1969, Rana born in Nazareth in 1975, and Hiyam born in Kufur Yasif in 1974, all political and women's rights activists, demanded that feminist organizations should transform and not duplicate already existing patriarchal structures (see Abu El-Asal, 2006; Ghanim, 2005). Ghadeer, born in Kufur Yasif in 1974, described how she benefited from the services of the aid centers, and how she attended meetings for gender empowerment and consciousness raising in Haifa. She put the onus on national and feminist organizations to deal with body politics and with what it means, in her case, to be a lesbian Palestinian. For women who were active in political parties, the emphasis was on the need to introduce quotas for political candidates, and create non-hierarchical structures that link the social with the political. They warned against relying only on civil society organizations to implement change.

Third-generation women defined themselves in personal terms while still describing their belonging to their communities and the larger Palestinian society. Many also defined themselves in comparison with the generation that preceded them, especially that of their mothers (see Henry, 2005; Wells, 2003; Hasso, 2001; Ransel, 2000; Wang, 1999; Bar-On, 1998). Women of different generations often tried to make sense of themselves and their conditions by drawing comparisons with women older and younger than themselves (Garcia, 2004). Reem, for example, emphasized throughout the interview how she structured her life in reaction to her mother's. She also recognized that she is the exact copy of her mother but in different colors. Reem, like Fida and Haneen, wanted her daughters to start where she finished and not where she started. She stressed the link between institutional and individual change, and feminist values and national collective identity. Her narrative, like those of many women from her generation, emphasized her constant search for ways to sustain her presence and expand the space available for change in the private and public spheres.

BELONGING, EXCLUSION AND RESISTANCE

The narratives of three generations of Palestinian women in Israel attested to certain continuities between these generational groups particularly as they relate to their belonging to the local Palestinian community and alienation from the Israeli state ethos. They went beyond a victim/survivor dichotomy, and rooted their discourses in their daily realities (Bardenstein, 1998). However, as women from each generation historicized and contextualized their narratives, they used different vocabularies to explain certain events in their lives. The narratives of women from the first and second generations focused on social dynamics (Jayussi, 2007). Without relating to a nostalgic and mythical past, they intertwined the present with the past to give mean- ing to these events and describe the effect they had on their lives. They transformed narratives of the past resurrected in the present into a story of remembrance, a process, a working through (Gertz and Khleifi, 2008; Beinin, 2005). Their narratives were deeply embedded in social and political events and locations that are particular to each generation.

The narratives of three generations of Palestinian women in Israel illustrated the constructed nature and historical constitution of public and private boundaries (Herzog, 2004a). Gender roles were spatially and politi- cally constructed, and women's access to the public sphere was still limited despite some strides made by third-generation women. The narratives described the limits and possibilities for change, and analyzed gender as a relation of power in family and state politics. They addressed the structural confines of their positionality and location as Palestinian women in a Jewish state. They also reflected on the contested nature of the relation between gender and nationalism and questioned the ethnonationalist and militarized nature of Israeli politics.

All three generations of Palestinian women interviewed emphasized the headway made by third-generation women in accessing education, working outside the home, and choosing their marriage partners. Third-generation women were born mostly after the Israeli state lifted its military rule over Palestinians in Israel in 1966, and came of age as the hegemonic power of the state was in slight decline (Pappe, 2006; Yiftachel, 2006). This in part allowed for a limited increase in public space for women to develop feminist consciousness and collectively call for equality in the private and public spheres. It also allowed for the development of more pragmatic approaches to dealing with Israeli state institutions. Yet, the majority of the women still felt alienated, albeit differently, by continued state discrimination against Palestinians in Israel and the politics of occupation in the West Bank and Gaza. They reiterated how the local remains their site of belonging and resistance.

By emphasizing their belonging to the local, women define the relation to place and space as constitutive and reflective of relations of power in society. These power relations are constructed by cultural practices and state policies of exclusion that are simultaneously resisted and accommodated (Peteet, 2005). In order to understand these, we cannot only focus on institutional politics but must pay close attention to the gendered politics of everyday life. It is imperative that we examine the private and the public as sites of contestation of social and political relations and not privilege one over the other (Afsaruddin, 1999). Acts of resistance in this context represent the search for personal and collective space. Jamileh who was active with the Communist Party since 1948, described how it took her until 1958–1960 to gain economic and social independence from her controlling uncle. She also described how she was fined and put in prison for one month as a result of her "disruption" of the celebrations in Nazareth of the tenth anniversary to the creation of the State of Israel. Some second-generation women described the modes of resistance that they learned from their mothers even under limiting conditions. Nahida remembered the pressure exerted on her widowed mother to work as an informant for the Israeli military regime in the 1950s, leading her mother to refrain from political activity and focus on social ones. Despite this pressure, Nahida described how her mother used to sometimes release words (*tfallit ḥakī*) about the political situation. Third-generation women described their resistance as being in continuity and in opposition to that of their mothers'. Many emphasized how empowered they felt that there were feminist organizations that offered institutional and collective frameworks for change. Therefore, the constraints and survival strategies used by women of all three generations play a major role in shaping their emergent identities and the boundaries that they construct and contest (Garcia, 2004).

The agency through which women accept, accommodate, ignore, resist or protest are embodied in power relations and oppositional practices (Macleaod, 1991). All women interviewed related to the local as their main site of belonging and resistance. Eyal Ben-Ari and Edna Lomsky-Feder (1999) refer to the territorialization of space in Israel as being Zionist where a naturalization of hierarchies of exclusion takes place (see Shihadeh and Sabbagh-Khoury, 2005; Bashir 2004; Sultany 2004, 2003; Benvenesti, 2000; Silbestein, 2000; Furman, 1999; Ben-Yehuda, 1999). Within this context, cultural definitions and social and political practices produce and reproduce the ethnonational and gendered divide of inequality in Israeli society, and the boundaries of who is included or excluded from these practices. Nuhad said, "My emotional belonging to my city substitutes for my lack of belonging to Israel." Rabiha, born in al-Taybeh in 1946, added, "Our life is in our village and the rest is for the state. . . . It is getting worse . . . No one dared open their mouth [during and after October 2000]." For Farha, the events of October 2000 exposed the limits of Israeli democracy. "It is as if the state was telling us: 'We can erase you at any point.' " Hala, born in Nazareth in 1960, was severely beaten by the police and border-patrol during the October 2000 demonstrations. She made clear connections between what took place in 2000 and 1948, and between her generation and that of her parents. "It is still the same. They want to terrorize you so you won't raise your voice. . . . It is occupation. . . . The way Israel treats us does not allow one to forget." As women from all three generations continue to address gender and national discrimination in their lives, it remains to be seen what strategies and modes of resistance they manage to employ on the personal and public level to contest and breakaway from these limitations.

NOTES

1. This article is based on research conducted in 1998, and intermittently from 2005–2009, with women from various backgrounds and social, economic, and political positions. Not all women interviewed belonged to the same familial generational groups. All interviews were conducted in Arabic and the names of the interviewees have been changed.

2. The majority of the women in this generation described their marriages as arranged, and three described them as forced especially that the husband was much older than they were. Nahla, born in al-Taybeh in 1925, said her marriage was *zawāj badal* (exchange marriage), "They did not use to ask the girl, may God not forgive them."

3. Studies by Sayigh (2007, 2002, 1998, 1996, 1993) and Peteet (2002, 2000, 1999, 1991) who interviewed Palestinian refugees in Lebanon, similarly emphasized the devastating impact of the 1948 war on their lives resulting in their dispossession and displacement.

4. See Michel Khleifi's 1985 film *Ma'lul Celebrates Its Destruction*.

5. These are Palestinian villages adjacent to Nazareth that were destroyed during the 1948 war.

6. Israel's national anthem.

7. I decided to include this interview as it marked the start of the British Mandate of Palestine.

8. For further elaboration on the rape of Palestinian women during the 1948 war, see Pappe (2007: 156, 184, 208–211); Slyomovics (2007); and Morris (2004: 220, 249, 419, 420).

9. Three first-generation women had the equivalent of college education and two finished high school. Of the twenty-three second-generation women interviewed, five went to the Teachers College to become educators. Four out of twenty-seven third-generation women did not gain a college degree, and two did not finish their high school education.

10. Haneen's mother, 'Abla, was recently elected together with Rihab to public office in their community.

FIVE

COUNTER-MEMORY

―――――――――――――――――――――

Palestinian Women Naming Historical Events

Fatma Kassem

> What is missing in your tale, Aunty, is that I must learn a language
> with which I can "speak." A language with which I can find my family
> "self." Language too has its dark nooks and crannies. I am now searching
> for those spaces in your tale and in everything around me.
>
> —Rhoda Kanaaneh, "We'll Talk Later"

This chapter attempts to create a public space for the voices of urban
Palestinian women in Israel. These women are engaged in daily struggles
against the erasure of their memories and histories both as Palestinians and
as women. Palestinian women from so-called mixed cities such as Lydd and
Ramleh are some of the most marginalized, as they have been entirely left
out of the formation of the collective Palestinian historical-political narrative and deprived of any legitimacy in the public domain of the exclusively
Jewish state. By documenting their accounts of historic events, subjectivity
is reclaimed and "their right to define their own reality, establish their own
identities, and name their history" is recognized (hooks, 1989: 42). Throughout
this chapter, I analyze the terminology and narrative of ordinary Palestinian
women from the cities of Lydd and Ramleh as they narrate historic events.
I show how they use particular words to establish the realms of personal
and collective memory while challenging both the delegitimization of their
history as Palestinians in a Jewish state and the absence of women from

national Palestinian history. Paying close attention to their choice of terms helps map the significance of events in their lives.

Sandra Harding argues that knowledge about women's lives and experiences is at best partial, and because women were objects of "otherness," research starting from their lives "can be made to yield clearer and more complete visions of social reality" (Harding, 1991: 126). The voices of ordinary Palestinian women challenge the canonic tradition that refuses to recognize them as "important agents [or] reliable reporters and interpreters of history" (Baker, 1998: 1). Only women who carry bombs in the name of the nation or who have experiences in battle or in the official "political" realm succeed in entering into the national discourse (Shohat, 2001). The active participation of women in maintaining daily life and attending to family and community needs remains unrecognized. Ellen Fleischmann notes the "surprising silence that shrouds the subject of Palestinian women in almost all historical writings on Palestine" (Fleischmann, 2003: 11), and Rema Hammami found that women were absent from studies of the Nakba and were mentioned only when cultural and traditional norms and practices were invoked (Hammami, 2004). This absenting of women from history is all the more limiting given that Rosemary Sayigh suggests that Palestinian women's narrations of the past are historically more accurate than those of men, because women did not perceive themselves as responsible for losing the homeland in 1948 (Sayigh, 1998).

Gayatri Chakravorty Spivak describes the subaltern woman in colonial situations as doubly effaced, "both as object of colonialist historiography and as subject of insurgency where the ideological construction of gender keeps the male dominant. If, in the context of colonial production, the subaltern has no history and cannot speak, the subaltern as female is ever more deeply in the shadow" (Spivak, 1994: 82–83). The protracted and bloody conflict between the Palestinian collective, to which these women belong, and the Israeli state in which they are citizens, multiplies their marginality. Thus, women's stories preserve them from oblivion and build "the identity of the teller and the legacy [s]he will leave in time to come" (Portelli, 1981: 162).

The cities of Lydd and Ramleh are located in the central part of Palestine/Israel in the coastal plain, close to the Tel Aviv-Jaffa metropolis. According to the website Palestine Remembered and data from the British Statistical Bureau and the Israeli Bureau, there were 18,250 people in Lydd in 1947, and only 1,050 remained in 1950. In Ramleh, out of a population of 16,380 only 400 Palestinians remained in 1950. Both cities became "mixed cities" in the state's official lexicon, a term reflecting their ongoing Judaization (Yacobi, 2003; Bashir, 2004). Around 20 percent of the current inhabitants of both cities are Palestinians who live in segregated districts and suffer from poverty and exclusion. Historically, the Palestinian national collective has focused on remembering Palestinian refugees and destroyed villages with less attention to the destruction of Palestinian cities in 1948. Israeli state ideology of expelling Palestinians from the cities that were to be reserved for Jewish immigrants halted Palestinian urbanization.

Some of the women in this study are original residents of Lydd and Ramleh who continue to live there today, though some of them were forced to leave their original homes and move into new ones, where they are now minoritized and ghettoized. Others in this study were uprooted in 1948 from neighboring villages like Zakariyya and towns like al-Majdal and were forced to move into cities where the vast majority of the original Palestinian population were expelled.

Between 2002 and 2004, I interviewed thirty-seven women (and six men) living in Lydd and Ramleh using the life-story method. Women's ages ranged from sixty-eight to eighty-four. Three of the women attended up to four years of formal schooling while the rest did not attend school and the majority were illiterate. I used the snowball approach to reach the women and conducted the discussion in Arabic in their homes. In most of the interviews, family members of different ages were present and some intervened occasionally by reminding the interviewee to add, reveal, or complete certain details. It became clear that I was not the first person to hear their stories, and that they had already been transmitted to the younger generation. Some of the interviewees wondered who would hear or read their stories, and whether telling them to me could harm their monthly elderly allowance from the state. I assured them that their identities would remain anonymous.

Ordinary voices such as those of the women in this study have to be heard "if we are to successfully challenge our oppression. This non-autobiographical mode of expression must be the collective experience of the people, not only of a few politicians and intellectuals. Otherwise . . . we will remain silent even as we speak, and paralyzed even as we act" (Warwar, 2002: 118). My aim is to make the voices of ordinary Palestinian women heard and their presence visible within the context of multiplied silence and deprivation resulting from Palestinian male dominance and exclusive Jewish state politics. However, the problematics of representation remain. Spivak questions the possibility of representation within the same collective group because of class and other differences. She argues that "the subject of exploitation cannot recognize or speak the text of exploitation of women, even when . . . the non-representative intellectual gives her room to speak" (Spivak, 1994: 84).

As I recognize that voices of "illiterate and ordinary" women could be silenced by educated women like me, I also recognize that the voice of the researcher writing these events is silenced by exclusion and delegitimization. Both sides struggle, albeit differently, to make their voices heard in a place where the right to speak is being constantly confiscated. Educated Palestinian citizens of Israel are largely absent from the Israeli academy. Palestinian women scholars whose work focuses on Palestinian historiography, including contributors to this volume among others, have found no place for their scholarly work in Israeli academic institutions. By conducting this research in the Israeli academy, I attempt to break the silence enforced on Palestinian women, both academic and nonacademic, as members of the Palestinian collective and as female citizens of the State of Israel.

Although I am Palestinian, I am aware of Spivak's questions of representation and Patricia Hill Collins' argument that "depending on the context, an individual may be an oppressor, a member of an oppressed group, or simultaneously oppressor and oppressed" (Collins, 1990: 225). Being aware of our different positioning and power relations, I do not pretend to represent these women whose take on historical events could be similar or different from mine. Rather, I seek to create (as much as possible) a legitimate place for their subsumed voices, a place in which their language can emerge intertwined with my own, demanding recognition, acknowledgment, and responsibility. As this chapter deals with narrative and because language is constructed within the masculine realm, women have continuously found themselves positioned outside of it yet "responsible for preserving culture" (Lakoff, 1975: 55). In narrating unresolved past events that directly shape their present lives, the language of older Palestinian women and their descriptions of historic events reflect the contours of the private and public spheres, and constitute a political mirror of their realities. Their terminology also edifies their roles as agents making history.

When I began my research, I telephoned Khawla, a woman from Lydd. I started the conversation by greeting her in Arabic. Khawla answered in fluent Arabic that left no doubt in my mind as to which language I should use during the interview. I followed a similar procedure with all the other interviewees, and they all responded by telling their life stories in Arabic. Once we set a time and place for our meeting, I asked Khawla for directions. As I did not understand her explanation and was afraid of getting lost, I asked for her exact address. "I live on Salah al-Din Street," she said, and immediately laughed and corrected herself: "No, don't say 'Salah al-Din Street;' no one will know where that is. They call it 'Herzl Street' today."

This replacement of the name of Salah al-Din, a figure drawn from Isalmic history, which symbolizes Arab, Palestinian, and Muslim territory (though Salah al-Din was not Arab himself) by that of Herzl, a figure from Jewish-Zionist history, is indicative of the ongoing Zionization of Palestinian/Arab territory, where renaming streets is a facet of the victorious Israeli ideology since 1948. Both names are those of men and relate to men's power on both sides. They extend from the Crusader era to the national modern Jewish state, illustrating how through commemoration, male dominance reproduced and reshaped history as "hu-man" history. However, Khawla's use of Salah al-Din's name resists the erasure of Palestinian history and the history of her street and city. It symbolizes resistance to Zionist renaming and expresses the need for recognition and legitimacy for collective Palestinian history and memory. This struggle takes place within the realm of language and is fraught with symbolic historical meanings where women seek a legitimate place in history.

"I'M FROM HERE," "I'M NOT FROM HERE"

When I asked Salma to tell her life story, she smiled and answered: "My life story? Who would be interested in that?" "Me," I said. "What do you want to hear about, exactly?" she asked. "What you want to tell me about," I replied. She looked me in the eye and said: "Do you want me to tell you about the time when we migrated?" "Whatever you want," I answered. Similar negotiations took place with the majority of women. Salma is from Lydd. She began her life story by saying: "I'm originally from here, and by origin we are from here." Most of the "original" residents of Lydd and Ramleh started their stories with "I'm originally from here." In contrast, women from both urban and rural areas who came to Lydd and Ramleh after the 1948 war started their life stories with the words, "I'm not from here."

When the interviewees say, "I'm from here," "I am *bint il-balad*" (literally, daughter of the city, or a local girl), or "we are *ahl il-balad*" (local people), they assert their right to the city irrespective of attempts to challenge it. By emphasizing the words "from here," they explain their sense of belonging to their city, notwithstanding the Zionist forces that conquered it in 1948. "I'm from here; we're not migrants" is the phrase used by Salma and her friends to mark the social boundary between native daughters of the city and the other Palestinian population groups that came after 1948. The women emphasize their local origins in order to distinguish themselves from the "newcomers" and create a separate social group. This was also evident when I asked them to refer me to refugee women in the neighborhood. Some of the "original" residents answered that they were not in contact with such women, or that they did not know any. These answers reflect the persistent tension between the original urban Palestinian population of Lydd and Ramleh and the population that came following the events of 1948.

Interestingly, the latter group of interviewees began their life stories by saying: "I'm not from here." For example, Fatma said: "I'm not from here; I'm from Zakariyya." Sara said: "We're not from here; we're originally from al-Majdal." This common opening sentence is not a direct response to "I'm from here." Rather, it indirectly represents the interviewees' perception of historic events and emphasizes their pre-1948 origins. What the interviewees are in effect saying is: "The reason I'm here now, when I'm not originally 'from' here, has to do with the 1948 war and the fact that the village or city that I came from was destroyed and its population expelled." The words "I'm not from here" also reflect the feelings of strangeness and alienation that these women still experience, notwithstanding the passage of a considerable amount of time, vis-à-vis the "new" place in which they settled after having been uprooted from their place of "origin." As Hillel Cohen points out in his study of internal refugees: "The majority of the refugees still feel like strangers or refugees in the places that absorbed them" (Cohen, 2000: 28). The fact that these women define themselves by means of negation—"I'm not from here"—indicates that they have not yet been fully assimilated in their new locations.

For both women's groups, the year 1948 shaped their lives and locations. The interviewees started their life stories by denoting territorial terms directly related to the 1948 events. "I'm originally from here" and "I'm not originally from here" are both personal and collective declarations. They are principally political and emphasize women's rights to place/territory in the face of daily attempts to delegitimize their right to homes, villages, and cities that they are not allowed to return to. Salma from Lydd said: "They ruined it [my house]. I will show you the place (she laughs); they ruined it and got us out." Salma continues to say: "No, they did not allow us to go back to our house." Salma's daughter adds: "No one could go back to their home; no one went back. . . . Jews entered into our homes and we were allowed to enter into ruined Arab homes in the old city."

The emphasis on origin is closely bound with the 1948 war as a crucial and constitutive event in their lives. Present life is shaped in relation to the past and the ongoing attempt of the Jewish state to pressure them out of their place. The way they define themselves shapes and is shaped by these past and present lived historical events. "I am from here" and "I am not from here" are deployed in a situation of ongoing conflict where the *watan*, homeland, is constantly under threat and the affiliation to the village or the city of "origin" is delegitimized.

DESCRIPTION OF THE EVENTS OF 1948: THE JEWS ENTERED AND TOOK US

A conspicuous element in the narratives of the women interviewed was the absence of the word "Nakba," a well-known, fundamental, collective term used by Palestinians to describe what took place in 1948. Only three of the thirty-seven women I interviewed mentioned the word "Nakba"; all three were political activists in the Communist Party. Halima from Lydd described the events as follows: "The English came in 1914, right? They took the country (*liblād*) in 1918, they moved the railroad away from here, from the city; they cut our land in the middle; and after that, the Jews came. When the Jews came, my brother . . . was twenty years old." Khawla from Lydd said: "I was ten years old when the Jews entered, and I had to carry the whole burden. My brothers were part of my responsibility."

The interviewees described the events of 1948 in words like "when the Jews entered," "when Israel came," "when the Jews took us," and "when

Israel took us." They used the words "Jews" and "Israelis" interchangeably to denote the conquering force. The phrase, "when the Jews came" is drawn from day-to-day Palestinian life. The verb "to come" (*jā'a*) is a primal, everyday word. In contrast to the women's terminology, most of the men I interviewed used terms such as "the Israelis conquered" or "the days of the Jewish conquest," which are formal terms borrowed from common public discourse in Arab media and political debates.

The term "Nakba" first appeared in a book by Qustantin Zurayk published in Beirut in August 1948. According to Zurayk, in *Nakbat Falastin*, the Palestinians lost control of the land on which the Jewish state was established and as a result, hundreds of thousands of Palestinians became refugees. Palestinian researchers—mainly men, politicians, intellectuals, authors, and poets—adopted the concept of Nakba, which became one of the most fundamental concepts of Palestinian collective awareness. Palestinian author Salman Natur wrote: "I belong to the generation born one year after the Nakba" (Natur, 1985: 49). By identifying himself in this way, Natur marked the identity of Palestinians relative to the Nakba: those born before it, those born during it, and those born after it (Natur, 1995: 16). In her doctoral thesis on Palestinian intellectuals in Israel, Honaida Ghanim (2004) illustrates the degree to which the Nakba was a fundamental event in their private and collective lives.

That the women in my study used the words "came," "entered," and "took us" rather than "Nakba" reflects the way in which they experienced these events, emotionally and historically. The choice of words is shaped by norms and values that control relationships between the sexes in Palestinian Arab society. The entrance was made without permission—that is, the Jews entered as uninvited guests and caught the Palestinians exposed and unready. This description is analogous to a phrase used to describe the wedding night. In accordance with Palestinian social norms, it is customary to say in spoken Arabic: "The bridegroom entered (*dakhala*) to the bride." The bride is supposed to be a virgin on her wedding night, and the bridegroom must penetrate her and pierce her hymen. Another phrase used for this is: "The bridegroom took the bride." Fatma from Zakariyya refers to "the day when Israel took us." Palestinian women from Lydd and Ramleh describe the events of the Nakba in terminology drawn from the private sphere and reserved for the relationship between men and women. Women who were born into a patriarchal language and grew up within its realm draw on it to describe their experiences. In my reading of the women's choice of language, the entry into cities or villages is linked to the penetration of the body, symbolizing the invasion of Palestinian homes and forced access to the most intimate and private areas of their lives.

The language reflects, on the one hand, the gender-related balance of power in Palestinian society, and on the other, the political balance resulting from the events of the war. According to Spivak, women are described in nationalist discourse as "Mother Earth" (Spivak, 1992). This symbolic construct is intended to link control of a territory with control of women's bodies and sexuality. The parallel between the two types of control is evoked by the interviewees, who describe the entry of foreign forces into their territory using the same terms as those for the physical penetration of women's bodies by men.

The bride often encounters the forceful penetration of her body on her wedding night without being told about intercourse as a result of taboos surrounding sexuality—this was especially the case for the generation of women I interviewed. Despite this, the bride overcomes the pain and injury of forced penetration and establishes a subject position and respect from which she grows a new family and life. The analogy on the collective level is that despite the traumatic conquest in 1948, the potential recovery from the traumatic events and the opportunity for resourceful creative action and social and political reorganization remains. The penetration/conquest does not entirely subdue the woman/collective of Palestinians. In this context, through the use of terminology drawn from the private sphere, Palestinian women draw an analogy to the trauma from which one must recover and start reorganizing and reconstructing along new lines—personally and collectively.

The use of the word "Nakba" in official Arab history typically represents total defeat where the possibility of overcoming the catastrophic event is negated.[1] The language used by the women I interviewed indicates that, consciously or unconsciously, they perceived themselves as still capable of action, choice, and control in their lives. Notwithstanding the ruin, destruction, and loss, they described how they managed to overcome and rehabilitate their lives, to rebuild their homes, families, and reestablish their communities. All of the married interviewees, for example, stated that "we raised the children and married them off." The women used other verbs that may be translated as "to establish a home" or "to open a house," and expressions such as "we were the only family who stayed here and now there are many of us" and "I am the only one who remained in the country and my children built their homes around me." Their private homes crumbled in 1948; their communities were ripped apart and dispersed. The establishment of a home of their own was actually a step toward reestablishing a community.

Palestinian women described the events of 1948 using everyday language that is far removed from both national Palestinian discourse and the Zionist-Jewish narrative about peasants with no connection to the land who left voluntarily. The fact that most of these women are illiterate and subordinate to Palestinian men has kept them at some levels "free" of Palestinian nationalist and Zionist discourses. By using private, familial terms, the women provide an alternative sphere of conceptualization. That the women refrain from using the term "Nakba" but favor cultural language drawn from the private sphere reflects and structures the reality of their lives as "ordinary" women and is linked to their absence from the political-national sphere.

THE TIME OF THE ENGLISH

Interviewees generally related to their individual lives and those of their families. At the same time, their memories hold a collective significance. Memories of the English were brought up by Fatin from Ramleh/Sdud using the following language:

> Our Palestinian people were always oppressed and discriminated against. Turkey conquered us and put the young men to death. My father-in-law was a fighter in Turkey. . . . After the Turks, the English came, and after the English, Israel came [she laughs]. During the time of the English, I remember our neighbor had two bullets, and they gave him two years [in prison]; they didn't find a gun or anything on him. . . . Anyone who was a revolutionary got hanged. There's a song—I don't remember it—about Palestinians who were executed in Acre, three of them. . . . The song is about the beginning of the English conquest where the English would execute any Palestinian who even breathed, or who was a revolutionary or anything like that. They say that the Palestinian people have always been discriminated against, have been humiliated throughout their life—since Turkey, and even before Turkey, and under those English, and now Israel. If only Israel had left the Palestinians in their own country! It exiled them [sigh].

Fatin uses the concept of "our Palestinian people," a statement that reflects Palestinian collective awareness. In her narrative, she uses the national term "Turks" and not "the Ottoman Empire." The English, in Fatin's memory, were oppressors who hanged and killed Palestinians for seeking liberation. She uses the name "English" and not "British." This is true of many of the women interviewed. They used these lay terms that describe the experiences of power in daily life rather than the formal political terminology.

In contrast to the Turks and the English, the entry by the Jews in 1948 "drove us out," and "dispersed us." In the interviewees' words, entry took place and was immediately followed by expulsion and exile—whereas, under the Turks and the English, the majority of the women continued to live their lives in their homes and in the bosoms of their families.

"REVOLUTION"

Da'asa from Lydd describes an experience told to her by her mother: "My uncle, Amin Hasuna, was ambushed at night on the way from Ramleh during the days of the English. The English commander, Totley, told him, 'Turn around.' He didn't agree and Totley shot my uncle in the back. The English used to pick us up in the fields, where the *fallāhīn* used to harvest grain. In those days, the revolutionaries would wear a black *jilbāb* [women's robes] and hide in the fields." When the women mentioned the days of the revolution against the British in 1936, they called the Palestinian fighters "revolution-aries." Though the women describe the Nakba in language drawn from the private sphere, they made considerable use of the word *thawra* (revolution) drawn from the official national and political sphere to describe the more distant events of 1936 and the revolt against the British Mandate.[2] The Nakba is more intimately tied to their present lives than the *thawra*.

Fatma from Ramleh/Zakariyya recalls: "I was young and I heard about the revolutionaries. They were in the days of the English, not in the days of the Jews. I would hear about them, rumors. I was small and ignorant. . . . Some of them were killed, a lot of them were killed during the days of the revolution. . . . They fought against the same English and a lot of people were killed, my God." Almost all the women who mentioned the English used the same terms for the fighters and the fight—"revolutionaries" and "revolution." Only one woman, Fatin, used the term, "the days of the strike." The words *al-thawra* and *al-thuwwār* are frequently used by Palestinians in the context of the revolt against the British in 1936. "Revolution" implies an ambition to effect a profound change in society; it implicitly justifies the act. The word "revolutionaries" also carries Palestinian dreams and hopes of ending the British Mandate. By killing the revolutionaries, or as Sara puts it, executing "any Palestinian who even breathed," the British killed the dream of Palestinians to liberate their country, making the invasion and dispersion of the Palestinians by the Israelis all the more inevitable.

THE DAYS OF THE ARABS VERSUS THE DAYS OF ISRAEL

Language changes and is updated in accordance with changing social and cultural circumstances (Hertzler, 1965). New social needs and cultural experiences expand, modify, and reshape the borders of language and its components. Layla (Lydd) recounts life under the British Mandate:

> At first, and during the days of the English, we were in the Orthodox Society Club at the Christian Center. There were English ladies who held exhibitions and organized outings. We finished school during the days of the Arabs, and the Jews came and we didn't continue the way we should have, there were no good schools anymore. I was in school before the Jews came in 1948. The [British] Government had a strong education system in the days of the Arabs. I studied from first until fourth grade at the Christian Center School.

While speaking of the dedication of the Christian Orthodox club, Layla sees the English positively. When speaking of the positive experience of her studies, she uses the words "in the days of the Arabs." Layla mentions the high standard of education "in the days of the Arabs" and not "in the days of the English." Layla does not perceive the Christian club and its establishment by the English as part of their missionary activity with imperialist objectives. When she speaks of positive experiences in her life, such as acquiring a good education, before the Jews came in, she generally uses the words "the days of the Arabs."

Alice from Ramleh confirms Layla's statement: "We were in the Tabitha School, the best school in all of Palestine and known throughout the world. The elite people of Jaffa would go there; anyone who had money would go there." Alice and her friends point to the decline in the standard of education after 1948 and the current poor level of achievement among the Arab population in Lydd and Ramleh. They spoke of "the days of the Arabs" whenever they spoke of any positive experiences under the British Mandate.

Nahla from Ramleh/Lydd added: "In the days of the Arabs, people were really simple, they didn't have numbers on the houses, they didn't have names for the streets [she laughs]. . . . In the days of the Arabs, when someone arrived, he would ask 'Where is so-and-so's house?' 'Where is Salma's house?' and everybody knew." Nahla's statement reflects the security she associates when she remembers these days compared to her present insecurity and estrangement. She also associates nostalgia for the closeness among the population, when everyone knew everyone else. She recalls: "We lived in a city where everyone knew everyone, there were no house numbers, no street numbers, and everyone knew Umm-Anis and everyone could direct you to her house." The past is important only to the extent of present-day belief in its existence (Grinberg, 2000: 13). Fatma, originally from Zakariyya, says: "We lived in the best possible way in Zakariyya, there was no gossip like there is today, no 'so-and-so' talk and no nothing. Nothing like that. And there weren't people who killed other people, and there weren't people who hit other people. We were like one family."

The women in a sense invent a myth of a cohesive social group that lived in safety and security, because that is how they relive the past today. Irrespective of whether or not that memory is factually correct, the solidarity and security depicted in that memory indicate the current absence of such feelings in their cities today. The words "the days of the Jews" appear in the context of the current insecurity, in relation to poor education and other forms of discrimination. The sense of security that prevailed in the days of the Arabs disappeared when the Jews came in.

The women described their lives under the British Mandate by means of active verbs that reflect vitality, and in the plural: "we lived here," "we worked the land," "we harvested," "we went to the fields," "we drew water from the wells," "we washed," and "we cooked." Fatma from Zakariyya says: "We stored the grain in pitchers that we filled with wheat, barley, lentils, chickpeas, beans, and corn. . . . The men harvested and the women gathered, and everyone would load together, until we finished." By means of such verbs, the interviewees expressed a certain degree of control over their lives and property. Though they described how the British performed searches, destroyed harvests, and killed many young Palestinian men, Palestinians had a measure of independence where they could move freely on their land and in the fields. The English, according to their statements, did not control their day-to-day lives. The presence of the English in the interviewees' lives increased following the 1936 revolution. Interviewees from both urban and rural origins mentioned executions in Acre and manhunts for the rebels.

The interviewees' longing for the past, and for the years of the British Mandate, expresses a distinction between British control of their villages and cities and Israeli control of those places since 1948. "During the days of Israel," they were driven out of their homes, and their families were exiled to other places in Israel or other countries. As Sara from Lydd/al-Majdal says: "The Jews exiled and dispersed us." They also make comparative statements in relation to their present-day lives in Lydd and Ramleh: "In the time of the English, we didn't have to pay [taxes] on the house or the land;" "We had a good living;" "If only they could have left us in our homes!" In describing their lives since the Israeli conquest, the women talked about the lack of personal safety and about rent, taxes, and the non-collection of garbage as a means of pressuring them to leave their homes.

Salma (Lydd) describes the change that took place with regard to land inheritance: "In the days of the Arabs, for example, if the parents had ten dunums[3] of land, they gave their sons two dunums each and their daughters one dunum each, and everyone got his or her portion. My grandmother inherited from her parents, and my mother inherited, too. During the days of Israel, they give the same thing to women as to men." Salma explains that it was necessary to go to court to prove how many family members remained in Israel, and the inheritance was divided according to the number of family members who became citizens of Israel. Inheritors still in the country could receive their land, but only after they released it by paying taxes.

At first glance, it would seem that the modern Jewish state introduced egalitarian values, because, according to Salma, in the days of the Arabs, daughters received less than sons, whereas "in the days of Israel, they give the same thing to women as to men." However, Salma tells of how the 1950 Israeli Absentee Property Law influenced her life as a woman. According to this law, Salma was entitled to "liberate" her share from her family land inheritance. However, because of the high taxes, she did not have the means to do so. She worked with her husband to "liberate" his share of inheritance. They both had to work hard to release his plot. Salma was left without the egalitarian share in the land that was due to her by law. Although "in the days of Israel, they gave the same to women as to men," she was unable to benefit from that equality. The Israeli Absentee Property law was put in place to ensure efficiency in controlling more territory, which in turn affected gender relations in Palestinian society and disempowered women.

Another account that highlights contemporary insecurity is Salma's description of how her daughter's husband was found dead:

> My daughter has six daughters and a son. Her husband died six months ago. He was drinking and using drugs and he died like that . . . she is working, poor one, with the girls. . . . Lydd is full [of drugs] but thank God our kids and their kids are not among them. It all depends on how you were brought up. Our kids and their kids are good, thank God. . . . Only he was like that. He was drinking and using drugs, so he became an addict like them, and they found him dead.

The drug use in both cities is one of the main problems that the Palestinian community currently confronts. Some of the interviewees spoke openly about this while others hinted at it or silenced it.

Palestinians in Lydd and Ramleh face additional problems that make them feel insecure. In particular, they are subject to spatial closure and are not given licenses to build houses on their land, and the municipality does not offer any adequate solution to their housing problems. The personal experiences of Salma and her daughter illustrate this. When arriving at her mother's house, Salma's daughter approached me thinking that I was a journalist interviewing her mother. She said:

> Not long ago, we had a house demolition here in Lydd, you may have heard about it. They destroyed the house of my nephew Samir. Journalists and people from the Ta'ayush movement were present. They destroyed so much. . . . I built next door and I have a demolition order. We built seven houses here. . . . Each house destroyed, the Ta'ayush movement would come and help rebuild it with bricks until it [was] complete. I built it with bricks then they told me to stop so I stopped. They did not tell him [Samir] to stop, they let him finish and then they [the Israeli authorities] came and destroyed it. . . . Even the army came, as if there was a war. They blocked the road from all sides. It was like a war . . . you can tell that something is going on in Lydd when they demolish a house (laughs). There is air and land patrol and they close all the roads . . . they destroyed a house that belonged to the Naqib family.

Salma, her daughter, and many other interviewees described the current daily social and political pressure on the Palestinian community in both cities.

They focused on drug use and home demolition that relate to Palestinians as criminals violating the law.

The current political situation in the occupied Palestinian territories was also on the interviewees' minds. Their discussions of the escalation of the Second Intifada highlight their conflicted position as part of the Palestinian people who are under Israeli occupation, and as citizens of Israel, the state that is directly responsible for that oppression. Many women drew an analogy between their experiences in 1948 and what is happening today in Gaza, Jenin, and other refugee camps while expressing their pain and solidarity with the Palestinian people beyond the cities in which they presently reside. Salma says: "People in Gaza have nothing to eat. . . . [The Israelis] are hitting them from the sky and that is sad. . . . What can a person do? A person can go out into the world and give thanks to God. My God, the people have seen a lot [of suffering]; they've seen a lot here." Other interviewees used similar expressions—sometimes directly, as quoted here, and sometimes indirectly, in coded speech, broken or unexplained sentences, generally accompanied by sighs and silence, such as: "What can a person say? God is great," or "Look around and see what's going on." Present-day political realities hang over the women's stories and evoke the distant events of 1948.

Fatma (Ramleh/Zakariyya) recalls: "At that time, girls had shame, people had shame. Heaven forbid, no girl would dare stand by the gate, or open the gate and sit outside, the way they do today. . . . May God forgive you." Fatma describes today's Palestinian women and people in general as shameless. Today, in the days of Israel, Palestinian men have lost control over women. Fatma reflects an insecure feeling of her generation who went through rapid changes in a hostile environment. Some young women pay a heavy price for their behavior—at times, it even cost them their lives in the name of "family honor." Such murders represent, according to Baxter, the collapse of the moral order and "the quintessence of a system gone terribly wrong" (Baxter, 2007: 753). "The days of Israel" are described as days with unsafe cities, where men have lost control and fail to provide security for their families.

Alice from Ramleh talks about women being murdered for reasons of family honor: "Women are being murdered every day, there is no judge and no justice . . . we never saw murder like this in the days of Palestine." The expression "every day" illustrates the lack of personal safety that Palestinian women experience in their day-to-day lives in both cities. The women's testimonies point to the political brutality and violence affecting family life and relations between men and women within the family. Veena Das (2000) describes how colonialism in India left behind a heritage of relationships characterized by bitterness and betrayal—not only between Hindus and Muslims, but between Indian women and men as well. Alice's outcry—"Women are being murdered every day, there is no judge and no justice"—expresses her protest at the crass breaches of social and political conventions.

CONCLUSION

When we remember our past we are telling stories about ourselves, to ourselves and to others. Women recalled historical events and gave them names that have particular meaning to them as women and as Palestinians in a Jewish state. The differences in the terminology used by the interviewees and that of the researcher result from the need of each, from her own position, to retain legitimacy and visibility as female, as Palestinian, and as an equal citizen. It is not a coincidence that I decided to analyze what the women were *not* saying, what I saw as "the missing words." When they said "when the Jews came" instead of "the Nakba," "we're from here" instead of "I am," or "the English era" or "the days of the Arabs/Palestine" instead of the "British Mandate," they expressed a sense of survival necessary to rebuild shattered and dispersed communities.

The women interviewed described the events of 1948 with cultural language drawn from the private sphere, while the 1936 revolt was narrated with words drawn from the public realm. Their speech patterns were complex and do not give rise to monolithic thinking. The fact that older urban Palestinian women use different types of language for different historical events tells us about the operation of power in different regimes and women's resistance to it. Though they do not use the political term "Nakba," they frame the Zionists in 1948 as invaders who penetrated without permission and violated the privacy of the home and land/country that was not empty, but full of Palestinian inhabitants. The invasion of the Jews was deep; family and community were uprooted and dispersed. The influence that the penetration/invasion still has on the daily lives of these women was marked by a deep sense of insecurity articulated around honor killings and drugs. Their past is present in their daily routines where history remains vividly alive. In the face of today's house demolitions, the past lives on in the present and influences the way they conceive and locate their personal and collective sociohistorical life.

These choices of language blur the gendered dichotomy between the private and public and the personal and collective. The women resist the Zionist historiographic narrative by describing the invasion and forced expulsion of 1948 as well as the ongoing exclusion and insecurity that they experience in daily life. Their language preserves historic events, hopes and disappointments, rivalries and loyalties within Palestinian society and in relation to the Jewish state.

NOTES

I finished writing this article during the academic year 2007–2008 in Berlin while I was a Fellow at the program "Europe in the Middle East—the Middle East in Europe" at the Berlin-Brandenburg Academy of Sciences and Humanities, the

Fritz Thyssen Foundation, and the Wissenschaftskolleg zu Berlin. I am grateful to these institutions, particularly to the Fritz Thyssen Foundation, for providing me with a scholarship that enabled me to work on my research.

1. For example, in the Nakba of the Baramikah, a prominent Persian family who gained influence and power during the Abbasid Caliphate in Baghdad in the eighth century, they were extirpated, imprisoned, and their property confiscated.

2. According to Ted Swedenburg, Palestinians illusively describe the *thawra* of 1936–1939 and constitute their collective memory despite Israeli attempts to erase it (Swedenburg, 1995). While women were marginal in his research, he argued that some upper-class women participated in part in the 1936 revolt. Women in the villages played more active roles in the *thawra* from within the private sphere. When the British discovered the importance of the private sphere, they started to invade homes and ruin the crops, oil, and wheat (Swedenburg, 1995; Peteet, 1991).

3. *Dunum* is an area unit equivalent to approximately 1,000 m².

SIX

BEING A BORDER

Honaida Ghanim

"You can be a citizen or you can be stateless, but it is difficult to imagine *being* a border."

—Andre Green in Etienne Balibar, *Politics and the Other Scene*

Abu Ahmad was twenty-seven when the 1949 Rhodes ceasefire agreement was signed between Israel and Jordan, leaving him on one side of the new border and his parents, brothers, and sisters on the other. For him the agreement was a private disaster that decontextualized his social map. Abu Ahmad found an extraordinary way to reconnect with people now on the opposite side. Every day he would sit for a few hours at the top of a rock in the eastern side of Tulkarim where he now lives, with his eyes to the main street that connects Tulkarim with his mother village Dayr al-Ghusun. He counted the passing cars: "Thirty cars passed today," he would say to his friends who thought he was losing his mind.

Fatmeh was thirty-five when the borders kept her on one side and her family on the other. But she was more fortunate than Abu Ahmad, since she had land next to her parents. In those early years, only a line through the field indicated the inside and outside, a line preserved by the Jordanian and Israeli security forces. Fatmeh and her mother used to pretend that they were digging the land as they whispered their news and updates to each other. Most of the time they were lucky. But if the Jordanian guards saw them talking, they would shout at the mother who was on their side: "How dare you talk to the Jews," meaning, of course, her daughter!

THE CONSTRUCTION OF INSIDE/OUTSIDE

Relying on self-reflection and stories from family, neighbors, and friends in my home village of Marjeh, in the Triangle region, I explore how Palestinians there created symbolic and substantive practices that aimed on one hand to recapture their social life as they lived it before the partition of 1948–1949, and on the other hand to resist the transformation of the military and political border into a social one. Palestinians in Israel developed symbolic and practical actions to cope with the 1948 partition of Palestine and the demarcation of new borders that resulted from the establishment of Israel and the Nakba of the Palestinian people. These included infiltrating, sneaking, smuggling, using specific signs and marks to pass messages to the other side, loud calling, or quiet whispering and talking to friends and family across the border (see also Mana', 2006; Sa'adi, 2006; Ghanim, 2007). The partition shattered clans and social entities, sent mothers away from their children, and separated brothers and sisters from each other. The daily life of Palestinians was turned upside down and regular social practices became risky and dangerous.

The creation of Israel, followed by the 1949 ceasefire agreement, divided Palestinian villages into two parts: those "inside" what became known as the Green Line would be under Israeli control and those "outside" of it would be controlled by Jordan or Egypt. Around 170,000 Palestinians (approximately 10 percent of the Palestinian population) found themselves to be "inside" the Green Line. The ceasefire agreement created a *de facto* border and, for the Israelis at least, the "Green Line" became synonymous with the border line that had to be controlled and preserved by all possible means, including military ones. However, as Illana Feldman explains, "the political and military demarcation of a border, of a new spatial arrangement and of a new category of 'outside' (and 'inside') does not proceed at the same tempo as social life, as personal connection and as communal identification" (Feldman, 2006: 14). In the case of Palestinians, the social and cultural borders stand in contradictory and controversial relation to the political and military borders. Unlike Israelis, the Palestinians saw the Green Line as a temporary obstacle that needed to be overcome and dismantled.

The contradictory role of the border turned it into a site of constant tension between the indigenous and colonial orders, between Palestinian villagers and the Israeli armed forces. While the new State of Israel was doing all it could to turn the border into an untouchable and prohibited zone that demarcated its sovereignty, villagers from both sides of the border were also doing their best to dismantle it. In the new order that followed the Nakba and the establishment of Israel, the border was a microcosm of the conflict par excellence. The zone was always haunted by the "return of the real," by the eruption of phenomena that were supposed to be repressed by the new order. The border was the sign of oppression but also a possibility of liberation, a sign of cutting but also of connection, of colonizing and of decolonizing, of death but also of life. Ironically the border was a site for the intensive practice of power but also intensive resistance.

For the Palestinians, the Green Line could not and would not be conceptualized as a normal fact or *fait accompli*. Between 1948 and 1967, Palestinians living in Israel under strict military control and surveillance consistently attempted to cross the border. Their aim was not explicitly political. They were merely trying to visit their families, harvest their crops, and purchase merchandise. "Infiltrating," "sneaking," "evading," and "penetrating"—all strictly illegal actions as defined by the Israeli state—were, in fact, their way of catching a glimpse, however temporary and curtailed, into their lives as they had lived them before that border brutally crossed them. The border came to be a place that the Palestinian ran up against, repeatedly passing and repassing through it, as when she is expelled or allowed to rejoin her family. It becomes, in the end, a place where she resides, almost a home.

MARJEH: THE NEW MAP

One of the villages affected by the new "border" was Marjeh, my home village. Following the Rhodes ceasefire agreement, the village was annexed by Israel in 1949. Marjeh is colloquially referred to as a *khirbeh*, or hamlet, by its neighboring villagers. It is somewhat smaller than a village but larger than a farm. Marjeh's inhabitants are the descendants of several Palestinian families from the larger village of Dayr al-Ghusun, adjacent to Tulkarim, who decided in the nineteenth century to settle on their various plots of land, including the plot of land that was to become Marjeh, in order to preserve and cultivate them. After annexation, Marjeh, which had hitherto been merely an extension of Dayr al-Ghusun, was transformed into something of an orphan whose parents had forcibly abandoned it. In the space created by the absent parent, Marjeh was forced to mature into an independent village. Marjeh is now located at the edge of the Green Line between Tulkarim city, located inside the 1967-occupied territories of the West Bank, and Netanya city inside Israel. Today, the place proudly proclaims its heroic ability to grow and develop into what is nearly a village, and even boasts of its achievements to its absentee parent.

My family, descendants of Marjeh, used to sit together on hot summer nights telling and listening to stories of the old days. On such nights, my eight uncles and their wives and children would gather together on the roof of our house, and grandfather would regale us with his life story. The stories, however, were always accompanied by a warning: we were cautioned against telling these stories to other people so as to protect our family's privacy and, most importantly, to protect us from the Shin Bet (Israeli General Security Service). The conflicted relationship between my family and the border made our very history—even basics such as who begat whom, where, and with whom—criminal from the point of view of the Israeli state.

My grandfather would stretch his arm out toward the east and say: "That light comes from the village of Dayr al-Ghusun, where I was raised by my uncle Ahmad after my father died and my mother remarried." This orphaned grandfather of mine, growing up in an orphaned village, carried his burden in the hope that, if nothing else, the situation of national orphan-hood would one day be sorted out. Ever since I was a child, I have seen him gaze eastward, ears glued to the radio, listening to BBC reports about a "solution" that grew more and more distant by the day. He consistently held on to his hope, by now Messianic, that some metaphysical, omnipotent power would restore normality.

For my part, I always wanted to explore the other side of his life, to understand how he came to be "here" and not "there."

"Grandfather, why did you come here?"

My father looked at me with something of a shy smile: "Sssh . . . Grand-father must not be interrupted while he is talking."

I fell silent but the question continued to trouble me, and I remembered to ask my mother the same bothersome question the following day.

"Your grandfather came here because he fell in love with your grand-mother, whose family owned much land here. They agreed that he could marry her under the condition that he dig them water wells. So, he came from Dayr al-Ghusun and began digging the wells. Then he bought an olive grove, married your grandmother, and they settled down here. Your grandmother gave birth to nine boys and two girls."

One of these children was my uncle Khalid, who crossed the border when he was thirteen and joined the Jordanian security forces. According to my grandmother, the Jordanians picked him up when he was shepherd-ing the family cows near the border. They took him to an army station, and asked him to name the people that used to cross the border from the Jordanian side to meet with Jews in the house of my uncle's neighbor, a well-known Israeli collaborator. My uncle agreed but asked for their protec-tion, and he joined them.

The question that occupied me next was: "How did Uncle Khalid manage to visit his family?"

"He would steal out, always at night, when there was a heavy rain. He knew that the Jordanian guards would leave their stands in the heavy rain. And he always knew how to evade the Jordanians and the Israelis. He used to wear women's clothes and cover his head, especially because he didn't want our neighbors to know that he had come to visit."

"Border fear" did not prevent him from "infiltrating" back to his mother. The border, which was supposed to disconnect him from his family, failed in its task. The darkness of night was his faithful ally, hiding him on his journey westward and back.

The French philosopher Gaston Bachelard (1969) claimed that darkness denotes the unconscious that cannot be civilized, its nature mysterious and even frightening. My uncle, though he had never read Bachelard, understood that only in the darkness/unconscious could he experience the normal/conscious. At night he became a ghost or a shadow, released from his physical presence, invisible to the Jordanian and Israeli border patrols.

Living on the border overloaded my family with stories of border passages, although not all of them concluded with the same kind of Hollywood-style happy ending as my Uncle Khalid's tale. This was certainly not the case for his maternal grandfather, Abu 'Ali. Even though he was not a prince on a white horse and his wife was not Snow White, my great-grandfather's story inscribed itself into my childlike mind as the quintessential story of love and desire.

LOVE STORY

Once upon a time, but not so long ago, when the "Jews" conquered the village of Qaqun, destroying its houses and expelling its inhabitants, several families from Qaqun escaped to Marjeh and found a temporary safe haven in the midst of the families of our village. One such family settled near grandfather Abu 'Ali's land. Several months passed, and grandfather Abu 'Ali, who was a lonely widower, decided to marry again. Su'ad, a refugee widow whose family was living near grandfather's land, seemed like a perfect match for him. She would not ask for a fancy dowry like young brides nor would she tire him with a variety of demands and requests as the daughters of settled families were accustomed to doing. She would accept him as he was. The perfect choice perhaps, but certainly not in the perfect context.

She was an illegal resident and an unwelcome stepmother. From the perspective of the Israeli authorities, she was a right-less refugee who had not received permission to stay within the borders of the Green Line. From the perspective of her stepsons, she was a stranger and a poor woman whose offspring threatened their inheritance. Su'ad, by no choice of her own, became the personification of the border, embodying the presence of the unwanted, the prohibited, and the banned.

Su'ad was able to handle the double pressure for the short period of one year and a few months. During this time, she gave birth to Ibrahim, her only son from this marriage. When she could not take it anymore, she ran away and crossed the border toward the Jordanian side. For several years, she settled in Shwekieh, the closest village to Marjeh. Su'ad, the persecuted wife, and Abu 'Ali, the frustrated husband, believed that this was the most tenable arrangement: she would rent a home there and he would come to meet her once a week. Crossing the border was just a technical issue, or at least that's what they believed until they were made aware of the problematics inherent in the border.

Abu ʻAli safely navigated the border many times with the aim of visiting his son and wife. Sometimes he spent a night, sometimes an entire week. As his number of successful "infiltrations" increased, rumors reached the ears of the Israeli and Jordanian authorities who began to pay attention to his movements. The first time he was caught, the Jordanians issued a warning. They stressed that if he did not heed it, the next time he was caught he would be sent to prison. Abu ʻAli promised to behave like a "good citizen" and made guarantees that he would not return without the necessary permission.

He returned to Marjeh, on the Israeli side, waited a couple of weeks and then decided to traverse the border again. He received his permission, as he had on all previous occasions, from himself. But his bad luck and the Jordanians' good informants proved to be a recipe for disaster. He was apprehended by the Jordanian security forces, who were extremely angry that he had broken his promise. They arrested him and sent him to jail—but not before they violently beat him. His encounter with the Jordanian judge who presided over his case became a cynical family story. When the judge sentenced him to three months in prison, Abu ʻAli asked for permission to address the court:

"Sir, I have a family that I need to feed—who will take care of them if I am in jail for such a long time?"

The judge responded: "Don't worry. God will provide."

But Abu ʻAli, who wasn't a very religious man, retorted: "Oh sir, if I, God, and the donkey barely manage to provide, how on earth is God going to manage alone?"

The judge obviously was not impressed by the argument and Abu ʻAli spent three months in a Jordanian prison. Having served his time, he was brought to the Israeli side. The Israelis, not wanting to be outdone by the Jordanians, proceeded to send him to an Israeli prison.

The prison experiences left Abu ʻAli—by then a sixty-five-year-old man—reticent to continue "infiltrating" the border. He decided to wait a few months and hoped that the Jordanians and Israelis would forget about him in the meantime. Several months passed and Abu ʻAli decided to attempt another "infiltration." Crossing the border was by no means an impossible task but circumventing the network of collaborators and informants on the Jordanian side was. Having spent only a few hours with his wife and son, Abu ʻAli found himself in the hands of the Jordanian army who had come to the house to arrest the entire family. Abu ʻAli was sent to jail. His wife and son were transferred to an unknown place. When he was released from prison, Abu ʻAli returned to the village to see his family but was told by a neighbor that they had been forced to move. He searched for them endlessly but never managed to find them. After the 1967 war, Suʻad and her son, Ibrahim, came to visit the family in Marjeh, revealing the story of their transfer to an area near Jericho. Abu 'Ali, who passed away in August 1967 without having seen his wife and son again, never heard the story.

For the people who lived in my village, the border was a physical sign of the reality of emergency into which they had been thrown. The border marked an abrupt severing from their pre-Nakba lives. It embodied both the forced cutting of family ties as well as the loss of olive groves that had fallen on the other side of the border. Palestinians did not simply accept the border that crossed them—though it did so violently and with powerful border patrols, prisons, population displacements, informants, and new criminalizations. Border passage stories like those from Marjeh are an important reminder that state-formation processes such as land annexation and line drawing are not as neat and seamless as they often appear to be.

NOTE

Parts of this chapter appeared in a different form in 2007 in "Living in the Shadow of Emergency in Palestine." In *The Partition Motif in Contemporary Conflicts*. Smita Tewari Jassal and Eyal Ben-Ari, eds. Pp. 283–296. New Delhi: Sage Publications.

III

GENDERING BODIES AND SPACE

Figure 4. Still of filmmaker's mother on her rooftop in Ramleh, from *The Roof* by
Kamal Aljafari, 2006. Courtesy of the director.

SEVEN

THE ROLES OF
PALESTINIAN PEASANT WOMEN

The Case of al-Birweh Village, 1930–1960

Lena Meari

The mid-twentieth century was a period of the accumulation of multiple and drastic changes in Palestinian political, social, and economic life. This period saw British colonization (1917–1948), Zionist colonial occupation accompanied by the expulsion of more than 750,000 Palestinians (1947–1949), and military rule (1948–1966) imposed on those Palestinians who survived expulsion and managed to remain within the borders of what became in 1948 the colonial State of Israel.[1] This chapter explores the lives of peasant women from al-Birweh village during the years 1930 to 1960 and the transformations in their roles that accompanied the changing economic-political regimes. Based on interviews with al-Birweh refugees, I analyze women's work roles during the years that preceded the destruction of their village by the Zionist forces in June 1948, during the expulsion from al-Birweh, and later when they settled in other Palestinian villages that survived destruction. In particular, I examine how Palestinian peasant women experienced and coped with changes relating to land ownership during this period—property law, land tenure, and land expropriation and reappropriation.

   I explore women's roles as part of the household economy and under the changing conditions of colonialism and modernization. In the process, I answer Scott's (1988) call to interrogate ahistorically fixed binary oppositions between categories such as male and female by seeing them as contextually defined and repeatedly constructed. I show that in contrast to the simplistic

119

unilateral historical representations of an inflexible sexual division of labor, sexual segregation, restrictions on women's movement, and strict separation between public and private found in the classical literature on Arab women (see Abu-Lughod, 1989), the division of labor in the Palestinian village of al-Birweh appears at different times flexible, contestable, and shifting.

In my analysis, dynamism, change, and conflict in the lives of the interviewees are evident. This serves as a corrective to ahistorical depictions of the Palestinian peasantry found in colonial, Orientalist, and Zionist literatures, as traditional, fixed, premodern, passive, and unproductive.[2] The active roles of women that I explore also challenge Palestinian national representations of peasants, and specifically peasant women, as passive icons of the nation.[3] They also implicitly speak to the marginalization of peasants' social history—not to mention peasant women's social history—in Palestinian national historiography with its focus on the political national struggle and its elite leadership.[4] I do so without bracketing off women as having separate histories and describe their lives as integrally linked to a larger social history.

METHODOLOGICAL CONCERNS

A number of methodological concerns about positionality, power relations, representation, and the relationship between theory and politics constitute an integral component of this study and its writing. Such issues have been widely discussed in the literature (e.g., Lal, 1996; Wolf, 1996; Visweswaran, 1994) and my aim in invoking them here is to stress their unresolved tensions and inevitable recurrence in fieldwork, and to illustrate the ways in which I struggled with them within my study.

In 2003–2004 I interviewed twenty Palestinian refugees from al-Birweh village (ten men and ten women) between the ages of sixty-two and eighty-eight, living currently in Makir, Jdaideh, and Kufur Yasif villages located in the Galilee area. The discussions were held in the interviewees' houses, often in the house yard where most of the interviewees spent many hours, especially during the summer. Some interviews included one interviewee while others included two or three, which added richness to the conversations by tracing collective memories as well as conflicts, debates, and distinct perceptions and interpretations. The interviews extended between two to three hours and were recorded and transcribed. Most of the interviews fluctuated between joyful moments when the participants remembered their youth and life in al-Birweh, and distressing moments when they expressed feelings of loss of a mode of life and a place that sustained it. While some interviewees depicted a romantic view of life in al-Birweh, others pointed to the distress and hardship they suffered in the village. This chapter reflects a minor part of these rich conversations.

Being a third-generation al-Birweh refugee myself constitutes a vital part of my passionate personal and political interest in understanding, documenting, and circulating the refugees' narratives and generating political action to enhance their just demand for return. My personal-historical-political subject position facilitated my access to the interviewees and increased the interest of most of them in sharing their experiences and telling me their histories. Yet differences in gender, age, appearance, education, and personality affected the rapport I tried to build with them. This illustrates that there is no pure insider, or for that matter, outsider status (Wolf, 1996). I asked my father to accompany me to speak with some interviewees and felt that, despite some education and gender differences, the fact that he himself had lived in al-Birweh made them more forthcoming. At the same time, his presence seemed to inhibit some from raising sensitive issues related to particular people they knew in common.

Oral history can provide a partial opportunity for subaltern groups to participate in the process of history writing, though not without the mediation of the researcher. Wolf (1996) indicates that feminists have preferred using qualitative research methods and have found that oral history is a particularly compelling and less obtrusive way to study disempowered women. Still, power relations are inherent within this method. I asked the interviewees to tell me their life stories instead of asking them structured questions. They relied on their memory and life experiences to build their stories. Remembering is an active process that rebuilds and reproduces experiences and does not simply echo them. Most of the interviewees used the term "story" (qiṣa) to refer to their narratives, stories they offered as real accounts of their lives. I approached the interviewees as storytellers since storytelling was a common practice among this generation of Palestinians steeped in oral culture. As a reflection of the power relations that still inhere in this method, each refugee's story is, however, transformed into a written, fixed, unlived text held within a theoretical framework. Thus, I do not claim to represent the refugees' voices. This study offers a tentative and partial account of al-Birweh refugees' lives, shaped as it is by my theoretical framework, which hopefully serves as an opening for further and diverse accounts to follow.

As a member of an academic institution I have, in addition to my personal and political concerns, a theoretical one that the interviewees do not share. Academia, with its particular "rituals" and symbolizations, is often remote from ordinary illiterate people's lives and institutionalizes power relations that represent them as passive objects of study. Most of the interviewees in this study were not interested in my theoretical questions such as those concerning the gendered division of labor. Rather, the majority of them were interested in going home to al-Birweh. Academic analysis is inevitably implicated in politics and is never pure or neutral. My methodology is not intended to displace politics to matters of stylistic conventions (Lal, 1996). The goal of this study is not only to evoke understanding, but also to provoke action and real-world interventions (Birth, 1990). In my study, analyzing and circulating the experiences of Palestinian refugees and struggling alongside them for the right of return is the only way to combine both forms of political intervention.

AL-BIRWEH VILLAGE

Al-Birweh village is located on a hill in a strategic location at the Acre–Safad–Shafa 'Amir junction in the Palestinian Galilee, nine kilometers east of the coastal city of Acre. It is surrounded by Wadi al-Halazon and the lands of the still-standing villages of Julis, Majd al-Kurum, Sha'ab, and the destroyed village of al-Damun. The village's location is strategic because it is situated on a plateau overlooking the plains of Acre.

Before 1948 the village's inhabited area included fifty-nine *dunums*. Its total land area included 3,031 *dunums* of nonagricultural land and 10,452 *dunums* of agricultural land used to cultivate wheat, barley, corn, sesame, watermelon, olive trees, grapes, and figs (al-Marashli et al., 1984; Dirbas, 1992). By 1945 Zionists had purchased 546 *dunums* of uninhabited area, while the remaining lands were owned by al-Birweh villagers and other Palestinian and Arab landowners (ibid.). The village included two olive presses, two public water wells, a mosque, a church, and one elementary school established in the Ottoman era. In 1945 the number of al-Birweh inhabitants was 1,460 divided into twenty-two families (approximately 1,330 Muslims and 130 Christians) (ibid.). The majority of villagers lived off of planting cereals and vegetables and raising livestock. They sold surplus products in the adjacent market in Acre.

Al-Birweh inhabitants were affected by and engaged with Palestinian political struggles against British colonialism and British support of the Zionist movement and some were even active in the leadership of the 1936–1939 Palestinian peasant revolution.[5] Most interviewees recalled an event named *waqi'at al-ṣabir* (the cactus event) that took place in August 1937 when revolutionaries bombed a British military jeep in a street next to al-Birweh. Seeking revenge, the British collected al-Birweh men, forced them to cut cactus plants, and then put them on top of the cactus. The interviewees remember that Palestinian men and women from Acre helped remove the thorns from the men's bodies. They also pointed to the roles of al-Birweh women during this period in transferring food, water, and weapons to the revolutionaries in the mountains. These modes of engagement differ from the activities of urban elite women who were involved in welfare activism, organizing demonstrations, and writing petitions against the Zionist settlers.

Al-Birweh inhabitants resisted the Zionist occupation and, after the fall of the city of Acre, they refused to surrender to Zionist forces and succeeded initially in repelling them. But the forces returned, expelled the inhabitants, and destroyed the village on June 24, 1948. Most of al-Birweh's inhabitants became refugees either in nearby villages in the Galilee or in

Lebanon, Syria, and Jordan. The Zionists established Ahihud and Yasur Jewish settlements on al-Birweh lands. The estimated number of al-Birweh refugees today is 15,000.

ECONOMIC CHANGES SINCE
THE LATE NINETEENTH CENTURY

In the second half of the nineteenth century, Palestine was mainly agricultural and 70 percent of its population was rural subsistence farmers (Gojanski, 1987). Land in the Ottoman Empire was initially communally owned (*arāḍi mashā'*). Every male in the village had a share in the land, an arrangement that made selling it difficult (Granott, 1952). With the Ottoman Tanzimat reforms and the growing European penetration into the empire, Palestine was incorporated into the world capitalist market as an exporter of agricultural raw products for European markets (Scholch, 1988). These transformations facilitated the accumulation of trade profit surplus in the hands of wealthy traders, thus increasing the economic gap in the Palestinian community between large landowners and poor, landless peasants (Scholch, 1988; Mana', 1999). The shift from subsistence agriculture toward exportation entailed a new form of land ownership through new laws. The most famous of these was instated in 1858 and encouraged private ownership benefiting wealthy families. Ordinary peasants were unable to provide documents in accordance with the new laws to prove their ownership or they did not want to register their lands for fear of taxation and compulsory service in the Ottoman army. The 1858 Lands Law aimed to fragment lands in order to increase state control and revenue from the collection of registration fees.

In 1917 the British army invaded Palestine. In the same year the Balfour Declaration was issued pledging the commitment of Britain to the Zionist movement and to establishing a Jewish national home in Palestine. British colonial rule aimed to transform Palestine's economy from agrarian based to industrial agricultural. Private land ownership continued to become more concentrated during this period. The British changed the Ottoman taxation system, which was based on tithe (one-tenth of the produce), to a fixed amount paid annually irrespective of production. It also defined land ownership according to modern survey maps to allow purchase, transfer, or expropriation of land (Abu-Sitta, 2004). These transformations benefited three groups that succeeded in owning large amounts of land: the local elite, urban traders and the monetary bourgeoisie, and foreign and Jewish capitalists active in the Zionist movement (Mana', 1999). In 1918, 70 percent of Palestinian lands were communal and in 1923 this decreased to 56 percent of lands and continued to fall to 40 percent in 1940 (al-Hizmawi, 1998). During the almost three decades of British rule, the Jewish population of the country increased ten-fold through immigration, while Jewish landholdings quadrupled (Abu-Sitta, 2004: 2). The increase in Jewish landholdings was coupled with a boycott of Palestinian-Arab workers and products (Sayigh, 1980; Smith, 1984).

The introduction of private property is often regarded as the foundation of [civilization] in the colonies necessary for their transition to modernity (Mitchell, 2002). According to Mitchell's analysis of the colonial context, "The principle of [private] property was presented as the opposite of arbitrary power or coercion . . . but it justified a violent exercise of power, and in fact was established by this violence" (Mitchell, 2002: 56). The economic and land changes effected by the British further impoverished Palestinian peasants, increased the numbers of the landless, and transformed peasants into proletarian laborers. Palestinian peasants suffered from triple pressures: the Zionist invasion, Arab feudal ownership of the land, and heavy taxation imposed by the British Mandatory Government (Kanafani, 1972).

In the interviews, al-Birweh refugees described the different socio-economic levels of villagers before their expulsion. Class distinctions were defined mainly by the size of a family's land holdings. Interviewees used the categories of large, medium, and small landholders and the landless. Abu S'ud, aged thirty-three when expelled by Zionist forces, says:

> Al-Birweh was an agricultural village and we had livestock. People lived off of planting and herding, and a few were employees and chiefs (*makhatīr*). People were divided into levels: those with large, medium or small landholdings, and the landless. Those with medium and small landholdings used to plant their own plots in addition to plots belonging to large landowners according to the *ḍamān* and *ḥiṣṣa* systems. *Ḍamān* means planting a plot for a certain amount of money, and *ḥiṣṣa* means planting it for a certain portion of the crops. Those who were landless worked for landowners. Women and men worked in agriculture. . . . The additional plots were owned by large landowners who didn't farm their own lands such as Shaykh Ibrahim al-Akki and the Baidun family.

In 1941 some "30 percent of the Palestinian Arab peasants owned no land, while nearly 50 percent of the rest owned plots that were too small to meet their living requirements"[6] (Kanafani, 1972: 23).

THE EFFECTS OF THE ECONOMIC
TRANSFORMATIONS ON AL-BIRWEH

The abovementioned transformations deeply affected al-Birweh village. Interviewees described the ways in which they encountered the new colonial rules. They remember that in 1928 following the "law of lands settlement" initiated by the British colonial government, committees appointed by British rule came to the village to register uncultivated lands under state ownership. Um Ghazi, a Palestinian refugee living in Jdaideh, told me that her family owned uncultivated land in the hills of al-Birweh and when the lands committee came to the village, the family asked other peasants to help them fence this area and plant it so they would not lose it. Abu Yasar mentioned another strategy to confront colonial rules; he said that when the British committees included local Palestinians, the latter used to help the peasants by registering lands as cultivated even if they were not. In addition, some *mukhtārs* warned al-Birweh inhabitants before the committees' visits.

The interviewees described the hardships of the landless who worked in the fields of other families either as permanent or seasonal workers. In al-Birweh, female-headed households were mostly among the poorest landless villagers. Um Nayif, born in 1938, provides an example: "My grandmother was originally from Suhmata village. After her marriage she lived with her husband in Abu Snan village. When her husband died she didn't go back to her original village because there were no job opportunities. She moved with her four children to al-Birweh. During the olive seasons she picked olives in return for wheat and corn. Additionally she used to pick whatever crops were left after harvesting."

The interviewees also pointed to the growing number of households that became landless or owned smaller properties because they lost lands as a result of debt. They also mentioned that a growing number of landless people or people with small landholdings started to work outside the village in British projects such as road construction or in the British military camps. A growing number of al-Birweh men worked in the oil refinery in Haifa. Most of them remember a famous and bloody fight with Jewish workers at the end of 1947, and that the British supported the Jewish workers.

Some interviewees pointed to the fact that women were also affected by the growing transformation of peasants into workers. Hajja Thrayya, born in 1930 told me: "When the British opened the Safad road, which passes next to al-Birweh, a broker used to come to the village and take men and women to work on the road. He used to take twenty to thirty women to move stones . . . the men and women used to register each working day and be paid according to the number of days."

Um Nayif and Hajja Thrayya provided two examples of the crucial contribution of Palestinian peasant women to the household economy. Um Nayif's grandmother decided, after the death of her husband, on moving to al-Birweh rather than going back to her original village because there were more job opportunities in agriculture in al-Birweh. This points to the important roles women played in sustaining their families during that period. Hajja Thrayya's account that women from al-Birweh worked in British infrastructure projects means that Palestinian peasant women's contributions were not limited to agricultural ones.

WOMEN'S ROLES IN AL-BIRWEH

The interviews revealed the importance of women's roles to the household economy. The simple form of agriculture in al-Birweh necessitated a large labor force and women constituted an important part of it. Um S'ud told me: "A woman had to work on the family land, she had to work because the family had to survive," and Hajj Ahmad said: "Women's role in agriculture was crucial and necessary, her contribution was essential for the family." The age of women, their strength, and the size of the household landholdings shaped their roles. Old women mainly carried out the household work and cared for children, while young and strong women from households with medium and small landholdings participated in agricultural activities. Women from households with large landholdings did not participate in agricultural activities since these households hired landless peasants to work for them. Women from landless households worked on other households' lands especially as seasonal workers. Abu S'ud said:

> Women used to perform important tasks; they had specific agricultural tasks and took care of the livestock. After milking they took the milk on their heads to the Acre market. Women worked all the time, old women took care of children while young and strong women had to work on the land. I had an aunt called Amina, she was old and unmarried, and she took care of all the children of the extended family in order to enable the young mothers to work.

Hajja Thrayya said that her family "owned large landholdings and about three hundred livestock." Her father hired people from the village to do the agricultural work and her mother had no agricultural role, but had extra household work because the status of her husband as *mukhtār* meant they hosted guests on a daily basis. Um Ahmad added that as a girl she used to work in agriculture with her parents and siblings, but after her marriage to her cousin she had to do more work because her husband's family owned a larger plot. She said: "My father-in-law died. My mother-in-law, my husband, his brothers and all the brothers' wives worked on the land. We were very happy. When we harvested wheat, uprooted corn, and cut watermelon, we used to sing songs . . ."

The interviews suggest a gendered division of labor; some activities were described as men's responsibilities, others were considered women's, while still others were joint. On women's responsibilities, Abu 'Afif explains that:

> Women were responsible for administering the house including cleaning, cooking, collecting wood and carrying water from the wells. They were responsible also for raising livestock, milking, curdling the milk and carrying it to Acre market. In addition women were

responsible for agricultural tasks such as collecting herbs and bunch-ing. There were tasks that women and men performed together such as harvesting and picking olives.

Um Nayif asserts this division by saying:

> Plowing and sowing were men's responsibilities. Women collected herbs and raised livestock. Men and women worked together in harvesting and picking olives. As for water, I remember riding my uncle's donkey to fetch water. Women used to walk and carry water jars on their head, unless they had a donkey.

In spite of this gendered division some interviewees described more flexible work arrangements. Abu Isma'il, born in 1922, told me that some-times men brought water from wells: "Women and children used to bring water, and sometimes men did. But if the man had other work to do, he wouldn't bring water." Um Ahmad said that her husband used to collect wood and her mother-in-law plowed the land: "After the death of her hus-band, my mother-in-law Fatima al-Zahra Ibrahim al-Hajo plowed her land using an ox. She sowed like men and used to ride her horse and go to the land at midnight. She also used to go to Acre and deal with traders and I became like her." Um Ahmad said that her mother-in-law was respected by all the villagers.

Despite the formal gendered division of labor declared by some inter-viewees, in practice, the division of work in al-Birweh was more flexible, with men performing tasks defined by most interviewees as women's tasks and women performing men's tasks. In addition, the roles of Palestinian peasant women undermine any kind of segregation or private/public divi-sion. Women went to the wells to bring water, worked on the farms, and collected wood. Um Zuhayr said that "A woman went wherever she wanted in order to bring water and wood. It was not a problem or a shame," and Um al-Abed added: "The girl was going with her neighbor to the land as if she was going with her brother." Women's movement was routinely expected to exceed the village borders. Women from households with small land ownership or from landless households used to go to Acre market carrying milk or vegetables to sell to traders.

WOMEN'S ROLES DURING THE NAKBA

After Britain ended its mandate of the area and the war broke out, Zion-ist military organizations expelled about 750,000 Palestinians and turned them into refugees. Al-Birweh was one of the villages destroyed in 1948 and its population took refuge in neighboring villages as well as in other Arab countries. The interviews reveal the magnitude of the roles played by

women during the Nakba and the displacement era and their contribution
to family survival. During this period, most men were absent either because
they participated in the resistance, were arrested, or because they escaped
from the territories controlled by the Zionist forces. Um Nayif narrated the
story of expulsion as follows:

> After the occupation of al-Birweh we moved to al-Bi'neh village.
> When the Zionist forces occupied al-Bi'neh, they killed three men
> in public and arrested my father. My brother 'Ali who was fifteen
> years old escaped to Lebanon while my mother took me and my
> siblings to the village of Sajur. We had two cows and a donkey
> and in Sajur; my mother sold the cows and we moved with her to
> Lebanon. We arrived at Rmaysh, the conditions there were hard,
> and we had to drink filthy water. We stayed fifteen people in one
> room. Then we were moved to Sur [Tyre] where we built with our
> mother a house of two rooms and planted vegetables. My brothers
> and sisters went to school, but I stayed home to help my mother.
> We lived for four years in Lebanon and after my father's release he
> began sneaking to Lebanon to visit us. In 1952 my father finally
> succeeded in arranging a reunion for the family and we moved to
> the Palestinian village of al-Makir.

The central role that women played in Um Nayif's story is not unique.
Abu Yasar told me about the role his mother played during displacement:

> After al-Birweh and the neighboring villages were occupied we took
> the road to the north. We arrived in al-Bqay'ah village and stayed
> under the olive trees. My father didn't accompany us; he joined
> the Arab troops in Sakhnin and Dayr-Hanna. We stayed with our
> mother, grandfather, and two uncles under very hard conditions.
> After two months, my uncles decided to move to Lebanon but
> we moved back with my mother to Dayr-Hanna to find my father.
> We passed through Rama village and stayed under the olive trees
> with our relatives. We arrived in Dayr-Hanna and stayed for six
> months under the olive trees, then we moved to another place in
> Dayr-Hanna and stayed under a carob tree in front of a school. We
> waited for refugee families to take the bus to Lebanon in order to
> take their place in the school . . .

These and other stories illuminate the magnitude of the burden Palestinian
peasant women shouldered after the expulsion from al-Birweh. It took most
refugees a few months to settle and during this period most women assumed
sole responsibility for their families' survival and were the decision makers
regarding the direction of movement.

WOMEN'S ROLES UNDER MILITARY RULE

After the Nakba and the establishment of the colonial state of Israel, the first Israeli parliament reaffirmed in 1949 a state of emergency rule intro-duced by the British. Using emergency regulations, Israel imposed military rule on the Palestinians who remained in the new state and created military zones around them. Military rule included 170 articles controlling almost every aspect of Palestinian life, including the regulation of their mobility, their expression, their right to organize and to own property (Jiryis, 1973). The state established legal arrangements in order to continue expropriating Palestinian lands. One such law enabled the Israeli government to confis-cate any land or estate owned by Palestinians who left their residence after November 29, 1947. This law encompassed Palestinians who had to leave their villages but remained nearby, in cities and villages included within the borders of the newly declared state. These Palestinians were declared "present absentees" (Sabbagh in Muhammad and Nazzal, 1990). As a result of this law, al-Birweh peasants lost their lands.

The interviewees revealed different strategies al-Birweh refugees used to survive post-Nakba and during the military rule era. Between mid-1949 and 1952, al-Birweh refugees depended partially on assistance from the United Nations Relief and Works Agency (UNRWA) until the Israeli government objected and claimed the Palestinians as its citizens. Another strategy was to plant lands confiscated by the state under the ḍamān system, that is, for a set sum. Abu Sʻud provides an example of both of these strategies used by al-Birweh refugees to survive after losing their lands:

> We arrived at al-Makir village in 1951. We settled in the house of the Afandi family who left Palestine during the Nakba. At the beginning we lived off assistance from UNRWA, and then we farmed land according to the ḍamān system. After the Nakba, the Jewish government controlled all the lands owned by Palestinians who had to leave during the Nakba, and distributed some of these lands to Palestinian refugees [to farm] according to the ḍamān system. They did that in order to dispossess the original owners of their lands. I took 170 dunums of land and started to plant the land with my wife. We employed women and children to work with us during their vacation. We planted watermelon, corn and garbanzo beans, which were crops that we used to plant in al-Birweh. We also planted tobacco and cotton, which were new crops. We needed to have a permit from a company and supply it with the crops.

The strategies described by Abu Sʻud show that women continued to be important partners in the agricultural work that constituted the main pro-ductive activity for family survival.

Another survival strategy mentioned by most interviewees was "sneaking"[7] to al-Birweh, which had been declared a closed military zone, and cultivating their lands. Um Ghazi told me that after her family settled in Jdaideh village, "my mother began to go with other women to al-Birweh in order to pick green beans and okra that they planted in the village, and I accompanied her. Once the Jewish settlers in al-Birweh surrounded the women and threatened to kill them. My mother began to scream and I was holding her dress and screaming too."

Um al-'Abed remembers that after settling in Jdaideh she and her family "used to go secretly to al-Birweh in order to pick cactus fruits and figs, to see our lands, and to visit the graves of our dead ones." After living for years in al-Birweh and planting its lands, the inhabitants became refugees in nearby villages. They could see their village and lands but were not allowed to go there. They endangered their lives by "sneaking back," yet most of the women interviewed took that risk.

The majority of refugees became landless and employed the strategies used by landless people in al-Birweh to survive either by working on lands owned by Palestinians in villages where they settled or by going to others' lands and collecting the few leftovers in the fields after the main harvest. The most controversial strategy that a minority of al-Birweh refugees used was to agree to the Israeli government's suggestion to exchange their lands in al-Birweh for lands that the government confiscated from Palestinians who were expelled from the country in 1948. These government offers aimed to simultaneously silence al-Birweh residents' demands for return to their village as well as to negate the return demands of the refugees whose lands were being traded. Abu 'Afif said that after his family settled in Kufur Yasif village, "My father exchanged his land in al-Birweh for a plot in Kufur Yasif. We took thirty to thirty-five *dunums* and continued to work all together in the land." On the other hand Abu S'ud says: "A lot of al-Birweh refugees settled in al-Makir village and the Jewish government pressured the refugees to exchange their lands in al-Birweh for lands in al-Makir. A few accepted, but I didn't agree." Al-Birweh refugees made these decisions under difficult conditions of extreme vulnerability.

The sweeping changes to land that resulted from the Nakba impacted women's roles dramatically. Many women worked post-Nakba on Jewish farms and their labor was made cheap. For instance, Hajja Thrayya told me that she was not used to working in al-Birweh because her husband was a large landowner, but after the confiscation of their lands she was obliged to work with him. On the other hand, some women who used to work in al-Birweh lost their productive roles in agriculture after losing the lands. Abu Isma'il told me that his sister used to work on the family land in al-Birweh but after losing their land she stayed home.

Many women worked post-Nakba on Jewish farms as cheap labor. Palestinian brokers who worked for Jewish farmers used to find Palestinian men and women, issue them work permits from the military ruler, and take them to work on Jewish farms or in Palestinian villages that were emptied of residents like al-Bassa. The most painful survival strategy was working for the Jewish settlers who controlled al-Birweh lands, sometimes the laborers' own land, as some women from al-Birweh had to do. Um Ahmad narrated her experience:

> When UNRWA stopped providing assistance I began to work with my daughters on our lands in al-Birweh, which were taken from us and given to Jews who came from Yemen. There was a piece of land that belonged to my husband and I used to plant it with cucumbers. One day I filled cucumbers in a bucket from the land and the Jewish supervisor called me a thief. I told him, "Go away, this land is our land" . . . a lot of women worked for Yemenite Jews on al-Birweh lands. Men were looking for work in Haifa or Acre.

The Israeli authorities provided women with job opportunities on Jewish farms, but not in companies and factories, which were restricted to men. Hajja Thrayya said that "the Israeli company Mekorot used to hire men but did not hire women, while in Bustan Hagaleel farm, men as well as women were hired." These hiring practices led to a new gendered division of labor during this period where men were given relatively more options, especially in urban areas, and women were largely limited to agricultural labor.

CONCLUSION

An analysis of the narratives of Palestinian refugees who lived in al-Birweh village before 1948 and then became refugees inside the borders of the newly declared state reveals the dynamic life of Palestinian peasants in general and the diversity of women's roles as shaped by their social background and political context. It begins to undo some of the stereotypical representations of peasants—including Orientalist and Zionist ones of women confined to private spaces then liberated by the benefits of colonialism and modernity, as well as nationalist romanticizations of Palestinian peasants and the underestimation of peasant women's productive roles.

The narratives suggest that men and women's activities in al-Birweh village during the early part of the period studied were characterized by some degree of flexibility in the division of labor. They demonstrate the significance of women's productive roles effected by capitalist and colonial policies during the Nakba and their contributions to family survival during expulsion and the period that followed. They also reveal the subsequent multidirectional changes in women's productive roles. Some women who were initially not responsible for productive activities outside the home due to their household's financial status were forced to work post-Nakba. Other women lost their productive roles due to deprivation and the confiscation of their lands, while still others kept on working in agriculture, including in jobs made available to women by the Israeli authorities.

The relationship of al-Birweh refugees to land and agriculture changed dramatically during the period under study. More than sixty years after their displacement, many al-Birweh refugees and their descendants continue to identify with their emptied village and its lands currently occupied by Jewish Ahihud and Yasur. Like internal refugees from 'Iqrith, Bir'im, Saffuryi, and other Palestinian villages destroyed during or soon after the creation of the Israeli state, they visit the site of their village, commemorate their lives there or those of their parents or grandparents, and tell and retell stories of their displacement. My study is a continuation of this struggle with a nuanced, class-conscious, and gendered approach.

NOTES

This chapter is based on my thesis for the master's degree in Gender, Law, and Development at Birzeit University–Palestine, 2005.

1. The formal citizenship given to Palestinians who survived expulsion by the new colonial entity established on the ruins of their lands and society is paradoxical politically and ethically. Zionists used the granting of citizenship status to a minority of Palestinians in order to deny the right of return of the majority of Palestinians.

2. On the representation of Palestinian peasantry, see Reiker (1992).

3. On Palestinian peasants as "national signifiers," see Swedenburg (1990).

4. On Palestinian national historiography, see Ibrahim Abu Lughod Institute (2004) and Hammami (1995: 9–10).

5. Al-Birweh residents active in the 1936–1939 revolution include Yihia Hawwash, Saleh Mahmoud Me'ari-Abu S'ud, Abd-al-Hamid Daher Me'ari, Mhammad al-Haj 'Ali, Mahmoud Judi, Yusef Taha, 'Abbas al-Shattawi, Fadil 'Eid, Yousif Mai, and Asad 'Atallah.

6. Kanafani elaborates that "According to a survey of 322 Palestinian Arab villages conducted in 1936, 47 percent of the peasants owned less than seven *dunums* and 65 percent less than twenty *dunums* (the minimum required to feed an average family was 130 *dunums*)."

7. Israeli authorities used the term "sneaking" to criminalize the Palestinian refugees' permanent return to their lands.

EIGHT

POLITICS OF LOYALTY

===

Women's Voting Patterns in Municipal Elections

Taghreed Yahia-Younis

In the discourse on local Palestinian politics, it is widely accepted that there is a uniform, categorically ascribed voting pattern by which voters support their family's political list, and that women vote in accordance with the men with whom they are identified—fathers, in the case of single women, and husbands, in the case of married ones. This view is widespread within the Palestinian population and the Israeli public, as well as in research (Abu-Baker, 1998; al-Haj, 1987; Rouhana, 2004). This chapter sets out to understand the electoral politics of women in one Arab locale and to empirically test the validity of this alleged uniform pattern.

Palestinian-Arab society in Israel is an indigenous, minoritized group discriminated against and excluded from national politics and centers of power. As such, its members' direct access to politics is largely limited to local-level municipal government. Through this venue, they can have a direct effect on decision-making (al-Haj and Rosenfeld, 1990: 48; Reuben, 1989: 5; Elazar, 1987: 22; Raiter and Reuben, 1993: 51), and thus promote private and group interests and rights, especially at the level of kinship groups, political groups, or coalitions.

I focus on the local political loyalty of women, especially those referred to as "strangers," as manifested in their reported patterns of electoral participation. In the local language, "female strangers" (gharībāt) is the term used to refer to wives from cities, towns, and villages other than that of their husbands where they now reside. As a researcher, I use the term "strangers" in its sociological-theoretical sense, to describe women in an exogamic marriage, whether of a different locale of origin, of a different *hamuleh*[1] (pl. *hamāyil*, the largest familial unit known in Palestinian culture), or of a different national-ethnic group. During elections, their political loyalty is debated by all sides interested in their votes. Female strangers are caught up in the paradox between the marginality and powerlessness attributed to women in the dominant public discourse, and the importance attributed to them as a statistical majority (80 percent of wives) in determining the results of elections. They also embody the contradictions between two patriarchal principles of belonging, those of birth and marriage.

I argue that gender poses a problematical factor in the *hamuleh*-based categorical voting and is an additional element in the system's dynamism and diversity. Political state processes and mechanisms uphold patriarchal-communal arrangements. They sustain and intensify the subjugation and control of individuals' political participation, and more precisely, that of women. The significance of the local government and the close competition over it increase the importance of each vote, making individual decisions, including individual women's decisions, at times decisive for competitors. Women's political loyalty is demanded by each relevant side and evokes vital debate. The principle of belonging by birth can be in conflict with the principle of belonging by marriage, making women's voting in general and that of exogenously married women in particular, problematic. Gender relations are not absolute nor do they stand on their own. They are affected by other factors such as power relationships between the couple's families/ *hamāyil* and personal traits.

THEORETICAL FRAMEWORK

Much research indicates that family members tend to vote in a similar manner. The voting patterns of couples were the focus of a recent comparative study conducted in Europe (Zuckerman, 2005). Other studies suggest that children also tend to vote as their parents do. In attempting to predict how women's right to vote will affect the political system in some Arab countries where this right has yet to be established, researchers estimated that women will vote as men do (Peterson, 1989). Studies on the elections for the first legislative council in the Palestinian Authority in 1996 reached similar conclusions (Abdo, 1999; Jad, 1996; Said, 1999). These studies reinforce the central role of the family as a socialization agent, including in the political domain. The argument that women echo their husbands' political views has, however, been widely criticized by feminist researchers (Bourque and Grossholtz, 1984).

The existing research on Palestinian Arabs in Israel stresses the strengthening of the *hamuleh* as a political institution at the local level, especially *hamuleh*-based political organizing and categorical *hamuleh*-based voting patterns, in contrast to its weakening as a social and economic unit (al-Haj, 1987; Ozacky-Lazar and Ghanem, 1994). Historically, the political importance of the *hamuleh* was replicated and reinforced by the Ottoman, British, and Israeli regimes (al-Haj and Rosenfeld, 1990). In 1948, the Palestinian-Arab population was suddenly turned into a minority, lacking comprehensive structure and political, intellectual, and national leadership. It is an indigenous group, minoritized, marginalized, and discriminated against in the State of Israel, which is defined first and foremost as the Jewish state. The state collective is figured as corresponding to the boundaries of the Jewish majority and excludes the Palestinian-Arab indigenous minority (Horowitz and Lisk, 1990; Kimmerling, 2004; Kemp, 1997, 1999), turning them into strangers in their own land (Yahia-Younis, 2006).

The *hamuleh* and the locality remained the two sources of belonging and solidarity for Palestinian citizens (Bishara, 1998). Starting with the establishment of the State of Israel, through the period of the military regime, and up to today, Israeli governments and institutions worked to segment the Arab population as a means of control. The division was based on ascribed lines: religious, geographic, and familial. Until the 1980s, the government and its institutions consistently suppressed Arab independent national political organizations, while promoting the *hamuleh* (Lustick, 1980). Historically, the category of *hamuleh* was Orientalized and fetishized by Israeli scholars as the basic unit of analysis of Palestinian society (Asad, 1975; Eyal, 1996). Residential segregation enforced by the state, together with the common constructed tendency of Arabs in Israel to live close to their extended families in their localities, strengthened this trend (see Abou-Tabickh, chapter 11 in this volume).

Dependency and co-optation were also used in this system of control (ibid.). Heads of *hamāyil* were used by the state to provide basic services, such as authorization to travel between villages, work, and seek medical attention. The heads were the sole communicators between the state and its Arab citizens (Cohen, 2006). The *hamuleh* served as a mechanism of patronage in a state of the ruling majority. Local government became of enhanced significance, and in fact, essential. By controlling or participating in the local government, the *hamuleh* emerges as a vehicle to obtain basic services as well as social and material resources for its members and coalitional partners from the national government, limited though these might be.

The saying "My *hamuleh* is my state," as one female respondent put it, powerfully illustrates this trend. Moreover, "the good name" (*al-ṣīt*)—the *hamuleh*'s reputation—is perceived as one of the few symbolic resources left to the Arab minority. Although this resource has gone through many cultural changes and has been reduced, it is still considered a relic to be maintained. This produces a situation at the personal level in which individuals strongly identify with the *hamuleh*, and hence, are politically loyal to it. This is even more so for women. Politically speaking, a "strong" *hamuleh* is able to maneuver opposite other *hamāyil* and, to some extent—in a reversal of Orientalist assumptions—is able to maneuver opposite the state. It provides its members, especially women, with, in the study respondents' words, a "back" and "support." A strong *hamuleh* can also potentially tackle the state's discriminatory policies and marginalization, or at least attempt to ameliorate them in minor local ways.

This reality powerfully shapes the local politics of Palestinian Arabs in Israel. Their average rates of participation in municipal elections is high (90 percent) in comparison to their participation in national elections (75 percent)[2] and to Jewish participation at both levels (85 percent and 80 percent, respectively) (Ozacky-Lazar and Ghanem, 1994; Rekhess, 1981:146; Stendel, 1992: 202, 284). All family members are expected to support the *hamuleh*'s political list and candidates, whether said candidates are family members or part of its coalition.

Contrary to the perception that the *hamuleh* is getting stronger, however, the multiplicity of candidates for mayors and town council members observed during the elections of 2003 indicates in fact just the opposite trend—the weakening of the *hamuleh*. This multiplicity is an expression of intra-*hamuleh* rifts and conflicts. Many *hamāyil* held primaries to choose their candidates. The primaries were a reaction, aimed at reinforcing the *hamuleh* as the dominant political institution (Herzog and Yahia-Younis, 2007). They excluded women not only from participating as candidates, but also as voters.

Women in particular are expected to vote for their families' lists and/or candidates (al-Haj, 1987; Abu-Baker, 1998) and those supported by the men to whom they are connected: fathers and husbands, brothers and sons. This support has been taken for granted, to the point that no empirical study of any kind has been conducted on the subject. Except for studies recently published (Yahia-Younis, 2001, 2006; Yahia-Younis and Herzog, 2005), the focus on women's voting has remained marginal and centers on a handful of politically active women (Abu-Baker, 1998; Abu-Oksa, 2003), or on women's status in general (al-Haj, 1987) and from an Orientalist approach (as in the work of Ginat, 1982). This oversight is even more blatant in light of the fact that social science research on the Arab minority has focused on their politics and national voting patterns, part of the state's desire to assess and control their political tendencies (al-Haj and Yaniv, 1983; Ozacky-Lazar and Ghanem, 1996; Ghanem and Ozacky-Lazar, 1999; Ginat, 1989; Jamal, 2002; Raiter and Aharoni, 1993; Rekhess, 1986; Stendel, 1992).

This study was conducted in 2002–2003 with ninety-two participants using in-depth interviews. The locale studied is nationally and religiously homogenous—all of its residents are Muslim Palestinian Arabs. It is heterogeneous in its *hamuleh* and family makeup. To date, there is no single family or coalition that is sufficiently large or powerful to determine municipal election results alone. Voting is unstable and dynamic, including among women.

THE RULE OR EXPECTATION:
"NORMATIVE" VOTING PATTERNS

Almost all of the interviewees pointed to the common expectation that women, as well as men, vote for their *hamuleh*'s lists and candidates. This is considered the normative voting pattern in this context. Each and every interviewee opened with a remark regarding the *hamuleh*-based nature of municipal elections among Arabs in Israel, including the locality studied, to explain the aforementioned expectations of women's voting. Patriarchy dictates a woman's political loyalty according to that of the men with whom she is identified. A single or divorced woman shares the same loyalty as her father and family of origin, whereas a married woman or a widow living among her husband's family shares her husband's family's political loyalty.

With phrases such as "as is known," "it is obvious," "we all know," "it is acceptable to think," and terms such as "consensus," "all of," and "the norm," the interviewees expressed the common perception of married women's normative voting patterns. One male interviewee said: "It is socially accepted in life that the woman and her husband vote for his family. Show me a candidate who doesn't count his votes by the household: the husband, his wife, and the kids," while another said: "The acceptable behavior is that the wife is subject to her husband. In general, the husband, liberal as he may be, will demand his wife's vote." Another way to express the rule was in short, definitive sentences, as one female interviewee said: "Wives vote as their husbands do." A woman who was born in another locality said: "The guiding [rule] is whatever the husband and his family decide. The man is the one who decides." A feminist activist added: "I think women are taken for granted."

"NO ONE IS IN THERE WITH HER":
EXPECTATION VERSUS REPORTED PRACTICE

The apparent lack of women's agency in this norm is disrupted by the findings of this study. It is commonly believed that women usually abide by the rule of voting with their husband's *hamuleh*. Interviewees did not hesitate to offer exact measures of the level of compliance with this norm. A young man married to a woman from a different locality said: "I give you that no more than five percent of women might go behind the husband ['s back] and vote for her father's family." One of the informants stated that "Eighty percent of all women vote as their husbands do." The lowest rate was given by a female interviewee whose political loyalty to her *hamuleh* of origin is a well-known fact in the community. She lowered the rate: "Almost half of the women, in my opinion, go by what their husband wants." A difference in the rate of norm compliance assessed by the men in the study as opposed to that assessed by the women reflects the difference in the two genders' assessments of women's power and the degree of manipulation attributed to them, as well as the level of control men can have over them.

Despite the existence of a clear rule, most of the interviewees limited its application. Their reservations show that although there is a norm, it is also violated. A principal finding is that violation of the norm is usually attributed to wives married to men outside their *hamuleh*, especially wives indigenous to the locality. For a better understanding of this finding we must ask: How are women's voting patterns depicted in the community's awareness, and particularly those of women from other *hamāyil*? Needless to say, there is no way to test the reliability of the answers, as the study is based on the interviewees' reports. The interviewees themselves are alert to this point, and statements such as "I can't tell you what she put in the ballot box," "No one is in there with her," and "No one can know" express this awareness.

The interviewees' reports regarding women's voting ran the entire spectrum, from full congruence with the expected norm to complete divergence from it. In addition to the normative pattern, I found several other nonnormative ones. These include a splitting one where a woman splits her two votes between her *hamuleh* of origin and that of her husband's. Other nonnormative patterns include "complete violation" where a woman votes differently for both the mayor's position and the list for town council than does her husband's family, "free" voting for candidates not associated with either family, "invalidation" where a woman deliberately casts an invalidated blank or double ballot, or abstention. It turns out that in voting, all women, and "stranger" women in particular, deal with the situation with complexity and do not blindly follow the expected norm.

MODELS OF MARRIAGE, CATEGORIES OF WOMEN

Given the potentially conflicting expectations from a woman's family of origin and that of her husband, I identified four possible models of marriage in the field of research: one endogamous (within the *hamuleh*), and three exogamous. Each model creates a distinct category of women. The endogamous model creates a category known as "women daughters of the *hamuleh*." The exogamous intralocality model creates "women daughters of other *hamāyil*," the exogamous interlocality model creates "the strangers" (*al-gharībāt*), while "*al-ajnabiyyāt*" is produced by marriage to non-Arabs. Table 8.1 illustrates their frequency based on a survey conducted during an early stage of this research and includes a random sample of three hundred households of the village studied.

As was found elsewhere (Granqvist, 1931; Rosenfeld, 1964; Ginat, 1982), exogamous marriages account for the majority of unions, in this case,

Table 8.1. Distribution of models of marriage in the village studied.

%	Description of Model	Category Created	Model No.	Type
20.3	Intra-*hamuleh*/Familial	Women "daughters of the *hamuleh*"	I	Endogamous
45.5	Intra-locality: spouses from same town/village belonging to different *hamāyil*	Women "daughters of other *hamāyil*"	II	Exogamous
33	Inter-locality: Arab spouses from different towns and villages	"*el-Gharībāt*"- Female strangers	III	Exogamous
1.2	Non-Arab women from different national-ethnic groups	"*el-Ajnabiyyāt*"	IV	Exogamous

approximately 80 percent of the total. I found that the type of marriage a woman identifies with is a primary factor in her voting choices.

Endogamous Marriages: Exclusive Loyalty

"The girls/daughters of the family" (*banat al-'ayleh*) is the common way to refer to girls, young women, and adult women born in the *hamuleh*, whether they are still single or married within it. In this study, the latter group constitutes 20.3 percent of all wives. The principal finding in relation to these women is that the "normative" voting pattern is perceived as practically the only pattern among them. They are positioned opposite all the women from outside the family. The argument is that "there is a difference between women who are daughters of the *hamuleh*/family and women from outside." More than anyone else, their voting pattern is deemed obvious. "If the married woman is from the family, there's definitely no problem. [She moves] from this house to the other," said a male interviewee. Their strong political loyalty was expressed by a young newlywed woman from a large *hamuleh* in the village:

> Of course for me it's easier. Since we are both from the same *hamuleh* I will not vote for someone else, I will not deviate. . . . A woman from the *hamuleh* treats the matter differently. A woman not from the *hamuleh* votes, doesn't vote, it doesn't matter to her. Those from within the *hamuleh* make a bigger effort. One helps to recruit votes, older women keep talking up their candidate: how good he is for all people and not just for them. . . . When the family's candidate won the elections the women of the family and those related started *dabkeh* [dancing] and singing, but those who were in the coalition weren't that interested.

According to the views expressed in the interviews, women who were born in the family and then married within it have a tendency to be politically loyal, a pattern that supposedly applies to all *hamāyil* and transcends education and age. Hence, the well-known conclusion in the literature, that the endogamous marriage pattern, which maintains "pure" patriarchal principles and strengthens family ties, increases the external control of women, and strengthens inner unity and solidarity (Rosenfeld, 1964: 105; Bourdieu, 1977; Granqvist, 1931: 80). Analysis of the interviews, however, reveals a much more complex reality.

Limited Loyalty

In contrast to the perception that an individual is blindly loyal to his or her family, it turns out that this rule is conditional. The principal conditions that arose in the interviews are the attitudes of the *hamuleh*/family toward its son/daughter, its characteristics, unity/fragmentation, familial closeness/distance between the candidates and the voter, peer pressure, a close race, and more. A male interviewee, son of a small family, who holds a bachelor's degree and is in an endogamous marriage, said, "The smaller the *hamuleh*, the stronger the family ties and the more compelling it is [for voting]." Unity is presented in the case of small families as political capital, in contrast to their overall small electoral power. Other interviewees expressed the opposite, more common view that, "In fact, a smaller family doesn't compel political loyalty and a defined voting pattern." There was no agreement among the study participants about the relationship between family size and unity.

Familial closeness between the candidate and the woman is another condition that compels loyalty. A female interviewee from a large *hamuleh* said: "If the candidate who is closer to me is good, then it is possible [that I will vote for him]." The internal structure of the *hamuleh*—fragments, branches, extended families, households, and nuclear families—impact this degree of closeness. A young newlywed, married to a young man from the same branch of her large *hamuleh*, said: "If there is a candidate from my family, I mean our branch, and the entire *hamuleh* supports him, I will support him. If not, and the family goes with another candidate, and we [our branch] have an interest in it, I will vote for him. If not, [I will vote] for the candidates as I see fit." A split can occur within the same section of a *hamuleh*. The division into branches makes the status of a woman from one branch married to a relative from a different branch similar to that of a "stranger." Her political loyalty becomes an object of struggles and pressure, especially when the two branches join opposing political lists.

Hamuleh leaders sometimes take a strategic position and collectively abstain from supporting a specific candidate for mayor, enabling a greater measure of "free" choice. A female interviewee in her fifties who belongs to a large *hamuleh* and is married to a relative, reported: "This time, in the first round, I voted as the *hamuleh* wished. It had an interest in the elections. In the second round, I didn't vote as the *hamuleh* wanted. No one would leave their families and go to another unless there is a problem with the *hamuleh*, a split. Women do not decide on splits. Where her husband goes, she goes."

Distinctions between branches and between the core of the *hamuleh* (*quḥ*) and its margins (*aṭrāf*) are often used to account for who is perceived to be politically loyal and who may deviate. "*Hamuleh* unity" is a myth that masks its divided incoherent nature. An older woman from a large *hamuleh*, married to a relative, said: "It's not connected; there are those from the *hamuleh*'s core who vote for someone who is not a member of the *hamuleh*. Frequently, there is head-butting, you have no idea." Internal distinctions (core/margins), personal disputes, meritocratic considerations (worthy/unworthy candidate), ideological bases for voting, all cause "violation" among men as well as women. People with no proven "blood relation" can undergo a social process to "become" a family for political reasons (al-Haj and Rosenfeld, 1990; Rabinowitz, 1998) such as dominant *hamāyil* absorbing smaller ones. Families can also fall apart for the same reasons.

A young male interviewee, in an endogamous marriage, said in the presence of his wife:

> It has happened that we've voted out of the *hamuleh*. We voted for the Islamic Movement and we didn't regret it. Both of us did, because we respected the man who headed it. I've personally never pressured her to vote, and never told her [whom to vote for] and I don't know [whom she voted for]. It is fundamental to me. I don't want to pressure her. The idea is to vote for whomever is most worthy.

And a thirty-year-old female interviewee, from a medium-large *hamuleh*, with a bachelor's degree, who is married to her cousin, said:

> Since I believe in the Islamic Movement, I voted for it, but in secrecy. When the family found out they were very angry. It was when I was a university student. I felt that for once, I would like to express my own opinion. . . . If there is another candidate, even from outside the *hamuleh*, who I believe is better and more fitting, I will take the risk and vote for him.

In the local discourse, it is widely accepted that women in an endogamous marriage are almost always politically loyal to the *hamuleh*. Nonetheless, the findings show that limited, conditional "violations" occur.

Arab Women from Outside the Locality—*Gharībāt*: A Dual Perception of Loyalty

"Normative" patriarchal arrangements compel wives to move to their husbands' locality (see Abou-Tabickh, chapter 11 in this volume) and to take on their last names (Yahia-Younis, 2006). Women from other localities make up 33 percent of all wives within the research site. The reports map their political loyalty as dual: on the one hand, as having "normative" political loyalty, and on the other as prone to "violation." This duality is produced by the intersection between being a loyal daughter-in-law to the husband's family and having a different family of origin.

In this category, the woman's *hamuleh* of origin is absent in her new place of residence and is not part of the local political system. Therefore, it is assumed that such women have no competing alternative. A man said in the presence of his wife, "My wife is from outside the locality. She's stuck (*rāḥat 'alayha*). It's one hundred percent certain that she votes with her husband's family." Another, married to a woman from this category, said, "She has no choice. The female strangers are very easy-going. [She] doesn't try to have an opinion. She goes in any direction her husband chooses." A woman said emphatically and concisely: "Where my husband goes, I am with him."

On the continuum of political loyalty, the interviewees rate the loyalty of women from outside the locality as second after "women who are daughters of the *hamuleh*," and infinitely higher than that of women indigenous to the locality, in an exogamous marriage within it. A female interviewee in an endogamous marriage said: "During elections they are even more fervent than us. They are fanatics for the *hamuleh*." These women's spatial strangeness is perceived as comfortable, since no conflict exists between the two patriarchal affinity principles—that of birth and that of marriage. Rather, the stronger the adherence to the family of origin, the stronger the feeling of belonging to the husband's family. This is not the case when a woman is indigenous to the locality, because then the possibility of a clash between the two exists, as discussed further on.

The interviewees admire the adherence and fanaticism of the *gharībāt* to their husbands' *hamāyil*/families, especially in light of their inherent strangeness. When a woman fulfills the desired model, she is frequently described with satisfaction and respect as "one of the family," "as if she is a family daughter," "you cannot tell her apart from the other women in the family." These reactions actually emphasize women's strangeness and make it all the more obvious.

Countless other statements point to the fact that *gharībāt*'s political loyalty is doubted, often based on the same factors used to explain violation among endogamously married women. A split within the *hamuleh*/family, for example, enables strangers not only to choose between sections, but also to choose not to choose. "If they do not agree among themselves, why should I go to vote?" said one woman.

Indifference and apathetical attitudes are attributed to women who are strangers, which become the basis for these women's decisions not to vote. A female interviewee in an exogamous marriage, who is part of a medium-sized family, said: "One of our neighbors, a stranger from [name of locality], says: 'Let them go to hell, I don't want to vote. Whoever wins, wins.' She doesn't care." A woman from this category said, "I don't care. Yet if my husband was [involved] in the elections [then] I would care." The decision not to vote can also be based on the type and nature of the ties: "Materialism diminishes family ties, makes a stranger not feel the same compelling bonds and sense of belonging. And in the end, either she votes or she doesn't. The percentage of non-voters is only growing," said a male interviewee.

"It Is Easy to Recruit Their Votes"

Gharībāt's votes are deemed easy to recruit by other lists whether ideological or *hamuleh*-based. One of the women interviewed, who takes an active role beside her politician husband said:

> It is easy to get the female "strangers" from outside the locality [to support any list]. They have no relatives or obligations; at most, they are committed to one side. I made a list of women and I want to call them. Last time, I sent a pen and a key chain with the [political] list's symbol to the women who are strangers, who were my husband's students. They know him.

Gharībāt's perceived objectivity allows for meritocratic considerations, referred to here as "knowing the candidate." Meritocratic considerations are possible especially if the woman's husband has no specific interest and does not demand that she vote in a certain way, a meritocracy limited by patriarchy. In cases where there is a split in the *hamuleh*, different sections take over command. Sometimes all the households decide that every nuclear family will make its own decision. Under these circumstances, everyone, including wives who are "strangers," enjoy more alternatives in voting.

Furthermore, women who are strangers are in a position to publicly challenge the *hamuleh*-based political system. A woman from outside the locality, with a highly developed feminist and national consciousness, said:

> This is not my family to begin with. I wouldn't even vote for my father if he is a traitor [in nationalist terms]. . . . It was very difficult for me that someone told me how to vote. My father-in-law said to me: "We don't care about the Islamic Movement. We are involved because of [name of his son]." There were three candidates: one from the Islamic Movement, one Zionist, and a third from a *hamuleh*. In the first round I voted for the Islamic Movement's candidate. I said that at least the Islamic Movement has a national basis. In the second round, I didn't vote [since there was no] good national or independent alternative. I am sure the average husband is not like mine when it comes to the level of choice he affords his wife.

Interviewees reported cases in which *gharībāt* women continue to vote in their locality of origin for their family of origin. One male interviewee said, "There are married women in [name of another locality] who continue to come [back] and vote."

Ajnabiyyāt

Ajnabiyyāt are women from outside the ethnic, national, linguistic, and religious group. Many of them in this locality were women from Eastern

Europe who married men who had gone to study in their countries. They constitute 1.2 percent of all married women in the study, the smallest of the four categories identified. The perception of their electoral behavior is dual. On the one hand, they are perceived as conforming. On the other hand, because of their multidimensional strangeness, their vote is simultaneously situated in the "violation" category. However, more diversity and variation were found in the motivations and considerations on which women in this category base their decisions. Their normative behavior can be understood as a way to deal with their ultimate strangeness as *ajnabiyyāt*, that is, as a mechanism that establishes belonging, both in the eyes of the community and in their own eyes. One female interviewee expressed herself disapprovingly: "When votes are counted, then the *ajnabiyyeh* is in the family."

In light of their position, some of these women do not view insistence on a different voting pattern as an issue worth the price they might have to pay, that is, disagreements and problems with their husbands and their families. One woman told me: "[Name of husband] says [who to vote for] and I don't say I don't want this or that. He says: 'We're going to vote.' That's it—we go."

Together with her conformity, the *ajnabiyyeh* wife will tend to say what bothers her about it: "I did not know the candidates and their backgrounds. To me they don't represent an ideology—right or left. . . . I vote with a bad conscience because I don't know who I'm helping to gain control of the government." The potential adjustment difficulties and alienation of some of the *ajnabiyyāt* turn the municipal elections into an opportunity for them to express their anger, their disappointment and their hard feelings toward their husbands or their husbands' families. This is true for Arab women as well. However, it is perceived more in the case of *ajnabiyyāt* because their marriages involve the crossing of many borders including those of kinship, geography, culture, language, religion, ethnicity, and social norms, on the way to ultimate strangeness. Moreover, when a woman from this category violates the norm, she tends to talk about it without hesitation, while indigenous women tend to hide this.

Though many of them hail from the former Soviet Union, the *ajnabiyyāt* often criticize the political system as undemocratic. Arab women on the other hand usually do not dare use democratic rhetoric without the support of a husband who embraces it. One woman said of her friend, from the same country of origin: "My friend, [her name], wife of [her husband's name], never goes to vote. She says they are not serious. Whoever has a big *hamuleh* wins.' "

A protesting comment was made by a new Russian-Jewish immigrant, married to a young man from the "margins" of one of the largest *hamāyil* in the locality: "Politics don't interest me at all. I don't talk politics with my husband. Why get into it and give myself a headache, especially in the village? Once there were elections, I don't even remember. I don't know this one or that one. The family cannot force me to vote for anyone. That is me. Other women and men—I don't know."

Despite the violation and challenges they present, women in this category are given little attention and more forgiveness in the local political discourse. A partial explanation for this is their statistical marginality in the studied population. They are also used by members of the community in a manipulative way. When they do not behave according to expectations, their political behavior is explained by their strangeness, in the spirit of "she is an *ajnabiyyeh*." When they behave "normatively," the community highlights that they conform despite their ultimate strangeness. In both cases the community aims to reproduce norms and surveillance upon indigenous women. At the end, the strangeness of the *ajnabiyyāt* is used to strengthen patriarchal principles and the existing social-political order. Violation is perceived as much more threatening when it comes from within, from Arab women.

"DAUGHTERS OF OTHER *HAMĀYIL*," BORN IN THE VILLAGE: DOUBTS, PRESSURES, AND CONFLICTS

Exogamous marriages within the community are discussed in the literature as building solidarity and social unity at the village level (Rosenfeld, 1964: 109; Granqvist, 1931: 88–91). Similar to the imaginary unity and insularity of the *hamuleh*, the openness and connections created by such marriages are perceived as constituting a broad social network with potential alliances and mutual trust. Nevertheless, the situation of women involved in this model of marriage is problematic in instances of competition between their two families. Their votes turn into a subject of contention.

According to the study findings, in the locality studied, women in exogamous intralocality marriages constitute almost half (45.5 percent) of all the married women, which is higher than the rates found in other studies (Rosenfeld, 1964: 108; Ginat, 1982: 86; Granqvist, 1931: 92). Concurrent kin strangeness and spatial proximity make these the closest strangers and thus the most threatening. High rates together with high risk of violation place these women at the center of local discourse on female voting.[3] The women's structural location places them under crosscurrents of pressure.

The interviews contained considerable discussion on this subject. One male interviewee said: "In general, a large number of them vote as their husbands do." More than in any other model of marriage, however, these close strangers have the highest perceived potential for and self-reported instances of breach of loyalty. This view is prominent in public debate. In this model, women are likely to encounter disagreements, conflicts, pressures, problems, and dilemmas.

Hamāyil differ in electoral size, social prestige, and influence and are positioned in a local hierarchy. Inter-*hamāyil* marriages result in power relationships between the woman's two families that become decisive in electoral behavior patterns. Four models of power relationships were found in the empirical data: 1) An advantage for the husband's *hamuleh*; 2) A positive balance in the power relationships, with both *hamāyil* possessing a great deal of electoral power, social prestige, and political influence; 3) An advantage for the woman's *hamuleh* of origin; and 4) A negative balance, that is, both *hamāyil* are marginal politically.

POWER RELATIONSHIPS WITH
ADVANTAGE FOR THE HUSBAND'S *HAMULEH*/FAMILY

Of the twenty-five interviewees who are married to spouses of other *hamāyil*, eight (five women and three men) have an advantage for the husband's *hamuleh*. All of the men in this model reported that their wives' loyalty was to the men's *hamuleh*. Three of the women said the same thing. One woman supported the *hamuleh* of her uncles on her mother's side, and no clear answer was obtained from the fifth.

Both men and women perceived the voting decisions of women in the model in similar ways. However, men used terms of dominance, control, and power to explain their behavior, while women relied on the social benefits achieved via their marriages—such as social mobility, a sense of belonging, pride, respect for the husband, and his importance—to explain their sense of political loyalty. Thus, an advantage for the husband's *hamuleh*/family involves the overlap of two structured hierarchies: *hamuleh* hierarchy and gender hierarchy. The first nourishes and reinforces the second. In this sense, this model contributes to the reproduction of the patriarchal order.

POSITIVE BALANCE IN THE
INTER-*HAMĀYIL* POWER RELATIONSHIP

Seven of the twenty-five interviewees in exogamous but local marriages (five women and two men) are positively balanced—their *hamāyil* of origin and by marriage are both strong. Three of these women reported that they voted for their husbands' *hamāyil*; one voted for her *hamuleh* of origin, and the fifth evaded giving a clear answer. One male interviewee said that his wife was politically loyal to his *hamuleh*, and the second said his wife was loyal to hers.

The interviews revealed that this is the most problematic model for the couple, primarily for the woman. "The women in this situation live in conflict. They are torn between the two *hamāyil*, especially when the race is close. It's not easy for them to see either their children or their brothers 'disappointed,'" said one female interviewee. This situation causes the involved parties, usually the husband and his family, to try to supervise her and control her vote. Simultaneously, by virtue of the system's recognition of the dilemma inherent in her position, it enables women's "legitimate violation." "The equality between the woman's *hamāyil* gives her a greater opportunity to reach a personal decision," said one interviewee.

Another interviewee said, "For mayor, I always voted for my *hamuleh*. The fact that there was no mayoral candidate from my husband's *hamuleh* [because of internal divisions] made it easier for me to support my family. For members of the town council, I voted with my spouse's family. Not because I was convinced by their candidacy, but because his family pressured [me] and my husband's standing was important to me."

An interviewee from the positive balance model explained:

> In the elections, I was on one side and my wife on the other. There's no dictatorship at home. As long as she can head a whole department at her work, what right do I have to force her to vote for a specific party? Freedom of expression for everyone. That is not a slogan, but practice. A person has to act in his home the way he states things publicly.

Specific couples in the positive balance kinship model attract the attention of people in the community during elections. One of the interviewees, who is from a small family and married to his cousin, said:

> The problem becomes difficult when there are candidates for mayor from the two *hamāyil*. We watched from afar how, in the same home, the brother of one woman ran for mayor, and her husband was active on the other side, and she was in conflict. That's when you sense that there is tension between the husband and wife.

The competition between the two *hamāyil* can embitter the woman's experience.

Conforming to the expectation of voting for the husband's family does not always solve the problems but often creates new ones. A woman's family of origin often expects her to be politically loyal to her father's *hamuleh*. Positively balanced power relationships between *hamāyil* are fertile ground for raising doubts and fears about the woman's political loyalty. One interviewee even described the extreme situation in which a woman can find herself:

> If the election becomes more difficult, prejudiced, with jealousies and suspicions, threats and use of violence, then the woman expresses interest in her family of origin. When the conflict is at its height, her family of origin plays a very important role for her. My wife's brother was a candidate in the elections. During that period, the house was filled with tension and emotions. When he withdrew his candidacy, she stopped showing any interest in the elections whatsoever.

The interviewee continued with a partial laugh: "That's the price that daugh-ters of leadership (*za'āmeh*) pay when they marry into families of leadership." And he indicated her possible reactions: "When the clash between her family and her husband becomes sharp, either she threatens that she won't vote, thereby punishing both sides, or she votes for them secretly."

In summary, a positive balance in the power relationships between *hamāyil* has a dual ambivalent effect on the perception of women's politi-cal loyalty. It provides women with a greater amount of free space, which is recognized by the community as "legitimate violation" on one hand. However, supervision and oversight of her is tightened, on the other hand. More than in any other model, the woman here is exposed to pressures from all sides, but at the same time receives understanding. This duality derives from the disjunction between equality of the *hamāyil* and the "normative" gender hierarchy between spouses.

HAMULEH POWER RELATIONSHIPS
WITH AN ADVANTAGE FOR THE WIFE'S HAMULEH

Five interviewees (three women and two men) were involved in inter-*hamuleh* marriages in the town with an advantage for the wife's *hamuleh*. All three women reported that they maintained political loyalty to their *hamuleh* of origin. The men evaded discussing their wives' votes, suggesting the likeli-hood that their wives' behavior contravened the norm, and that they were disloyal to the husbands' *hamāyil*.

Women in this model are the first to be labeled as disturbing norma-tive loyalty. The situation was thus described by one interviewee: "The problem [exists] when the woman is from a large *hamuleh* and is very proud of her family." And the problem is aggravated "especially if she moved to a socially inferior family in the same locality." Because then, "her family of origin tries to get her vote." The model of power relationships in which the woman's *hamuleh* has an advantage places the *hamuleh* hierarchy of the couple in contradiction to that of gender. The community tends to show flexibility and understanding for the couple's situation. The wife's behavior during elections is recognized as "legitimate violation." Normative arrange-ments enable the woman, and sometimes even her husband and his family, to vote for her family.

According to one woman:

> My husband and I agree that I always vote for his *hamuleh*'s candidate for membership of the town council, and for my *hamuleh*'s candidate for mayor. I do it out of love for my family, and also because, usually when they're on the town council, they treat everyone fairly. They don't give favors only to members of their own *hamuleh*.

An informant frames his wife's support for a different candidate by saying, "We gave freedom." I argue that in this model of marriage, egalitarian rhetoric is a product of the normative nature of the violation of the rule of voting for the husband's family.

Paradoxically, under these same conditions, some husbands try to impose normative loyalty at any price. Men in the model of marriage with an advantage to the woman's *hamuleh* do not feel comfortable, at least not in regard to local elections. When members of the community have the impression that the wives of certain men control voting, the men are described as "weak," "a man who is not a man," "a loser." Fear of the stigma, which can be affixed to both husband and wife, along with the contradiction that is characteristic of this model, explain the men's stubborn efforts to impose rules on their wives. One of the female interviewees said:

> My sister [full name] never dared to express loyalty to her *hamuleh* of origin, even when someone from her *hamuleh* of origin ran for mayor. Her husband didn't even want to know that she was planning to vote for their [her family of origin's] candidate. He always drew her and his family members to the opposition's side. He didn't like being identified with his wife's *hamuleh*, which is nevertheless closer to him in many respects.

This model still presents an opportunity for empowering women. Within it, they challenge the binary perspective of gender/power that attributes power to men and weakness to women. Thus, they are able to express their loyalty to their *hamāyil* of origin, for the most part without risking exclusion from the husband's family. When the wife's *hamuleh* has the advantage, power relations are beneficial for her in general and in local elections in particular. They enable the definition, recognition, and acceptance of what I term "normative/legitimate violation" at the systemic level. More than in any other model, women in this model enjoy the freedom to express their political loyalty to their family of origin. This arrangement supplies women with important resources in the form of influence, prestige, and support. Women benefit by taking advantage of these resources in their relationships with their husbands, in the community in general and in elections in particular. Still, the effort to impose normative behavior at any price also exists.

NEGATIVE BALANCE IN INTER-FAMILIAL POWER RELATIONSHIPS

Five of the twenty-five cases of exogamous marriage in the community (three men and two women) belong to this model. Three cases, two men and one woman, reported a free vote by the women, not necessarily for someone from either of the two families. The third reported that he controlled his wife's vote, made in favor of a candidate from a large *hamuleh*. The second interviewee reported that she voted with her family of origin.

Theoretically, negatively balanced power relationships guarantee the freest vote possible for both the woman and her husband. Marginality and the resulting lack of involvement in politics on the part of both families enable them to be released from commitments. However, an up-to-date reading of local politics suggests that the situation is more complex. Parties' struggle to remain in power in local government has brought about the involvement of marginal groups who, in some cases, can potentially swing the elections. This situation turns into an opportunity for small families to move from marginality toward the center. The internal organization and relationships of marginal families become of utmost importance, so that they can act as a pressure group or as coalition partners with bargaining power. In such a situation, women's votes, like those of men, are needed.

When a small family has any interest in local elections, it organizes and acts more strictly. "A small family counts every vote and supervises it. The loss of one vote leads the family to suspect women who are strangers. . . . One father asked his daughters who married into a small family to vote as their husbands do, so as to avoid problems. That way, they leave no room for doubt," one male informant reported.

CONCLUSION

While this research provides an empirical base for the general perception of *hamuleh*-ascribed voting in municipal elections, it also reveals its complex nature. It suggests a duality in the perception of electoral behavior and political loyalty, especially for women who are strangers, but also for others. Electoral behavior is gendered and the dimension of strangeness is a major factor in shaping it. On the one hand, women are viewed by the public and by researchers as maintaining electoral normativity, yet they simultaneously attribute electoral violation to them. Wives who are strangers from outside the family, locality, or ethnicity who make up the majority of wives are marked as the primary violators of this rule. They challenge the sociopolitical voting order.

This study problematizes the concept of *hamuleh* in connection to electoral politics, especially along feminist lines. By showing different component groups, the category of "women" is deconstructed. Normally regarded as a monolithic, coherent, primordial unit, the *hamuleh* emerges as socially constructed of distinct components (Rabinowitz, 1998). In addition to nuclear families, extended families, branches, fragments, and "blood" versus "fictive" kin, the category of women married into the *hamuleh* must be added to this list. Distinction between women is placed at the center of public debate during municipal elections and is used to redefine the *hamuleh* boundaries.

When attending to women's voting, inherent paradoxes in the socio-political structure and the patriarchal order—at both the Israeli macro and the Palestinian intracommunal levels—become apparent. They bring out multiple tensions such as that between membership by birth versus by marriage, the free choice or ideological versus ascribed principles of voting, forces and power relations at the macro level versus at the intracommunal level. These tensions allow, even compel, electoral normativity *and* violation with a continuum of possibilities in between.

Due to local government's essentiality to the population studied, and the close competition in the elections, voters' behavior, particularly women's, is supervised and controlled at times quite intensely. On the one hand, Palestinian citizens' overall marginality, exclusion, and estrangement reinforce conservative cultural patterns. On the other hand, the same real-ity is a source of subversion on several levels. The patriarchal logic enables exogamously married women to expand their ability to negotiate within this power structure. Though the breach of gender roles is an outcome of patri-archal, group-ascribed characteristics that give the wife an advantage over her husband, it is still enough to challenge voting, sociopolitical, and gender norms. They manage to increase their possibilities and to make the best of a structure perceived as confining their opportunities (Kandiyoti, 1988).

NOTES

1. This word and several others are transliterated from the colloquial.

2. Though the rates of Palestinian-Arab participation in municipal elections are high, their rates of participation in national elections, as well as Jewish partici-pation at both levels, have declined over the last decade.

3. About the connection made between strangers and danger see Ahmed (2000: chapter 1).

NINE

THE SEXUAL POLITICS
OF PALESTINIAN WOMEN IN ISRAEL

Manal Shalabi

Over the last three decades, Palestinian society in Israel has undergone
intense changes on a number of fronts, including attitudes to sexuality.
These changes are welcomed by many members of society, and are critiqued
and rejected by others. The subject of sexuality is considered sensitive and
threatening and is thus frequently silenced. It is also muted in academia
where it is a highly neglected area of research. This study is one of the first
to attempt to examine the processes by which Palestinian women in Israel
formulate their sexual outlooks, including the personal and sociopolitical
components of those processes.

My research is grounded in the meaning that the women participants in
this study give to sexuality, oppression, and liberation, and how they define
and experience them. Palestinian women in Israel give the word "sexuality"
a wide array of significance, including genitalia, gender, a woman's body,
the sex act, one's relationship to sex, "the oppression I suffer as a woman,"
love, romance, sexual orientation, femininity, fear, embarrassment, and taboo.
Utilizing in-depth interviews and focus groups with Palestinian women, I
present some of the participants' outlooks on sexuality, and the meanings
and life experiences they ascribe to it. In particular, I analyze the power
dynamics of silencing and the ways in which women cope and resist.

While Palestinian society can certainly be characterized as patriarchal,
it is not a homogeneous, closed, or absolute social order. Hisham Sharabi's
concept of neopatriarchy (1988) conveys some of the heterogeneity and
changing structures of Palestinian society in Israel, yet attention must be
given to the power of individuals in strategizing to gain power and autonomy.
My analysis takes into account traditions and norms as well as constant

change, social structure and agency, and overarching conditions together with disparity and complexity. Thus, this study shows that the binary division of sexual freedom versus suppression is too simplistic and one-dimensional. It looks at a number of levels in which social power operates, including Palestinian women's relation to each other, to Palestinian men, and to Jews in the Israeli state.

The experiences and practices of the women in the study were highly varied. Some led independent lives, lived alone, were educated, and yet did not dare speak about the subject of sexuality or their own sexual experiences. Other women found a way to cope with the rules of society through stretching the limits and maneuvering through them. Rather than focus on sexual intercourse exclusively, the women refer to a range of other behaviors that sexually satisfy them and enable them to connect to their intimate selves. At the same time, the majority of the interviewees spoke about a "red line" that cannot be ignored. This limit, though varied from one family to the next, can still be considered uniform in that it links conformity to sexual norms with social value. Although some of the interviewees spoke about crossing this boundary, most of them maintained the clear norms concerning these "red lines."

METHODOLOGY

The study conducted in 2007 included semi-structured taped interviews and three focus groups. The interviews were conducted with twelve Palestinian women, including married, divorced, single, and widowed women ages twenty-five to fifty-five. The group of interviewees was heterogeneous not only in terms of age and family status, but also level of education, geographical residence, socioeconomic status, religious affiliation, level of religiosity, and as found by the study, in terms of sexual attitudes and practices. The identification of the Christian, Muslim, and Druze women who participated in the study ranged from being very religious, to secular, to atheist. Five of the interviewees were academics with university degrees. Six worked outside the home, and the other six worked inside. Two were feminists active in social issues and one was a political activist.

The process of finding interviewees was long and difficult, as was the recruitment of participants for the focus groups. It was particularly difficult to find highly educated women considered leaders and agents of social change who would agree to participate. Many women expressed willingness to be interviewed but later cancelled or did not show up for the interview.

The qualitative interview method used in this study allowed for a collection of the women's life narratives, and broad information about their sexual experiences and their perceptions of themselves. It should be noted at the outset that indicators such as education, social status, and level of religiosity did not necessarily affect the sexual attitudes and practices of the participants in any predictable way. For example, I found that some of the less-educated women expressed greater openness concerning their sexuality and in terms of participating in the study.

In addition to the semi-structured interviews, I conducted three focus groups on the subject of sexuality. The first focus group included girls aged fourteen to eighteen, the second included young women students attending university, and the third was a group of married women. These participants were contacted with the help of social workers from their cities and villages.

The fact that I am a woman, a social worker, a Palestinian, a committed feminist, and a political activist shaped my relation to the topic as well as to the study participants. In this regard, my positionality placed me as an insider in relation to the women and increased my access. Yet it also increased the potential for the women to experience more shame and fear in connection to some of their more socially controversial experiences. Since I identify as a radical feminist and am associated with the activities of the Palestinian feminist movement in Israel, some of the women made an effort to impress me by repeating what they considered to be feminist positions. Others sought to challenge what they interpreted as my morals. Both the attempts to impress and criticize me were catalysts for our discussions of sexuality. My background influenced my communication with the women as I was familiar with Palestinian language on the topic, including some of the more euphemistic references.

SOURCES OF COMPLEXITY

Palestinian women in Israel are in the contradictory position of having new opportunities on the one hand, and being forcefully excluded and controlled on the other. Patriarchal social norms together with a patriarchal and ethnocratic state collude to limit them. But social norms valuing education, the penetration of consumer capitalism, and liberal democratic aspects of the Israeli state offer them certain choices. Thus, the interweaving of ethnonational status and gender control simultaneously aggravate their oppression but also create historical opportunities for a significant number of them (Sa'ar, 2007).

The State of Israel promotes a hierarchical order of gender-ethnicity-nationality, which discriminates against and excludes Palestinian women both as women and as part of an ethnic minority. The state works to reinforce Palestinian male patriarchal control over women within their families and communities while simultaneously dramatizing their gender "backwardness" to prove their inferiority (Sa'ar, 2007; Abdo, 2004). Thus male dominance is interwoven with other control mechanisms related to ethnic-national status. These complex encounters create different versions of male dominance at each level of society, in the family, ethnic community, workforce, and government bureaucracy.

As an "ethnocracy," the interests of the dominant ethnic group in Israel, that is, Jews, dictate the character of public policy in most fields creating stratification and widespread segregation (Yiftachel, 1999). The ethnocratic goals of the state and the merger of religion and state led to the imposition of military rule over Palestinian citizens until 1966, the occupation of Palestinian territories in 1967, the expropriation of Palestinian land and work resources, and the proletarianization of the majority of the Palestinian population. As a result, Palestinians today live primarily in segregated, underdeveloped, and underserved communities. They remain stuck at the lowest and middle socioeconomic levels. The price for this difficult situation was paid for by women, principally in the fields of education and employment. The 1990s brought about a slight change, with some improvement in the quality of life, as well as women's entry into white-collar positions (Sa'ar, 2007).

Along with the destruction of the agricultural base of Palestinian society and the creation of an impoverished and dependent, largely male workforce, the introduction of universal education—though at an inferior level in Palestinian communities—has created educational opportunities for some Palestinian women. The extended family structure was weakened, the birthrate dropped, and women were no longer required to stay at home and take care of children (al-Haj, 1987: 111–112). On the one hand, a woman's respect is predicated on her sexual modesty, which she is expected to express in modest dress, refraining from intimate relationships with men, and not living away from home. Yet girls and women adopt various practices that they use to maneuver and stretch the limits of patriarchal rules. This is apparent in the growing number of female Palestinian students who study outside their hometowns, some of whom live in dormitories or rented apartments. Young Palestinian women are managing to seek empowerment in academia and many have also opted to remain single for a period of time (Haidar, 2005b).

These changes do not cause essential transformations in society's perceptions of women's status, but do show some modification in the old norms. I found a great deal of complexity in the interviews and focus groups. This is a product, in part, of what Suad Joseph refers to as the agency of individuals within the patriarchal order of society (Joseph, 1999: 3–17). It also derives from structural contradictions. Alongside the difficult picture of subjugation and self-alienation, the high heterogeneity of Palestinian society creates different and even conflicting norms. Thus, it is legitimate for women to leave the home in order to work and study, but the opposite norm also exists, which prevents them from leaving their homes for other purposes or controls their movement when they do. Such contradictions create various situations in which some women are simultaneously prevented from leaving their homes in certain contexts, and are encouraged to do so in others.

VIRGINITY: TRUE OR FAKE

Social concepts like *hishma* (humility), *sutra* (modesty), *'ayb* (shame), *harām* (forbidden), and *hijāb* (veil) mold the sexual behavior of Palestinian women and men. A woman who is not yet married is supposed to be a virgin. Such a woman, regardless of age, is commonly referred to as *bint* (girl), an appellation that signifies an inferior childish state before sexual awakening. Some families even consider torn hymens and having premarital sex as social and religious crimes. In the official Palestinian discourse, virgins are in great danger: loss of virginity threatens the family's honor, the young woman's reputation, and could endanger her life (Sa'ar, 2004: 13). All of the women who participated in the focus groups, with one exception, spoke of the importance of remaining virgins until they got married. The one exception was a student who indirectly spoke of her sexual experiences but did not directly say that she had sex, even in response to a direct question by another participant.

Despite the expectation that women should maintain their virginity until marriage, many of them undergo various stages of sexual awakening. Most single women technically meet the expectation of carefully guarding their virginity. A comparison between the norm of virginity and daily life, however, shows that the dividing line between being a virgin and not, between sexuality and pre-sexuality, is tortuous and winding and is subject to maneuvering and negotiations. Women's sexuality in general, and virginity in particular, are complex and multidimensional (Sa'ar, 2004: 15).

On the one hand, the prohibition of premarital sex can cause some women to develop a fear of having sex (Abu-Baker, 2004: 229). Others decide to lose interest in it. Samar,[1] a single, twenty-seven-year-old lawyer, lives in a village with her parents and says: "The truth is . . . I've never tried to have sex. I never felt that I couldn't sleep at night because I didn't have sex. When I was engaged, I didn't have sex with my fiancé, I didn't allow him to even ask me to, I wouldn't have let him. Why? Where are we? I know where the line in the sand is, and I never crossed it. There is a price to pay in this world and I'm not willing to pay that price."

In Palestinian society in Israel, the ideal virgin is not only someone with an intact hymen, but one whose sexual desire has not been aroused and who is sexually ignorant. Many of the single women in the study said that not only were they physically virgins and had not consummated the sexual act, but they also prevented petting and almost any other form of touching by men. The fact that they work outside the home, drive cars, enjoy themselves, and are independent made them suspect. They hesitate to engage in sexual activities because the price they are likely to pay is harmful to their good names (ibid.: 19). According to Khulud, one of the participants in the student focus group, "The truth is that when I hear about the hymen, I don't even know where it is. Leave it alone. You know what? I don't know exactly what my genitalia look like."

Samira, thirty-seven years old, is a registered nurse. She is single and lives alone in a mixed city. She said:

> I can tell you that Arab girls are sexually oppressed, but there are women who aren't. Most women are sexually oppressed; they can't even talk about the subject. As for me, I began to have sex at the age of twenty-nine. My sister, too, had sex with her husband before they were married. Of course, I didn't tell my family, but I have a brother who is very open, and he knew. He has no problem with it. He also knows that I live in a rented apartment with a Jewish male roommate. Even though he's not my boyfriend, that is considered taboo in our society. The truth is that I was raised in a regular, simple home. My parents aren't highly educated, but they were permissive. You could say that we had freedom.

Many women have sex, but do not allow vaginal penetration, and so they remain virgins in society's eyes, though not "true" virgins. This choice, of not being a "true" virgin, in which the woman tries to maintain her virginity and good name, can also exact a price. They adopt "fake" virginity in order to prevent conflict with men and their partners in the "hard truth." Mernissi writes about this practice, which is widespread in Morocco, as allowing women to engage in some form of sexual activity while satisfying the basic needs of the patriarchal family (Mernissi, 2004: 241). Thus they live passively with the collective and remain ostensibly in agreement with its norms.

Rather than being submissive victims of patriarchal society, women are often active strategizing agents, maximizing the benefits they can obtain from the system within its existing limitations. Kandiyoti calls this feminine strategic pattern a "patriarchal transaction" whereby women actively support the system that perpetuates their collective inferiority in exchange for personal benefits (Kandiyoti, 1988: 276–277). They develop personal strategic expertise and attempt to maximize their autonomy, as is the case with Palestinian women who are technically but not "truly" virgins. Many of them simultaneously negotiate the patriarchal structure, socioeconomic power dynamics, their loyalty to their community, and their contestation of social and sexual boundaries. I argue that many Palestinian women are sexually, socially, and economically active, and are, in fact, not punished for their behavior but given considerable freedom of movement.

MOTHERS AND FATHERS

The emphasis on virginity and sexual honor is transmitted to women by their families. All of the women, with no exceptions, spoke about clear, unequivocal familial messages that forbade them from having sexual relations. Families also enforced a number of other behaviors related to sexual practices, such as walking carefully and "honorably" in the street, and refraining from leaving the house, contacting boys, or wearing revealing clothing. The participants said that these messages were given to them directly or indirectly principally by their mothers; it was always the mother who made sure to pass on the message to her daughters.

Ghada, thirty-one, who lives alone and is a feminist and activist, said:

> I was raised in a home where my mother is Catholic and my father Maronite. My father's amazing, and very liberal. Despite that, we never spoke about the subject of sex, and when I would hint about it, they would ignore it and continue to discuss something else. My mother always told me to sit properly, don't spread your legs when you're sitting. I never understood why she said that.

Samira, the nurse, stated: "My mother always said to me, 'Be careful, be careful of the boys, don't trust them, and be careful that you don't make a mistake.' " Like Ghada and Samira, all of the women in both the interviews and the focus groups said that they received clear messages about sexuality primarily from their mothers. The majority of the interviewees perceived their mothers as more strict, and spoke about special, close, and more open relationships with their fathers.

Mona who is thirty-two and single explained:

> My father is an open man. When we were little, he would tell us about adolescence and he was very clear. I feel very comfortable with my father, more than with my stepmother. I remember when I was a teenager and had a crush on somebody, I would tell him and he would accept it in a very nice way. He directed me and helped me a lot. I felt very comfortable with him. He taught us that we should express our opinions and that we should respect each other.

Mothers were discussed as strict figures, responsible for educating the children, particularly the girls, while fathers were described as more supportive. This contradicts the widespread belief that in a patriarchal society, the father is the source of fear and subjugation. The father was described as a positive figure, and in some of the interviews, even as enabling and supportive. The reason for this is that the mothers would be blamed if they failed in their child-rearing task or in their role of maintaining the family's good name, since they are expected to control what happens in the home, including their daughters. Mothers are thus recruited as subjugating agents to help the men limit and control the women in the family (Srur, 2000: 62).

Ghada added, "Sometimes I blame my father for the education he gave us, because he gave us awareness, knowledge, and alternatives. The father is a central figure in a woman's life; if the father isn't supportive at home, the mother cannot be supportive. The father is the supporter, he's the man." Fathers are part of the same patriarchal order but often they do not get their hands dirty. The one who does the direct subjugation is the mother. This may explain why the interviewees generally portrayed their mothers as mean, coarse, and patriarchal. Returning to the concept of the patriarchal bargain, mothers can be understood as actively supporting the system that entrenches their collective inferiority in exchange for benefits at the individual level—of being esteemed as good mothers.

Of course women's positions, including those of mothers, tend to be more complex and deeply contradictory. Sahar, one of the interviewees, idealizes her mother because she accepted Sahar when she told her she was a lesbian. This contradicts her mother's extreme reaction when she caught Sahar masturbating in the shower when she was eight years old.

BETWEEN TRADITION AND MODERNITY

The notion of modernization preoccupies Palestinians both materially, ideologically, and culturally. As a minoritized community within an ostensibly Western state, they are forced to deal with the pro-Western mythical narratives of modernization as well as its material effects. They do so by embracing some aspects while rejecting others, and at times deploying a traditionalist counter-narrative (Kanaaneh, 2002: 165). Kanaaneh argues that changes resulting from "modernization" of the body among Palestinians in the Galilee have been enthusiastically sought after on the one hand, and criticized and distanced on the other (Kanaaneh, 2002: 167). This is also true in relation to sexuality. For example, many interviewees claimed modernization was responsible for providing women with opportunities for higher education and for living outside the family home—which many evaluated as positive. Other interviewees, particularly a group of students and young women who participated in the focus groups, spoke about the negative aspects of "Westernization" in relation to sexuality, including Arab girls' imitation of Jewish girls and their "embarrassing" behavior and revealing dress.

In response to the question "What is sexuality in your eyes?" Nawal said: "Women throughout the world have lost control over their bodies in the new commercial era, where sex products are marketed and women's bodies are used for advertising." Nawal spoke about this with strong revulsion, as she felt that such advertising exposed her body and not just the bodies of the models. Most of the women in the study raised the issue of "modern" values and regarded such changes as negative because they represented the potential loss of Arab values.

Palestinians come in daily contact with Jews, both in government institutions and in other prosaic transactions. In the context of Jewish economic dominance and Jewish society's attempted self-representation as modern, Western, and non-Middle Eastern, some Arabs view Jewish society as a role model in terms of freedom and "modern" life and thus copy certain Jewish norms in the hope of "modernizing" themselves. In many cases, youngsters attempt to reverse the Western or Israeli stereotype of them as "traditional." Simultaneously, the opposite tendency is for Palestinians to express the desire to hold on to so-called traditions that maintain the cohesiveness of their society against the values and policies of hegemonic Israeli society (Srur, 2000: 84).

Sahar, thirty-one, who is a lesbian, grew up in an Arab city, but now lives in a city with a mixed Jewish-Arab population. She tells of her experience: "I came out of the closet at age twenty-eight, a difficult experience. The person who accepted me the most was my mother; she was amazing in her acceptance. My mother wasn't exposed to Western society. The first time I began to understand that I'm a lesbian was at a conference in Germany, when I realized I had a crush on someone there, and I spoke to her about it. A short time later, I met my partner, who lived in Tel Aviv." Like many other Palestinians, Sahar's view of the influence of the "West" is contradictory. On the one hand, she attributes her mother's acceptance of her sexual identity to the fact that she has not been influenced by the West. Yet, it is in a "Western" context (Tel Aviv and Germany) that she chose to come out of the closet and felt encouraged in her sexual identity.

Hana' is a widow, age forty-six, and a mother of three who claims to "maintain the traditions," and is considered a leader in her local community. Hana' continually tries to compare the situation of Palestinian women in Israel with that of Jewish and Western women: "Not only are we, Arab women, subjugated; Jewish, Western women are, too. They suffer from deep subjugation and there are many cases of murder because of infidelity, which is the other side of the coin to murder in the name of 'family honor' in our society." Her comparisons emphasize the universality of the subjugation of women and minimize the influence of Jewish society on Arab women.

Some of the study participants wanted to minimize, negate or deny the influence of so-called Western culture on Palestinian lives, preferring to maintain supposedly traditional norms. Others attributed great importance to Western influence on the lives of women in general, and on their own lives in particular. Although the women in this study did not talk directly about politics, it was obvious that the interviewees and focus group participants took palpable political positions concerning the subject of modernity and the changes taking place in society. Their positions were rife with contradictions. On the one hand, they aspired for certain types of change, and on the other, they wanted to maintain the interests of Palestinians in Israel.

COPING WITH NEEDS

Jumanah, thirty-one, who lives with her mother in a village and works at odd jobs, describes the contradiction in her experience as follows:

> I had a boyfriend who always wanted me to have sex with him, and I repeatedly refused. I refused because of religion, *haram*. He has to be engaged to me, or be my husband, for me to have sex with him. When I refused, he left me. A short time after that, I met someone else. I loved him, and we had sex, but we didn't consummate the act. I was very fearful, and was of two minds. On the one hand, it's not accepted, and on the other, sexual, emotional, and physical needs do arise at this age, and I really wanted to try to have sex, and I told myself I'd try. It's not dangerous and doesn't cause pregnancy nor tear the hymen. I live with this contradiction all the time, and it drives me crazy.

A conflict between maintaining the "line in the sand" and finding a way to express sexual needs was evident in many of the interviews.

Samira said:

> Since I broke up with my boyfriend, I haven't had sex. That's almost four years. I had sex from age twenty-nine to age thirty-two, and since then I haven't had sex. I relate this to keeping myself. You can't give yourself to every man, you understand? At age twenty-nine, I met my boyfriend, and because our relationship was serious and we wanted to get married, I did it. Before that, I hadn't had sex because I wanted to keep my hymen intact.

While most of the women emphasized their premarital virginity, some of the women spoke about fulfilling their sexual needs and about sexual practices that satisfy them without intercourse. 'Ibtisam, a forty-two-year-old woman, told me, "I love my body. I love to pamper it. I love it, and really enjoy it when people compliment me."

The women in the study spoke about fear, deep prohibitions, and obstacles. Even the women who spoke about having sexual relations did so very cautiously. Some of the women are afraid of having sexual relations, do not masturbate, recoil from their own bodies and are disgusted by them, and refrain from going out because of the rules of society. Others are in the exact opposite situation. They have sexual relations and experience their sexuality in various ways. The women spoke about all types of practices that satisfy them sexually including sex on the internet, masturbating, fantasizing and dreaming, dressing the body, showing legs, personal and intimate contact with a friend of the husband, and speaking about sex.

Religion among Palestinians is sometimes used to justify certain practices, even when that religion does not formally stipulate them. For example, from 1986 to 2005, some eighty Palestinian women were murdered in Israel because of "family honor" (Ghanim, 2005). These women were killed by their male family members to supposedly cleanse the family honor, but without proof of actual sexual transgression, and in contradiction to religious beliefs and values. Some of the interviews touched upon the perceived significance of religion in relation to sexuality. Despite differences in the sexual practices of the women in the study, and the openness of some of them to practicing their sexuality, most of them mentioned the word *haram* (religiously prohibited), and two of the Christian women used the term "sin" when they spoke about their initial perceptions and the messages they received at home. Hana' told me: "I haven't had sex since my husband died twenty-one years ago. I was widowed at age twenty-three. I don't experience my sexuality. I have a need for sex, but I can't do it, because of the religious and social obstacles." Similarly, despite the official sanction by Islam for giving and receiving sexual enjoyment (Ahmed, 2000; Ilkkaracan, 2002/2003), expressions of passion even by wives are socially suspicious.

One cannot make simple assumptions about the relationship between religion and sexuality. Su'ad, forty-one, a religious woman who wears a headscarf, is married, and the mother of three said:

> I like it when my husband pampers me, but he doesn't. Nor does he compliment me; he's not romantic. I enjoy romance and compliments. My husband's friend always tells me that I'm the most perfect woman on earth. I feel safe with this friend and tell him about my sex life, and he tells me about his sex life as well. I like it when people pamper me. My husband knows about this, but he's not jealous, and that's what drives me crazy. Even my oldest daughter noticed that I'm close to this friend, and she always tells me that I'm in love with him. I don't know if I'm in love with him, but I enjoy talking with him and being close to him.

SOCIAL AND POLITICAL RELATIONSHIP TO THE BODY

The study participants referred to their bodies in similar ways. Words like disgust, distance, alienation, danger, and revulsion typified the way in which some of the women and teenagers expressed their feelings about their bodies.

Simultaneously, more than one of the interviewees mentioned liberating motifs concerning their bodies, such as divorce or marriage, maturity, psychological treatment, having sexual relations, ending a pregnancy, and coming out of the closet.

Most of the teenagers and women spoke about feelings of revulsion, embarrassment, danger, distance, and/or love of the body, especially during adolescence. This was expressed in the fact that the women, consciously or subconsciously, refrained from touching their bodies, from looking at their bodies in the mirror, and from masturbating. Some of the interviewees attributed this to unique experiences: adolescence, divorce, unhealthy marriages, sexual harassment, abuse, and violence. They tended to emphasize changes in their perception of their bodies at different stages in their lives.

For other women, the sense of distance and alienation from their bodies is related to the violence they experienced in their lives, whether physical or sexual, that affected them and their perceptions of sexuality. For example, one of the interviewees spoke about being raped when she was a child and how the experience caused her to hate her body and distance herself from it. Another interviewee spoke about experiencing physical violence at the hands of her brothers and mother.

Ma'adi (2004), a researcher who studied the significance of the body for peasant women in the Shawiya region of Morocco comments that:

> Refraining from looking at their bodies, and ignorance about the body's parts and genitalia reflect the socialization process of society's fear and continuing concern about the woman's body, and primarily women's virginity. . . . This turns the woman's body into a site for supervision and inspection, entailing at its zenith "closing" the woman's body, which creates a strange relationship between the woman and her own body. It creates various contradictions in bodily practices. On one hand, it is her body, and on the other, it is the subject of supervision and inspection by others. (Ma'adi, 2004: 72–75)

Ma'adi's discussion is relevant to Palestinian women in Israel, despite contextual differences. Like in Ma'adi's research, the relationship of the interviewees to their bodies is full of contradictions. On the one hand, some expressed love and closeness to their bodies at this stage in their lives. On the other hand, they were embarrassed to look at their bodies in the mirror. Another manifestation of this charged and ambivalent relationship is that some of the women who characterized themselves as less distanced and disgusted by their bodies said that they shower often throughout the day. Maha said: "I love my body, my genitalia, my breasts, my belly. After I separated from my husband, I became more open. I see today's woman as strong in everything, including sex. I really love my body; I nurture it and shower one hundred times a day."

A significant number of the interviewees spoke about not loving their bodies because they were fat or skinny. This attitude developed, for the most part, as a result of the messages that they received from their families and society which ridiculed their appearance. In extreme cases, this caused women to hate their bodies. The positive feelings of some of the interviewees toward their bodies existed alongside difficult feelings of disgust and self-alienation and were reportedly the result of exposure to processes of empowerment and independence that they went through. These factors served as the basis for closeness to and satisfaction with their bodies despite all the criticism they faced.

'Ibtisam, forty-two, a married woman and mother of two children, who had been raped as a child and had recently undergone psychological therapy, said: "When I was little, I wouldn't look in the mirror. I was afraid of the mirror itself. I would get into the shower at night, and was afraid of the flushing noise the toilet made. Today, after all the treatment I really love my body. I stand in front of the mirror and like to look at myself. Sometimes, I pamper myself and tell myself how beautiful I am." Hanan said:

> I underwent a very long process regarding my body. Once, I never paid attention to it; it didn't even exist for me. It only existed for eating and drinking. The subject of sex didn't exist. There was a great deal of danger in my relating to my body; I always related to it unwillingly, with embarrassment. Today, I love my body although I don't have the legitimacy to love it. I fear giving it legitimacy because that is perceived as something negative. When I was twenty-two or twenty-three and after completing university, I began to look at my body in the mirror.

Jumana added: "What a difficult question! I never thought about my body. When I think about it, it's in relation to hygiene. I don't look at it in the mirror. I don't know the reason for that, but I don't look. I remember once that I sat opposite the mirror and looked at myself because I wanted to see all the parts of my body [including my genitalia], and see where they are, and I felt revulsion and disgust at the way it looked and its color."

Contradictions thus also exist in the way women relate to their bodies. In the group of teens, one of the participants got angry when I asked the question about their bodies and said, "Why do we have to deal with that subject? I don't look at my body in the mirror. I focus on things that are much, much better. My studies are more important to me." As is common among this age group, most of the participants spoke about distance from and dislike of their bodies during adolescence.

INSERTING THE SEXUAL INTO PALESTINIAN POLITICS

This study was designed to examine the attitudes of Palestinian women in Israel toward their sexuality, and the processes through which these attitudes were formed. Sexuality is considered a taboo subject. Yet simultaneously, women have some space for maneuvering and applying various versions of the norms, and stretching the limits placed on their sexuality. The women who participated in the study spoke of these abilities but also of their need to survive in a patriarchal system. Palestinian society often views women as weak and powerless, but many of them cope with the power arrayed against them by negotiating with patriarchy as a way of opposing it.

The women spoke of fears but also of desires, of danger but also of curiosity, of being unprepared but also of liberation and openness during certain periods of their lives. Their narratives portray segmented biographies. Childhood and adolescence are described as periods of ignorance, while adulthood is considered a more liberating period when consciousness and choice increase. The life stories map trajectories from childhood to adulthood, from ignorance to consciousness, from distance to closeness, and from passivity to active sensuality. A number of factors are associated with these individual transitions including marriage, leaving the home and family, discovering the body and exposure to sex, and the legitimacy that women receive from being older and especially from being married. The end result is that sexuality is not necessarily always traumatic, but that reality is more varied.

I found that the women participants have a broad range of sexual practices. Fear of the social sanction against women's sexual activity outside marriage causes them to find other ways and strategies to cope. The subject of sexuality is taboo not only at the individual level of practice, but also at the level of social discourse. Even empowered activists in society do not dare to raise the subject or place it on the public agenda to be discussed openly and clearly. In her book A Rocky Road (1998), Khawla Abu-Baker identifies the pragmatic strategy adopted by Palestinian women in Israel that takes into account existing social structures rather than a revolutionary approach that fights against these structures. The first and principal struggle of most women political leaders was their right to continue their education and acquire academic degrees. In this, they received familial and social support because it did not conflict with existing values and religious principles of either Muslims or Christians. Women's academic education was translated into social and political power, which enabled them to intervene in the social agenda and values of Palestinian women—though not in relation to sexuality (Abu-Baker, 1998).

Whether hidden or stated outright, Palestinian women aspire for more freedom to choose in their lives—aspirations that at some level reflect a feminist approach and a desire for "women's rights to define themselves through the rejection of given standards" (Abu Rabi'a, 2005). It can be said that women utilize power from within; they use "power in a way that is socially acceptable, such that it is seen as a contribution and not opposition." They use traditional structures as they actively cope with their limitations (Abu Rabi'a, 2005: 91).

Women's experiences of sexuality documented in this study reflect their positionality within gendered, familial, economic, and political power structures. Responsibility for the contradictions in women's sexual experiences is complicated, interlacing internal aspects of the Palestinian collective and external ones relating to the state in which that society operates. I found that alongside the limitations women face, many lead extremely varied lives. Therefore, it is not possible to generalize about their sexualities or the choices they make.

I maintain, like other radical feminists, that so long as there is no essential change in gender relationships within the family, and as long as relationships between men and women are unequal, women will not be able to be socially, economically, and politically free (Tong, 1989). My study shows that factors like academic education and participation in the work-force do not guarantee achievement of women's independence and sexual freedom, as illustrated by Samar, who says she knows where the line is and is not willing to pay the price of crossing it. The case of Su'ad, the religious housewife, who apparently displayed the most openness, both in what she said and in having a romantic relationship with her husband's friend, clearly demonstrates the complexity of conceptualizing sexuality and contradicts all common stereotypes about women from various groups and backgrounds.

With the exception of the organization Aswat, the subject of sexuality has not been adequately addressed by the Palestinian feminist movement (Aswat, nd). This is also echoed by the women who participated in the study, who criticized the feminist movement for not investing enough energy in this subject. Most of the efforts of Arab feminists in Israel today are directed at exposing political subjugation and in working on domestic and sexual violence. For the most part, they focus on issues like inequalities between Palestinians and Jewish citizens, poverty and the lack of employment opportunities. Living in a subjugated Palestinian community, political discourse is virtually the only one given public legitimacy. Though the issues of equality with Jews and of violence are undoubtedly important, sexual discourse is absented from the political and social agenda. The subject is taboo such that political activists are afraid to touch or deal with it. Yet if the issue of sexuality is not integrated into agendas of political change, no real transformation in social and gender relationships will occur (Accad, 2004: 51–53). Understanding the importance of sexuality in subjugating women and the centrality of changing gender relationships is a necessary step in building strong foundations for change in the social, economic, and political realms. Key to this is a complex and nuanced understanding of women's intimate sexual experiences.

NOTE

1. All participants in the study have been given pseudonyms.

IV

MIGRATIONS

Figure 5. Filmmaker Ibtisam Maraʻana from Fridis and Suʻad George, now settled in the UK discuss their dreams, opportunities, and the state. From *Paradise Lost* by Ibtisam Maraʻana 2003. Courtesy of director.

TEN

PALESTINIAN PREDICAMENTS

Jewish Immigration and Refugee Repatriation

Areej Sabbagh-Khoury

In the early 1990s a massive number of immigrants were brought to Israel from the former USSR in what was the largest wave of immigration in the history of the State of Israel since 1951. More than 350,000 immigrants arrived at the end of 1991, equaling 6.5 percent of the total population at the time (Yonah, 2004: 195–196). This chapter examines the content and contours of the Palestinian discourse in Israel in response to this influx of immigrants.

Drawing on interviews with twelve political activists, the main question I explore is whether this vast wave of immigration led Palestinians in Israel to raise questions regarding the state's policies of immigration and the Palestinian refugees' right of return, and the factors influencing Palestinian political discussion of the subject. Though a Palestinian discourse on refugees is certainly present in informal politics and in literature, poetry, and art, I sought its expression at the formal level of political parties. The massive size of the wave of immigration in the 1990s might be expected to reawaken memories of the Nakba, and of the hundreds of thousands of Palestinian refugees who were expelled from Palestine in 1948 and in 1967. It stands to reason that it would constitute a trigger for Palestinians to discuss the ban on the return of Palestinian refugees, which, perforce, renders the practice of the Jewish Law of Return morally unjust.

Jewish immigration to Palestine as part of the Zionist project began in the nineteenth century and greatly increased with the creation of the Israeli state and the passing of the Jewish Law of Return. In contrast to previous waves of Jewish immigration that occurred when Palestinians in Israel lived under direct military government, the wave under discussion took place after Palestinians began to "recover" from the trauma of 1948. It happened as a new independent Palestinian leadership emerged and new institutions of civil society crystallized. It also occurred at a time when the Israeli Communist Party (ICP) experienced substantial changes such as the loosening of the grip of Jewish party members over its institutions (Sabbagh-Khoury, 2006: 28–31) and the collapse of the Soviet Union that theoretically would allow for clearer national Arab voices to increase in volume and scope within the party. All of these factors support an expectation of strong Palestinian public political objection to this wave of immigration.

Al-Ittihad is a newspaper published by the ICP and the affiliated Democratic Front for Peace and Equality (DFPE), which has played a central political and cultural role among Palestinians in Israel for many years and is the only Arabic daily newspaper in Israel. Kul al-'Arab is a more populist and independent weekly newspaper established in 1987. An earlier review of these two Arabic newspapers between 1989 and 1991 showed that there was a great deal of discussion concerning Jewish and non-Jewish Soviet immigration during the three years I sampled (Sabbagh-Khoury, 2006). Articles in those newspapers criticized the negative ramifications of immigration for Palestinians in terms of employment, land expropriation, the settling of immigrants in the Palestinian Territories occupied in 1967, and the displacement of Palestinian citizens from villages defined by Israel as "unrecognized." Numerous articles reflected the opposition of Palestinians to these oppressive practices. Nevertheless, and contrary to my initial expectations, I did not find evidence of explicit opposition to the practice of immigration itself.

There was no direct political opposition to the immigration of Jews (and non-Jews) as an instrument of "maintaining" the Jewish majority in Israel. Likewise, there was virtually no discussion of the logical connection between Jewish immigration and Palestinian refugees' return. In more than 350 articles that appeared during this period in al-Ittihad addressing Jewish immigration, only seven referred to the issue of the right of return. Of the seven, only two made a direct connection between Jewish and non-Jewish immigration and the right of return. The other five mentioned it in passing. In Kul al-'Arab, of the 157 articles dealing with the wave of immigration, only two addressed the right of return, and the issue was not a central focus of either article (Sabbagh-Khoury, 2006).

In search of explanations for this apparent silence in the Arabic press, I conducted interviews with prominent Palestinian leaders and political activists. I was interested in the reasons and explanations for what I perceived as a bewildering anomaly. This chapter analyzes the results of these interviews and offers an account of Palestinian discourse on the subject.

THE ISRAELI DEMOGRAPHIC DISCOURSE
AND POLICIES OF IMMIGRATION

Jewish immigration commenced in an organized manner, on a low profile, during the period of the Ottoman Empire, and continued in increasingly large numbers during the British colonial period in Palestine (Khalidi, 1997; Hourany, 2003). The Zionist movement acted to establish a Jewish national homeland by increasing the number of Jews in Palestine, and by curtailing the number of Palestinians within it (Yuval-Davis, 1987; Masalha, 1997). With the establishment of the State of Israel, the exile of the majority of Palestinians in 1948, and prohibition of their return, the immigration of Jews to Palestine became standard practice, and constituted the central axis for maintaining a Jewish majority (Lesch and Lustick, 2005).

The Israeli state perceives the Palestinians as a "demographic" threat, and attempts to ensure a Jewish majority. Israeli policies to maintain this so-called demographic balance between Palestinians and Jews are reflected at both the national and regional levels. At the national level, the Jewish state, its institutions, and quasi-governmental organizations (e.g., the Jewish Agency) work to bring Jewish immigrants to the country, support higher Jewish birthrates,[1] and reduce the number of Palestinians and the Palestinian birthrate (Masalha, 1997; Zureik, 2003). Fertility policies in Israel, which were shaped and developed as early as the 1950s, were engineered toward achieving these objectives (Yuval-Davis, 1987; Kanaaneh, 2002). At the regional level, the state seeks to encourage and strengthen Jewish settlements in areas where Palestinians constitute a majority (Falah, 1989a, 1989b; Masalha, 1997; Bashir, 2004; Khamaisi, 2003).

Legal tools comprise a central element in the demographic project of maintaining a Jewish majority. These include the Law of Return and the Citizenship Law, which together constitute the legal basis for immigration to Israel and for immigrants to become citizens. The Law of Return of 1950 gives almost every Jew around the world the right to acquire instant and automatic citizenship in Israel (Weiss, 2001; Jiryis, 1981). At the same time, the Citizenship Law and its recent amendments curtail the ability of Palestinians and their descendants to return as well as to unite with their families in Israel (Kretzmer, 1999; Jiryis, 1981). A large percentage of the immigrants from the former Soviet Union actually did not define themselves as Jews but nevertheless enjoyed the privileges associated with "return," privileges not available to Palestinians.

The demographic framework and the view of Palestinians as a demographic threat have existed since the state's inception, but this discourse was intensified after the al-Aqsa Intifada in 2000. At that time, a number of prominent Jewish politicians openly called for the deportation of Palestinians, both residents of the Occupied Territories and citizens of the state. Others called for a population exchange, in particular, handing over the Triangle area and its Palestinian residents to the Palestinian Authority in exchange for other territories (*Haaretz*, March 22, 2002; Arieli et al., 2006). In July 2003 the Law of Citizenship and Entry into Israel was passed. The law "prohibits the granting of any residency or citizenship status to Palestinians from the 1967 Occupied Palestinian Territories who are married to Israeli citizens" (Adalah, 2009a). At the time, several Israeli and international human rights organizations protested that the proposed law was a form of institutionalized racism and infringed upon basic human rights. The law was nevertheless passed.

In addition to its intensive preoccupation with demography, Israel refuses to recognize its responsibility for the refugee problem; dominant Israeli historiographies instead hold the Arab and Palestinian leadership responsible for the refugees' dispersion in 1948 (Rouhana, 2005: 268; Khalidi, 1998: 238). The idea of the return of Palestinian refugees touches upon deep-rooted fears among Israelis (Khalidi, 1998: 235). According to Israeli sociologist Yehouda Shenhav, most Jewish Israelis treat the return of Palestinians as a black box or a sealed-off package, refusing to consider options of interpretations and negotiations of the issue (Shenhav, 2005: 225). This was manifested in Ehud Barak's strategy of negotiation at Camp David in 1999, in which he refused to conduct any serious discussion about the repatriation of refugees.[2] In other words, the official Israeli position refuses to return the Palestinian refugees to their homeland, even as part of a peace agreement with the Palestinians (Khalidi, 1998; Zureik, 1999; Rouhana, 2005).

METHODOLOGY

I conducted twelve in-depth interviews with political activists, utilizing a semi-structured questionnaire designed to probe the potential for linking Jewish immigration and Palestinian return. Though this is a relatively small number of interviews, they can nonetheless suggest important directions for future research. I chose interviewees from three principal political factions of Palestinian society in Israel: the ICP and the DFPE, The National Democratic Assembly (NDA), and the Islamic movement's Northern Islamic Branch, which boycotts the Israeli parliament elections. The Southern Islamic movement participates in Parliament and was not included in my study because of the similarity of its political and nationalist positions to those of the other political factions studied ('Ali, 2004: 156). The larger and more influential Northern Islamic movement (Salah, 2007), however, has significantly different views and calls for the establishment of institutions independent of the state ('Ali, 2004: 152).

The political movements or parties included in the study were selected to meet two criteria: 1) that they oppose the Zionist ideology of the State of Israel; and 2) that they constitute a central stream among Palestinians in Israel. For example, the Abna' al-Balad, Sons of the Village movement, meets the first criterion but not the second. I also did not interview activists affiliated with what is referred to as "the Arab-Israeli trend" (see, e.g., Ghanem, 2004: 244–251; Ghanem, 2001), which constituted roughly one-third of the voters in 1999 and 2003 (Rouhana et al., 2004: 66). Activists from this group are, for the most part, leaders of extended families and ethnic groups whom Israel has fostered and nurtured (Ghanem, 2004: 246–247; Rouhana, 1997: 96–97). They demand equality for Palestinian citizens of Israel, while accepting the premise of a Jewish Zionist state. The exclusion of this group is not intended to dismiss the possible tangible benefits gained by their strategy. Rather, I chose not to interview them because the return of refugees is marginal to their agenda.

The interviews were conducted in 2005, about a decade and a half after the immigration wave from the former Soviet Union. Many changes occurred in the Middle East and globally in the intervening years, changes that impact the political experiences of Palestinians in Israel and the interviewees' views of present and past political realities. Despite this limitation, this was the most useful methodology available to me to supplement the evidence that emerged out of my earlier analysis of newspapers. My sample is clearly biased toward those who might perceive the refugees' return as an important issue. My goal was not to have a representative sample of Palestinians in Israel, but rather, to understand the structures behind the silence manifested in the newspapers.

I chose twelve activists, four from each faction: two men and two women. The aim was to interview known activists, but not Knesset members because the latter are usually cautious about their responses since they serve in official positions within the Parliament of the Jewish state. The age range for interviewees spanned from thirty to fifty. The interviews were conducted in February and March 2005, and lasted for forty-five minutes to an hour each. They were taped and transcribed with the consent of the participants, who also chose the sites in which the interviews took place.

ABSENCE OF EXPLICIT OPPOSITION TO IMMIGRATION

When asked about the Palestinian position regarding immigration from the USSR, all the interviewees said that Palestinians in Israel opposed it. However, in their opinion, this opposition did not go beyond forewarning of its consequences to Palestinian society. The interviewees offered several reasons for this absence of direct opposition to immigration. The first reason is the sense of powerlessness and inability to influence discriminatory laws including the laws of immigration. As Fadi[3] says, "I think that is the prevailing feeling, the inability to influence the dominant view. The sense is that the maximum that we can do as a society is to demand that [immigration] not occur at our expense, that lands will not be expropriated, and that there won't be calls to throw people out of their jobs."

The feeling of powerlessness to oppose immigration is augmented by the balance in international power relations. Some of the interviewees explained that Palestinians in Israel perceived immigration as a combined by-product of the Nakba, the "international imperialistic game," and the Palestinian defeat, which they are unable to influence. According to Fadi,

> The Palestinians see [this immigration] as part of the Nakba, that is, we accepted the Nakba and its results, and this is part of the result. A powerful state was established which can impose its authority over the region, and that is related to the larger external colonial project. The fact that Jews have come as far as here is part of the international game following the collapse of the Soviet Union, and the USA pressuring the USSR to allow Jews to leave. That is, Arabs do not see any option in affecting this reality. . . . I think this is the prevailing mood of lack of influence on what is happening.

Another reason for the lack of direct opposition to immigration is that in their relations with the State of Israel, Palestinian citizens only raise those issues that affect their daily lives directly. Subjects that do not touch them directly or that are not an organic part of the relations between the Palestinian citizens and the State of Israel, like the issue of Jewish immigration, do not constitute, according to some of the interviewees, a central component of the political discourse of the Palestinian minority. In Shirin's words, "We, the Arabs . . . always speak of what we dub the Palestinian right to define themselves, their collective rights, their civil rights, the intersection, contradiction or overlap between their being citizens and their being a national minority. We developed all of these subjects. . . . We did not explain what we mean when we say a "democratic state," or how we see the collective rights of the Jews." Interviewees from the ICP and DFPE emphasized the "marginality" of the issue of immigration compared to other central issues that the Palestinians addressed, among them the First Intifada in 1987, the Gulf War in 1991, and the Oslo Accords signed in 1993. According to some of the interviewees, addressing these subjects distracted attention from opposing immigration. It is important to note that most Palestinians in Israel and elsewhere sided with Iraq in the Gulf War, a position derived from Iraq's support of the Palestinian Liberation Organization (PLO) (Ehrlich, 1993). This position was perceived by the Jewish majority as treason and therefore reinforced a sense of fear among Palestinians in Israel.

Another model of fear stems from the oppressive practices of the military government (1948–1966). Some of the interviewees mentioned the military government as a reason for the absence of opposition to Jewish immigration. According to Hussein: "Today, in fact, the military government still lives within us. The fear stems from the fact that the emergency regulations are still in effect and determine the type of political activism we were allowed to engage in. Anyone who went beyond that circumscribed area paid a price."

The objectives of the military government, as in other colonial situations, included suppressing political organization on a national or nationalist basis (Gil, 2005: 126; Ozacky-Lazar, 2002; Bauml, 2002; Lustick, 1980: 51–69; Jiryis, 1966: 52). The era of the military government was a principal, decisive factor in forming the political discourse in Palestinian society, and its consequences were considerable even after the military government was removed. During the 1960s, then prime minister Levi Eshkol expressed his aspirations to turn the military government into one that "sees but is not seen," that is, to create a situation in which the military government exists and fulfills its functions, but direct contact between its officers and soldiers and the population is limited (Bauml, 2002). In fact, the visual power of the military government was replaced over the years by the more sophisticated visual power of aerial photography of Palestinians during demonstrations and the establishment of surveillance police stations in Palestinian towns and villages, among others.

The military government affected the discourse of Palestinians in Israel, causing what I see as a proactive "self-censorship" effect. Palestinian society used control and defensive mechanisms toward discourses that were tagged "unwise" or "unpragmatic." Continued pressure from the military government—arrests, intimidation, punishments, dismissal from work, informant planting—sent a message to Palestinians about the limitations of what was permitted and prohibited in political discourse in Israel.

The experiences Palestinians underwent during the military government and thereafter created a tremendous and continuing effect on Palestinian discourse, even for those of subsequent generations who did not directly live through the military government. Though only some of the interviewees personally experienced the period of the military government as children, others were affected primarily through their parents who cautioned against the consequences of political involvement. The shadow of fear in which Palestinians lived during the period of military government became an "internal silencing mechanism" similar to Foucault's Panopticon effect (Foucault, 1979). Even long after the military government was officially abolished, Palestinians still suspect the presence of an informer or other control mechanisms in their midst. Moreover, Palestinian citizens were killed in the Kufur Qasim massacre in 1956, on Land Day in 1976, and during the October Intifada in 2000 (Bishara, 2002). The state has used force against Palestinians in different incidents like in al-Ruha in 1998 when Umm al-Fahim residents protested land confiscation (WRMEA), in Umm al-Sahali neighborhood near Shafa 'Amir in 1999 when Palestinians protested the demolition of homes under the pretext that they were unauthorized (Kabha, 2004), and elsewhere. Most large demonstrations among Palestinians have been met with police violence. This in turn creates valid fears about opposition to

Zionist hegemony. In fact, Palestinian movements that publicly protest the Israeli definition of the state as solely Jewish were persecuted, delegitimized, and sometimes outlawed. This was the case for example with the al-'Ard movement (see chapter 1 in this volume), the Sons of the Village movement, and the political trial and persecution of the NDA and its former political leader, Azmi Bishara.

According to some of the interviewees, Jewish immigration to Israel is considered a "sacred cow" in the Israeli arena and is related to what is termed in the Jewish discourse as "national security." Indeed, in a discussion conducted in the Parliament in March 1990 on the "expressions of Arab residents of Israel against immigration," Jewish Knesset members made it clear that Arabs were forbidden to touch the issue of immigration. The minister of interior at the time, Zevulun Hammer, threatened to revoke the citizenship of Arabs who opposed immigration (Sabbagh-Khoury, 2006: 135–144). Palestinians were silenced on issues considered taboo by Israelis, even if this silencing is not totalizing or irreversible. The study participants saw the immigration of Jews, the refusal of the return of refugees, as well as other issues touching the heart of the Zionist consensus, as "red lines" Palestinians were "forbidden" to cross. This affected the explicit and implicit discourses on immigration policies. Rather than explicitly oppose Israeli immigration policies, Palestinians reversed the logic of causality and criticized its consequences. Their politics in this regard can be characterized in Gramsci's (1971) terms as a "war of movements," which for the most part focuses on resisting oppressive practices (e.g., expropriation of land, the dismissal from work) without challenging their origins.

Fear also stems from Palestinian economic dependency. Zureik (1976; 1979) points to the destruction of the Palestinian economic structure in 1948 and the creation of what he labels as "internal colonialism." One of the principal components of this new system was the enforcement of a capitalist economy on a "traditional" social order. Lustick (1980) similarly argues that Israel implemented policies designed to make the Palestinian economy dependent on state institutions and on the Israeli business sector, as another means of controlling Palestinian society (150–198). Fear resulting from this economic dependence is expressed by Fatma:

> Lack of courage! Today, the newspaper owner wants to live. . . . If a newspaper owner wants to present a subject daringly—his newspaper can be closed and he will lose his livelihood. Even for me, as an individual, if I had a business or some independent enterprise or private clinic, I would have to be very flexible. I would adapt to the laws and the existing situation. That is, I cannot make the effort and establish a specific business and simultaneously oppose or be in opposition to state entities.

The fact that consumption patterns of Palestinians are almost totally dependent on the Israeli state and the Jewish business sector amplifies their sense of fear. They are at risk of having to pay a heavy price for political activism, the price of facing an economic boycott by Israeli companies and the Jewish majority as was the case after October 2000. Thus, socioeconomic limitations affect political discourse and sometimes shape its contents.

The internalization of fear is not an unalterable process that totally prevents explicit collective opposition and resistance. Domination and resistance are inextricably linked, and the political situation is not completely controlled by fear or acquiescence. Opposition among the Palestinian minority against Israel's oppressive practices and discriminatory definition as a Jewish state has in fact persistently increased. For instance, despite the imposition of a military government, the Democratic Front grew in the late fifties as an umbrella organization of Arab nationalists in Israel, in cooperation with the communists. Later, the al-'Ard movement was established. Cohen (2006: 180–181) argues that throughout the fifties and sixties, Palestinians sharply opposed the state and its practices in dramatic ways. The Sons of the Village movement explicitly opposed recent Jewish immigration. In the mid-1990s, opposition to the definition of Israel as a Jewish state was expressed by the NDA, which demanded the transformation of Israel into a "State for all its citizens." Furthermore, in 2006–2007, three documents were published by NGOs and political representatives calling for the transformation of the Jewish definition of the Israeli state and proposing alternatives to prevailing power relations between the Palestinian citizenry and the Israeli state.

A final reason noted by interviewees for the absence of explicit opposition to Jewish immigration has to do with the ideology of the ICP and DFPE, the primary political party among Palestinians in Israel at the time. The party's discourse represents attempts to survive the predicament of the Jewish state and to protect Palestinians against the oppressive ethnonationalist policies. Consistent with its historical position, the party focused mainly on the notion of differential citizenship and inequality in the Jewish state (Bishara, 2002: 91–92, 130), but did not directly challenge its character. The party opposed immigration in the newspaper *al-Ittihad* (1989–1991), primarily in terms of the price exacted from Palestinian citizens (Sabbagh-Khoury, 2006). Having been closely linked to the Soviet Union, the party was defensive given the increasingly large groups of Jewish and non-Jewish immigrants arriving from precisely the country whose political ideology and principles were the source of the party's ideology and principles (Rekhess, 1993: 211–212). Thus, despite the loosening of Jewish control of the party, its discourse did not significantly challenge immigration policies or tackle the refugees' right of return (Sabbagh-Khoury, 2006: 28–31).

PERCEPTION OF THE ISRAELI LAW OF RETURN

In answer to my question "Should Palestinians in Israel oppose the Israeli Law of Return?" most interviewees answered in the affirmative. They described it as a "colonial and racist law" and said that it should be abolished. Some opposed the term "Law of Return," because they did not see the immigration of Jews to Israel as a "return to the homeland." Nevertheless, this opposition was never translated into a central political demand among Palestinians in Israel. According to some of the interviewees, this was the case because given existing power relations, Palestinians, as a minority group, cannot change the Law of Return. Such a demand, they argued, is likely to hold up or roll back gained political achievements. Other interviewees pointed out that opposition to the Law of Return is subsumed in opposition to the Jewish nature of the state, as in the NDA's call to transform the State of Israel from a Jewish state into a "State for all its citizens." According to this position, in a "State of all its citizens," no immigration laws that favor one national group would exist.[4] Other interviewees attributed this lack of direct opposition to the Law of Return to the overall absence of a political strategy among the Palestinian parties, organizations, and the High Follow-Up Committee concerning the future of Palestinians in Israel and their relations to the state.

The fear factor was again evoked to explain this silence. The interviewees stressed that fear was reinforced after October 2000, especially fear of the General Security Service (GSS) and institutionalized persecution. In this context, Salwa argues that "the public discourse today is weary of the national discourse and is afraid of a return to the military and GSS government." A return to practices of the military government and GSS political persecution of Palestinians and their leadership is not hypothetical. In March 2007, the Ma'ariv newspaper published the contents of a discussion held by the head of the GSS, Yuval Diskin, with Prime Minister Ehud Olmert, in which Diskin, responding to the three aforementioned NGO documents, said that Arab citizens are a strategic threat. In response to a letter from the editor of Fasl al-Maqal, the newspaper of the NDA, Diskin wrote that the GSS is "obligated to remove subversive activities by sources interested in harming Israel as a Jewish and democratic State, even if their activities are carried out using democratic tools" (Mahsom, 2005a: 1).

Some of the interviewees even expressed fear that parties that opposed the Law of Return would be outlawed. Two of the Islamic movement activists did not provide clear answers to the question of whether Palestinians should oppose the Law of Return. Hussein answered, "I do not have an answer to this issue." When I asked him if Palestinians should oppose the Zionist ideological principles, he answered affirmatively. And then I asked him why they did not oppose the Law of Return. He answered:

There is an exaggeration in the perception of the Palestinian individual and where he is willing to stand. The Palestinians in this country as well as the political parties are unable to address psychological issues. . . . The ceiling for political parties is not much higher than that of the public . . . and it follows the street [public opinion]. Another thing is the obsession with survival and fear of persecution, the fear of expulsion. Recently, there has been a discussion of the issue of transfer and exchange of populations and of the demographic threat. During the last four to five years, since the al-Aqsa Intifada, they are speaking about the subject differently, violently and openly. That is more frightening and causes the ceiling on political discourse to descend even further.

Some of the interviewees stated that Palestinians should not oppose the Law of Return. Fatma, an activist in the Islamic movement, answered by saying, "That is related to the political future of the entire region. If there is a Palestinian state and the right of return is permitted, why would we care about the right of return to the State of Israel, to the Hebrew state?" This interviewee perceived the "return" of Palestinian refugees as limited to a future Palestinian state in the areas occupied by Israel in 1967.

Na'ila said that opposition to the Law of Return is likely to be problematic. "I would not suggest to any party to oppose Jewish immigration in the present political climate." She continued: "In the same way that I want the right of return for Palestinian refugees, the Israeli Jews think of and articulate it as their right to return. I don't want to base my right on negating theirs, although I do want to dispute it. I say that my discourse has to argue with the Law of Return." Palestinians in Israel, until recently, often worded their position on Jewish collective rights somewhat ambiguously.

PERCEPTIONS OF AND DISCOURSE ON THE PALESTINIAN RIGHT OF RETURN

All interviewees expressed their hope that a full right of return for Palestinian refugees will be achieved in the future, and some thought that the rights of refugees could not be relinquished. For others, the return of refugees is a right that Israel should be required to recognize in order to acknowledge its historical responsibility for the refugees' displacement. In this context, Hatim said:

I do not see the possibility of applying it in the near future and think that Palestinians have a problem fulfilling it. Because generations have grown up in exile, the right of return is important for them as a dream, but they will not be in a hurry to exercise that right.

Nevertheless, the right itself has to remain a basic demand. First, because it locates the historical narrative in the correct context, that of 1948, an expulsion occurred here, and a whole people were uprooted, and so it is about their right to return to their homeland, or finding a humane alternative to the right of return. Second, this right must be placed on the political agenda, in order to remind Israel and its politicians of the original injustice that was perpetrated when the state was founded. . . . That is likely to have ramifications for us, Palestinians in Israel. If they recognize this sin, it is possible that it will lead them to readdress the problematic ideology underlying Israeli demography, and think of Israel not as a Jewish state but as something else: a Jewish state and something else or perhaps not a Jewish state at all.

Na'ila said that Palestinians are afraid to present a real solution to the issue of the right of return, because that entails facing the reality in which six million Jews already live in Israel. Demanding the full right of return, as she sees it, is an ideal that ignores the existing reality. As far as a solution is concerned, she says,

> We still have areas that are not populated, and can be built on. . . . Some will probably have to remain in Palestine. . . . Most likely, some will choose not to live in Jaffa but nearby, in the vicinity of Jaffa. . . . That is, the distinction must be recognized between the operation, the practical effort, and the right. The right is a basic, human one, and should be referred to as such in our speech. . . . The right of return is presented in an ideal way. . . . That is why a large number of people are afraid of it, because it is as if I am putting somebody in place of somebody else.

Na'ila seems to accept the Israeli discourse in linking the refugees' return with the expulsion of the Jews. She refers to the Israeli fear of the return of refugees, and describes the Palestinian demand for the return of refugees as utopian. According to her, Palestinians in Israel do not speak about the right of return, because they are afraid that it will be perceived by Israeli Jews as a demand to expel Jews from Israel. Na'ila says that a distinction should be made between the right and its implementation. She is unwilling to relinquish the right, but is willing to discuss the ways in which it should be implemented.

'Ala' distinguishes between the rights of internally displaced refugees and the rights of refugees in exile. He says that internally displaced refugees have to return, but that not even a fifth of the refugees outside of Israel will return, and most of them will "return to the 1967 borders," because "there will be a political solution." Even though he hopes that all the refugees will return, he does not foresee this as attainable due to power relations between Israelis and Palestinians.

The interviewees provided several reasons for the absence of political discourse concerning the right of return during the period of immigration from the USSR. The first is that the right of return is part of the broader Palestinian question. Some interviewees noted that Palestinians perceive the issue as related to the solution of the Palestinian question, and that the PLO was the only representative for drawing the general contours of the resolution of the Israeli-Palestinian conflict, including the right of return. Others pointed out that Palestinians in Israel have no influence on the negotiations between Israel and the Palestinian Authority, and that the issue of the return of refugees does not constitute a component of their discourse within Israel. There has been an increasing preoccupation with the right of return in the political discourse of Palestinians in Israel after 2000. The right of return stood out as an issue in the general Palestinian discourse only after the 2000 Camp David Summit, which in turn increased its visibility in the Palestinian discourse in Israel.

In addition, the return of refugees would alarm and stir up negative reactions among the Jewish majority, where it has become the "nightmare of Jewish society," so to speak. According to Ra'ida, demanding the refugees' return is likely to raise opposition among Jews in Israel and would damage Palestinian efforts to establish a Palestinian state. Other interviewees said that the return of refugees was pushed to the corner for pragmatic reasons. In its place, Palestinian discourse addressed daily needs, fulfillment of ongoing demands, and the establishment of a Palestinian state in the Occupied Palestinian Territories. Thus, according to Zahi:

> The Arab public has come to the conclusion that it has to find just methods [to solve] the issue. Of course, these methods are relative. Pragmatic methods mean that the conclusion has been reached and the establishment of a Palestinian state, with its capital in Jerusalem, should be demanded today. They say that the issue of refugees will most likely frighten the Jewish public and the world, and that it should be put aside. The focus instead should be on establishing a Palestinian state.

Hussein and Na'ila attribute the absence of the Nakba and the attempt to repress dealing with its ramifications to the fear of re-expulsion. Hussein expressed it this way:

> First and foremost, we want to remain here with the nightmare and fear that pursued us since 1948. We still have the story of 1948. The truth is that we internalize it and live with it. . . . That is how we lived and lied. We lived and tried, in very wise ways,

> to run from the effect of these hard questions concerning the right
> of return and other issues. . . . Who today is willing to deal with
> the right of return, when Israel speaks of the right of return as a
> strategic threat to its existence?

Another explanation was the lack of national political awareness among Palestinians in Israel during the 1990s. Some interviewees also mentioned that
Palestinians addressed other exigent issues like the expropriation of land and
the dismissal of Arab workers and hiring of Jewish immigrants in their place.
'Ala' noted in this context that the "subject of the right of return was not
the first priority of Palestinians in Israel." Palestinians in Israel have always
searched for ways to minimize the negative consequences of state structural
discrimination, and they did the same during the recent immigration. The
issue of refugees was delayed but not dismissed as a strategy of persistence
so that Palestinians can cope with the state's daily oppressive practices and
influence their fate within the limitations imposed on them.

CONCLUSION: SPLIT CONSCIOUSNESS

The relationship between Palestinians and the Israeli state was shaped firstly
through the trauma of the Nakba and the subsequent threat of another
expulsion. The events of the Nakba engendered revolutionary changes in
the demography, geography, and the architecture of Palestinian physical
space, and turned the Palestinians in Israel into a national minority. Yet
Palestinian discourse in Israel, much like the general Palestinian discourse,
did not collectively raise the issue of the Nakba in the public sphere until
recently. It was only in 1998 that the Association for the Defense of the
Rights of the Internally Displaced Refugees organized the first Nakba march.
Since then parades to the destroyed villages take place every year on Israeli
Independence Day and different groups organize memorials to the Nakba. Up
until then, those who had been displaced would more privately visit their
villages on this day to mourn and relive the memories of their expulsion from
their villages. Sanbar points out that "paradoxical though it may seem, as
long as their exile remained absolute the Palestinians said practically nothing about their exodus—only about its consequences. It is as if the trauma
they experienced had made them mute" (Sanbar, 2001: 93). This truncated
discourse suggests a notion of split colonial consciousness.

This chapter presents the voices of Palestinian political leaders on
issues regarded as taboo in Israeli discourse; they offer their perception of
historical justice in relation to Jewish immigration and the repatriation of
Palestinian refugees. It locates and theorizes a principal source of tension
in the majority-minority relations in the State of Israel by giving voice to
the subordinated Palestinians on the Israeli state's policies of immigration.

This is to overcome an oversight in existing studies, which refer to Israeli policies of immigration and Israeli demographic practices, but do not delve deeply into the multiple layers of Palestinian discourse about them. The findings of this research are, however, specific to the Palestinian political leadership. Further research is required to explore whether generalizations can be made to the larger Palestinian society in Israel.

Though they all came from parties that criticized the exclusionary Zionist foundation of the state, the interviewees expressed a variety of opinions on the Israeli Law of Return and the Palestinian right of return. Using Bhabha, I argue that under Israeli internal colonialism the discourses of the colonized are rife with contradictory logics, conflicting desires, and bewildering anomalies of the double silence on hegemonic perspectives related to Jewish immigration and refugee repatriation.

I found a strong divide at the core of the interviews. Previous seminal work in postcolonial literature focused on a dichotomous colonizer-colonized relationship. Franz Fanon, for example, focused chiefly on the consciousness of the colonized whereas Edward Said's earlier work generally analyzed the colonizers' consciousness (Moore-Gilbert, 1997: 116; Fanon, 1990; Said, 1978). Bhabha (1994) on the other hand, offers a model that links the two and examines the "forms of multiple and contradictory beliefs" among both the colonizer and colonized (Moore-Gilbert, 1997: 116). He highlights the tensions, disturbances, and fractures within colonized discourses (Bhabha, 1994: 116). Similarly, Spivak's skepticism regarding the ability of the subaltern to speak (Spivak, 1994) suggests that when we speak about the voices of colonial subjects we, to some extent, romanticize their resistance to colonial violence. Palestinians on the one hand resist the Jewish state, and on the other, want to participate in its developed economy. Colonial subjects live simultaneously in several political spaces and develop a multifaceted, sometimes contradictory, consciousness because of their compound living circumstances and political exigencies.

In this vein, Raef Zreik (2003a, 2003b) describes two dominant alternating drives prevailing in Palestinian politics since 1948: the "Pole of Justice" and the "Pole of Power." According to the "Pole of Justice," Palestinians sense profound feelings of injustice that resulted from the trauma of 1948 and from discrimination against them produced by the establishment of a Jewish state. The "Pole of Power" results from the sense of powerlessness and inability to affect the existing reality. This strategy is founded on a "pragmatic" evaluation of the limitations on the Palestinian minority's abilities in comparison to the power of the state. Following Memmi (1991), a sense of weakness influences Palestinian perceptions of the existing political reality, as is the case in every colonial system. Thus, Palestinians manifest a colonized consciousness, split in this case between justice politics and everyday existence. I found both poles reflected in the interviews, sometimes invoked by the same person.

Different processes may be at work simultaneously, including self-censorship, denial, fear, or the dictation of economic interests. All these processes work together, and none can serve as the sole explanation. Foucault (1995) emphasizes that subjugation in the modern era involves constant subordination, control, and monitoring of subjects of the state. I contend that the oppressive practices that the State of Israel has used against Palestinians over the years—starting with the Nakba and followed by the military government and its transformation to less-visible forms of control—created fear among Palestinians with a prolonged deterrent effect. While not irreversible, this effect lowered the threshold of demands made by the Palestinian minority for many years. Self-censorship operated even when the oppressive Nakba practices were not actually implemented. The very fact that Palestinians thought that such practices could be expected was enough to forgo opposition to issues considered taboo in mainstream Israeli discourse.

As a result of the collective trauma experienced, the Palestinians repressed dealing with its collective ramifications and consequences, including Jewish immigration and the Palestinian refugee issue. They tried to survive and resist the state's oppressive daily practices and discrimination and maintain their presence in the homeland, while fearing further transfer.

Fear alone cannot explain the entire phenomenon of the absence of a discourse on the repatriation of refugees. Otherwise, the gradually intensifying discourse on the right of return since 2000 cannot be accounted for. In the historical conditions and political circumstances of the late 1980s, the prevailing political movements at the time did not articulate the question of the return of refugees. Although the state employed tremendous power, it failed to achieve its aim of capitulation on the issue of the right of return. Most Palestinians still hold the view that the refugees should return to their homeland regardless of the prevailing power structures between Israel and the Palestinian Authority.[5]

NOTES

This chapter is based on my master's thesis "Between the 'Law of Return' and the Right of Return: Reflections on Palestinian Discourse in Israel." I would like to thank Yehouda Shenhav, Nadim Rouhana, Rhoda Kanaaneh, Isis Nusair, and Sherene Seikaly for their valuable comments.

1. It should be noted that the pro-natal policies for Jewish women are also differential. Melamed (2004) points out that the policies adopted by the Israeli establishment were conducive to increasing the Ashkenazi Jewish population and limiting the number of Mizrahi Jews when possible.

2. As evident in the title of this chapter, I prefer the term "repatriation" over "return." Repatriation is a term accepted and used in the global-comparative lexicon. It refers to a person who returns to their native country or citizenship, having left it either against their will or as a member of a group that left for political, religious,

or other pertinent reasons. Repatriation emphasizes that Palestine was, and still is, their country and homeland.

3. The names of the interviewees are pseudonyms.

4. The NDA Party began to address (via former member of Parliament Azmi Bishara) the laws of immigration. However, this position does not yet form a central demand of the party. See the speech by Bishara in the 106th meeting of the 15th Knesset, on May 7, 2001. See also the position paper "Return and Citizenship" that Bishara presented to the "Law, Constitution and Justice Committee" in the discussion of a constitution for Israel in April 2005. For the full text of the position paper in Hebrew, see Mahsom (2005b: 2).

5. In a survey among Palestinians in Israel conducted by Mada-al-Carmel in September and October 2005, 70.3 percent of the survey's participants would grant all refugees the right to return to Israel, or offer them the choice between return and proper compensation (Rouhana and Sabbagh-Khoury, 2009).

ELEVEN

WOMEN'S MASKED MIGRATION

Palestinian Women Explain Their Move upon Marriage

Lilian Abou-Tabickh

Palestinians in Israel follow the rule of patrilocal marital residence according to which newlyweds join the husband's natal house. Upon marriage, a Palestinian woman is displaced from her natal family and her residence is changed to her husband's. Despite the massive numbers of women moving, their migration remains invisible. The transformation of women's residence upon marriage is in fact not commonly recognized as migration. The custom of patrilocal residence is accepted without question by Palestinian society in Israel, and is a conventional, regular event for young women and men. Only rarely are women required to explain this practice. Similarly, the literature on Palestinians in Israel argues that they migrate at low rates despite economic factors such as high unemployment, low income levels, shortages of land, and population growth. This literature thus overlooks women who have always migrated.

Researchers have characterized the Arab family in the Middle East as patrilineal, patriarchal, patrilocal, and endogamous (Sa'ar, 2001; Barakat, 1993; Sharabi, 1990, 1987; Kandiyoti, 1988, 1977; Granqvist, 1935). The rule of patrilocal residence is a common and deeply rooted custom in Palestinian society and, as Rula[1] states, "is very difficult to change." Lama adds: "Even if there were arguments about where to live, that wouldn't help nor change things." Therefore, it has become a naturalized practice, and women generally don't even think about or question the reasons for it or its ramifications. This essay examines the link between the naturalization of gender roles and the invisibility of women's migration upon marriage.

This chapter offers a corrective to this problematic oversight and suggests a gendered analysis of patrilocal residence. Using in-depth interviews, I explore how Palestinian women in Israel who marry and move to new Arab locales in Israel explain their moves. The participants in the study used various emotional, cultural, economic, and familial explanations for this unique form of migration. The study, however, is not limited to revealing Palestinian gendered disparities, but takes into account present events as well as the history of the Palestinian people, revealing deep structures of inequality, anchored in state definitions and practices.

ON MARRIAGE RULES AND PATRILOCAL RESIDENCE

The near-universal demand for a joint home on the part of a married couple involves uprooting and displacement from other homes (Murdock, 1949:16). The newly married husband and wife cannot both remain living with their parental families; one (or both) of them has to move. Patrilocal[2] or virilocal[3] residence patterns are more common than are other types of residence (Murdock and Wilson, 1980: 33). Claude Levi-Strauss and several ethnologists agree that one of the most basic and important structures in society is the rule of residence (Levi-Strauss, 1969: 150). Residence allocation is considered the most basic fact that determines origin, power, and inheritance rules (see also Gough, 1971; Marx and Engels, 1955). Murdock and Wilson maintain that generally, rules of residence reflect economic, social, and cultural conditions. When given conditions change, residence rules and the local kinship system also tend to change, resulting in a reorganization of the social and economic structures of society (Murdock and Wilson, 1980: 17). Marshall Sahlins explains that in addition to its economic advantages, the extended patrilocal family—made up of the patriarch, his wife, married sons and their wives and children—has political advantages by the very fact of its complexity. Such a structure fosters solidarity among patrilineal family members, acquiescence on the part of the younger generation to their elders in the family, and separation of women from their families of origin, so as to give birth to their husbands' heirs (Sahlins, 1968: 64–65; see also Ember and Ember, 1971; Otterbein and Otterbein, 1965).

MIGRATION OF PALESTINIANS IN ISRAEL

This chapter suggests a gendered analysis of patrilocal residence. Therefore, based on in-depth interviews, I define the move of women to their husbands' homes and communities on their wedding day as masked migration. In this section, I examine the overall internal migration of Palestinians in Israel since the state was founded and its various motivations and unique directions, in order to locate this phenomenon in the larger socioeconomic and political order.

George Kosaifi (1980) states that the internal migration of Arabs in Israel cannot be explained in terms of the usual migration from village to city, that is, using primarily socioeconomic factors. The reasons for internal migration do not lie in the attractiveness of urban centers in terms of health, education, and employment. Rather Palestinian internal migration in Israel has to be understood in relation to the colonial policies of Israel—and particularly, the expropriation of land. The pattern of migration principally reflects the unique political conditions under which Palestinians live and the policies of Zionist settlement on Arab land (ibid.: 22–36; see also Lipshitz, 1991). The Zionist movement has sought to Judaize the land and this process has involved major changes in the geographical landscape: massive transfer of lands to Jewish ownership and control; the building of Jewish settlements; the destruction of the majority of pre-1948 Arab villages, towns, and urban neighborhoods; and limiting the areas and development of Arab locales (Morris, 2005; Bashir, 2004; Shafir, 2004; Yiftachel and Kedar, 2003; Falah, 1989; Zureik, 1979).

Before the 1948 war, Arab-Palestinian places of residence in Israel had a hierarchical structure: central cities (such as Jaffa, Haifa, Jerusalem, and Acre) absorbed migrants from, and were the administrative and economic centers for, the surrounding agricultural villages (Khamaisi, 2000: 79–80; Khamaisi, 1998: 111). This process of migration from the village to the city stopped, for the most part, in 1948 (Meyer-Brodnitz, 1983: 110). During and after the 1948 war, the Arab population in the cities and a large portion of the villages were deported, uprooted, and displaced. In addition to becoming refugees outside the emerging borders of Israel, another portion of the Arab population who lived in communities that were destroyed became internally displaced refugees. Thus, the migration of Arabs to urban areas or Arab villages in Israel was spurred primarily by war and subsequent Judaization policies (Morris, 2005; Yiftachel and Kedar, 2003; Khamaisi, 2000, 1998; al-Haj, 1988; Ben-Artzi and Shoshani, 1986).

Azmi Bishara describes how, with the founding of the state and the establishment of Jewish cities, agricultural settlements, and industry, and the massive expropriation of Arab lands, the Palestinian village lost an agricultural economic base vital for its continued existence (Bishara, 1998). Despite this, Bishara explains, migration of Arabs from the villages to Jewish cities did not grow (ibid.: 8), and the increase in population was not accompanied by substantial migration from the villages to the cities or between villages, as is often the case in other parts of the world, but was absorbed by the village itself (Khamaisi, 2000: 79–80; Gonen and Khamaisi, 1992: 8). The internal migration of young, primarily educated people to Jewish cities and those with mixed populations is statistically negligible (Khamaisi, 1998: 152; see also Haidar, 2005a; Gonen and Khamaisi, 1992). Maps of Palestinian neighborhoods continued to show development in the 1950s and 1960s, whereby extended families spread out and built on adjacent pieces of privately owned land that were not confiscated (Khamaisi, 1994b). By contrast, since the mid-1980s, new housing has tended to be built far from the extended family because of the scarcity of land on familial territory, though the preference is for construction in the villages themselves, and not in other villages and towns (ibid.; see also ACRI, 2001).

The government's policies of concentrating the Arab population in the smallest possible number of settlements—primarily because of political territorial considerations (Khamaisi, 1998: 113; Falah, 1989: 232)—and the limitations imposed by the Israeli military administration on Arab mobility maintained the spatial distribution created by the war in the peripheral areas: in the Galilee, the Triangle, the northern Naqab, and in cities with mixed populations (Khamaisi, 1998: 111, 119; Gonen and Khamaisi, 1992; Kosaifi, 1980:21).[4] In addition, Jewish settlements refuse to accept Arab citizens as homeowners, as happened with the Qa'dan family in Katzir and other couples who wanted to live in Misgav, Rakefit, Mei Ami, Karmi'el, and Ma'alot (Adalah, 2007a, 2007b, 2007c; HRA, 2005; Sultany, 2005). The Israeli Land Administration discriminates against Arabs in the issuing of licenses to build in Jewish settlements, even when the land is privately owned by Arabs, as happened in the settlement of Kammun (Adalah, 2004, 2005).

Jewish settlement and Judaizing policies continue to be top priorities of government decision makers and planning and land use institutions, although instead of the expression "Judaizing the area," they have started using terms such as "improving the quality of life" (Hamdan, 2005; see also *Haaretz*, 2007). In addition to land policies, the political status of the Palestinian citizens of Israel, the structure of the employment market, the ways in which the local economy is organized and poverty administered, the types of residences made available to particular populations and the policy of settling the Jewish population in widely dispersed strategic locations are all aspects of the colonial system in Israel (Massad, 2006:13; Shenhav et al., 2004: 191; Zureik, 1979). These conditions constitute breaches of section thirteen of the Universal Declaration of Human Rights, which guarantees the right of every person to freedom of movement and housing (UDHR, 1948). These policies illustrate the role the state plays in women's migration movements and in maintaining the patrilocal residence rules. The custom of patrilocal dwelling makes the situation of Palestinian women twice as difficult, because they are doubly denied the freedom to choose their place of residence.

INVISIBLE MIGRATION

The literature on the migration of Palestinians in Israel does not examine gender, and addresses the Arab population as a national collective in which the migrant man or male refugee is the norm, with a focus on historical events and the lack of citizens' rights. Women's change in residence upon

Table 11.1. Sources of increase in Arab population by region of residence: 2001. (Haidar, 2005a: 36)

Region of Residence	Population at the Beginning of the Year	Natural Increase	Total Increase	Population at the End of the Year	Unexplained Gaps
Total	941,841	29,186	31,090	972,359	1904
The Galilee	533,960	14,260	14,832	548,220	572
The Triangle	216,339	6,786	7,124	223,463	338
The Naqab	111,812	6,117	6,565	118,377	448
Mixed Cities	79,730	2,023	2,569	82,299	546

Note: Figures have been recalculated by the author, as the original table contained some errors.

marriage does not even merit mention, and is not called migration. For example, in his book *Arab Society in Israel*, Aziz Haidar identifies the sources of increase in the Arab population by region (see table 11.1). According to this data, unexplained gaps exist between the total increase in the population in one year and that due to natural increase. This gap is not listed in the table and is not clearly identified or explained.

Table 11.2. A sample of internal migration balance in Israel, by sex and locality: 2006. (CBS, 2006)

Locality	Men Enter	Women Enter	Men Leave	Women Leave
Abu Snan	46	94	37	81
'Iksal	17	60	15	38
Tur'an	16	40	23	57
Jaffa of Nazareth	66	136	99	139
Kabul	16	36	17	48
Kufur Yasif	36	77	48	81
Kufur Kanna	43	93	42	84
Mi'ilya	7	14	9	22
Mghar	45	68	76	92
Mashhad	23	37	10	36
Nazareth	187	364	541	730
Sakhnin	46	95	48	92
'Ilut	18	35	9	31
'Ayn Mahil	10	26	11	37
'Arrabeh	30	74	39	66
Rameh	24	53	45	62
Rayneh	129	213	71	114
Shafa 'Amir	114	193	72	136

Note: For additional localities, see internal migration balance within Arab localities according to the Central Bureau of Statistics: http://gis.cbs.gov.il/website/Localities_2006/viewer.htm.

Hundreds of Arab women, then, are displaced from their place of origin every year (see table 11.2). According to Central Bureau of Statistics data, the highest rate of internal migration among Arab women is in the fifteen- to twenty-nine-year-old age group. Given that very few women change their residence for reasons other than marriage (many who move to study do not register a change of location), the gaps in the statistics largely reflect the rates of women's migration with marriage. One can read women's migration upon marriage into these sets of data, though Haidar and Khamaisi do not identify it as such.

PALESTINIAN WOMEN IN ISRAEL

Conservative social structures and the racist state reinforce each other and collude to limit Arab women's rights to housing, as well as their choices and opportunities in other spheres. Palestinian women in Israel are a diverse group: differences among women in the same family, in the same village or town, or between villages or towns, are sometimes small and sometimes mani- fold and unbridgeable (Sa'ar, 2001: 728). Nonetheless, many Arab families discourage their daughters from living outside their local areas or villages (Mahsom, 2005; Espanioly et al., 1997: 86–73), and the state has built higher education institutions only in Jewish areas and thus often at a geographic distance from Arab locales. In addition, the various government ministries do not provide adequate scholarships, financial support, or dormitory options for Arab students. A combination of gender restrictions on movement and gender roles, together with government discrimination and a subordinated school system produce low levels of academic achievement among Palestin- ian women (Haidar, 2005a: 33; Working Group Report, 2005; Espanioly et al., 1997: 86–73; Bader-'Araf, 1995: 215). Despite the growing trend of Arab women working outside the home, women composed only 18.7 percent of the Arab workforce in 2001; over half of these women work within their own villages, and their salaries were the lowest and their working conditions the poorest (Haidar, 2005: 53, 186; see also Touma-Shukha, 2007).

Socially, Palestinian women face attempts to restrict their move- ment, dress, and cross-gender friendships. They are obliged to maintain certain norms, follow stringent behavior, and fulfill a range of roles that are required of them by the patriarchal system (Hasan, 1999: 269; see also Zinger-Harouti, 2008; Keinan and Bar, 2007). In the event that these are breached, punishment can be swift. Between October 2000 and February 2009, seventy Arab women in Israel were murdered for what is called "fam- ily honor" (Masarweh, 2009; Ghanim, 2005; Vailer-Polak, 2009). Though they are required to carry the "burden of representing" collective identity (Yuval-Davis, 2001: 127), Samar Khamis notes that Palestinian women are generally absent from the national scene and are distanced from positions that serve as platforms of public expression (Khamis, 2005: 1). The state of education, employment, and violence among Palestinian women is linked to the social and structural limitations on women's lives. These conditions form the context in which women migrate, and are reflected in the interviews regarding their patrilocal migration.

The average age of marriage for Palestinian women is 22.2 (Haidar, 2005a: 44).[5] With the rule of patrilocal residence, marriage means a much greater change for a woman (Abou-Tabickh, 2008; al-Haj, 1987: 108–113; Kandiyoti, 1977; Granqvist, 1935: 144–145). She leaves her own family and familiar environment, is relocated to the home of her husband's family, and has to adapt herself to a new status regarding the members of her new household (Abou-Tabickh, 2008: 61–97; see also Granqvist, 1935: 141–145). Moving to her husband's home and family, which is sometimes a "hostile environment" (Kandiyoti, 1977: 72), means that a woman will always live among people who see her as a *gharība*, a stranger, and who, for the most part, will never let her forget that (Abou-Tabickh, 2008: 61–77; Yahia-Younis, 2006; Granqvist, 1935:144–145). This displacement, loss, and alienation are difficult with many potential ramifications. For example, many women who worked before they were married lost their positions due to their move as was the case for women in this study, and some did not find work after completing their academic degrees because of lack of employment positions in the Arab villages of their husbands, where positions are frequently linked to family connections (Abou-Tabickh, 2008: 78–88).

This study, conducted in 2006–2007, draws on seventeen semi-structured interviews with Arab-Palestinian women in Israel who, upon their marriages, migrated to the home communities of their husbands in the Galilee. This is a phenomenological study that seeks to learn about patrilocal residence as the participants in the study understand, explain, and analyze it. The women interviewed differ from one another in their education and professional training, economic status, place of origin and destination, age, and religion.

ONE RESIDENCE RULE, DIFFERENT STORIES

The participants offered various explanations for their moves upon marriage and their discourse was multivocal. For every hierarchy that shapes experience, there is more than one story created within us (Benjamin, 2003: 4). As women, for example, we can observe the world and experience it by accepting hierarchies and simultaneously relate to the world through feminist interpretations with their challenging perspectives (ibid.). Human interpretation is dynamic and back and forth movement between positions is not uncommon, because more than one story can appear reasonable (Griffiths, 1995; Davies and Harre, 1990).

One of the explanations provided by the participants for patrilocal residence is an emotional one. Heterosexual love between a man and a woman is highly valued locally, even though it is not usually fulfilled sexually before marriage (Sabbagh, 1996). When they were asked how they explain their move to their husbands' communities upon their marriage, the first answer that all the participants in the study gave invoked this notion of romantic love. Such interpretations draw on a construct of love as "the most important thing in the world, and every other consideration should be sacrificed for it, including material considerations" (Iluz, 2002: 16).

Sana, a teacher by profession, moved to Sakhnin from the city of Haifa fourteen years ago. Muna, a librarian and mother of three, moved from Acre to 'Iksal ten years ago. They both explain their moves in almost identical terms and reinforce the view of romance as irrational, unconditional, and not meant to be profitable (Iluz, 2002: 16). Muna stated that "Where didn't matter to me . . . the important thing was to live and be with him. That is, from my point of view, it wasn't important whether it was 'Iksal or Acre. Wherever he decided to live, whether Haifa or Acre, I would have agreed. I loved him to the point where I didn't think about anything else."

The explanations about love, as they are presented by the participants in the study, can be seen as containing elements of daring and revolt and as an individual choice in a society in which endogamous marriage is idealized. Though such endogamous marriages are in the minority today (see chapter 8 in this volume), families seek to be involved in the selection of marriage partners for their children. Still, in my view, this is a revolt against the existing socio-emotional order that simultaneously supports patriarchal values by maintaining the existing patrilocal order concerning residence. The link between love and culture in the context of housing thus reproduces existing power inequalities.

While the first interpretation that all of the study participants gave for their moving was love, the women also added other explanations, which at different points complemented and contradicted one another. Some of the women divided their explanations into two periods: before and after they "sobered up." Over the years, and with more experience, these women came to the conclusion that the principal reason women move upon marrying is the man's relationship with his family and community.

In addition to accounts of irrational love, capitalist values have penetrated into cultural practices, and have imbued the discourse of modern love with individualism and utilitarianism. These values allow individuals to view love relationships through the business world's logic of profit and loss (Iluz, 2002: 186). After Safa' explained that she moved from her beloved hometown of 'Ilabun to Nazareth because of her love for her husband, she noted that she made the move not only for him and because of him, but also for herself: "To tell you the truth, I didn't think that I could find a man with whom I'd be as close as I am with Farid, to be myself so totally. And that was the price I paid to be with him. That is, I profited in my feelings, and I fulfilled my emotional desires, but I also paid a price. . . . The price was that I left the town that I loved so much in order to come here and live in his town. I didn't do it because of him. I did it because of me." Yasmin, who was married at age twenty-four and moved from Nazareth to Abu Snan, maintains that she moved to her husband's locale because he owns land there, on which she can build the home of her dreams. In her words: "I don't like living in an apartment building. I like living in my own home, in a private house. These are things that are more important to me than getting used to people in a new place. . . . what caused me to come live in Abu Snan was the piece of land that he has, on which I can build a house to my liking." According to Bourdieu, social acts "adjust themselves to economic situations, even when they are apparently non-utilitarian . . . and are directed at non-material things that cannot be easily quantified" (Bourdieu, 1977: 171).

Many of the study participants perceived the patrilocal residence rule as natural fate and unchangeable. This sense is created by the prevailing cultural and social structures and is part of a cycle in which structures form people's practices and people's practices reestablish structures (Giddens, 1984: 25). Culture and marriage patterns are re-created by the thoughts and actions of the women themselves. Not only did the study participants display knowledge about cultural structures, but they also acted according to its requirements, took responsibility for it, and cooperated with it. Thus, in the words of Suha from Nazareth-'Ilut: "We move to them because we belong to the men. We suffer from that, but continue to do it. . . . We continue because of the power of continuity that suggests nothing else." Women's sense of not having other options is reinforced by gender roles in marriage, subordination within family structures and spatial limitations imposed by state policies.

PATRILOCAL RESIDENCE

Differential Inheritance

Resources, and land in particular, play a central role in the cycles of producing and reproducing the patrilocal residence rule. Differential inheritance practices for men and women rely on the patrilocal residence rule to continue transferring capital and land to men, which in turn justifies the continuation of transferring assets solely to men. May said:

> When there's a piece of land, it's much easier and cheaper to build on it, and when there's already a house built, there's nothing to be done . . . it's customary for women to give up their portion of the inheritance. When my father died, my sisters and I quickly went and signed a waiver to the rights to the houses, the fields,

the warehouses, the cars. . . . I don't know. We didn't ask. . . . Even though each one of them [her brothers] has a house, and we, the girls, do not.

Question: "Why did you all sign?" May answered:

We signed because we wanted to show them that we do not covet their assets. . . . A day won't come where we'll say that we want our parents' house. . . . That's our mentality . . . retarded. And when we asked why he [the brother] is so quick to deal with inheritance matters and ask us to sign the waiver, he got angry, and my mother got angry, and said that we should be ashamed that we covet their assets so much. According to Shari'a [Islamic law], a daughter is entitled to half of what a son is entitled to. Not only is that unjust, but the woman doesn't even get that. That's our mentality in everything related to inheritance. And if the woman dares to demand [her rights], then her brother and parents condemn her, are angry at her and break off ties with her. It's sad.

Since 1995, civil law in Israel officially placed the family court system, which requires an equal division of inheritance between the sexes, beside the religious courts. Marital matters in the Palestinian community, however, were kept under the jurisdiction of religious courts until 2001—since the state chose to view these matters as basically part of the "traditional Palestinian cultural domain." In 2001, a campaign run by a coalition of Palestinian women's groups and organizations for human rights helped pass an amendment to the family court law. This amendment enabled the family court system to adjudicate in marital matters, except for marriage and divorce. The amendment guarantees access to the civil judicial system, which is relatively more sensitive to women's needs and seeks to promote equality between the sexes (WGR, 2005: 48–50). Despite the existence of such laws on the books, the authorities implemented them weakly. The civil law of inheritance for the most part did not change the practice of inheritance, and men continue to deny their sisters' share in inheritance and build on the land of their fathers (see Abou-Tabickh, 2008: 42–47; 'Athamneh, 2007). Furthermore, civil law does not take precedence over a will. Fathers can continue to write their wills, leaving everything to their sons and depriving women of the protection of the civil law.

Through inheritance, parents who believe in the superiority of sons over daughters re-create the conditions that make the woman's move possible and generally certain. This inequality is not inevitable; it is a result of the specific social relationships that organize it (Young, 1992: 117–119). Negating women's inheritance perpetuates the pattern of men residing adjacent to their families, and prevents women from having the right to choose their residences. Gender is central to decisions about dividing assets, and assets are central to women's decisions to get married and to move.

Commodification in Service to the Land

Patrilocality in essence involves the trade and exchange of women by men (Levi-Strauss, 1969, 1960: 283). The participants' explanations nevertheless reveal that they are not exchanged or traded by anyone as they all freely chose their spouses. However, the family's role in denying the women's share in assets as well as the spouses' ownership of property involves an exchange in which Palestinian women get homes and Palestinian men get women. This exchange is evident in the following interview:

> Question: Why did you choose to live in Nazareth?
> 'Ula: Because I didn't want to live in a rented place . . .
> Question: [Your husband] had a house?
> 'Ula: He didn't have his own house, but there was an empty apartment in his family's building, in which we could live until we built or bought our own home. . . . And if I had wanted to stay in my home community, I would have had to live in a rented place, and I'm against renting.
> Question: The existence of the house was in fact decisive?
> 'Ula: I didn't care where we would live. What was important to me was that we wouldn't rent.

On the surface, this sounds like a good and simple arrangement, a type of mutual trade in which the man provides the home and the woman leaves everything and moves to his home. However, the stories of the study participants demonstrate that in reality the situation is different. It quickly becomes apparent that the exchange is not simple, because the parties involved are not really free or equal. The interviews indicate that women had limited power to set conditions concerning the home in which they will live. Some of the men only had pieces of land that could be built on, while construction itself was carried out by the couple after marriage. Other men did not prepare a home, but lived in a vacant apartment in their family's building. In those cases, the women as well as the men were partners in constructing their joint home. Some of the men prepared the framework for the house, and construction was completed after the wedding, with money earned by both the husband and wife. Thus, according to the marriage agreement, the man is required to build and provide a house, but in many cases, he does not fulfill his obligation. The women, in any event, carried out their obligations and moved to their husbands' homes, without setting any conditions relating to the size, location, or quality of the house.[6] To me, this is an exchange in which the woman relocates in return for a piece of land, and enters a home that the man continues to control as his own property. The man can justify his wife's move to his home on the basis of an incomplete gift. The women enter in the transaction without knowing its full details and consequences.

Based on Mauss's ([1923] 2005) framework, I propose that we view the home that the man prepares for the wedding as a gift that encompasses three obligations: the man is obliged to give, the woman is obliged to receive, and then the gift must be reciprocated. It cannot be refused, because of the obligation to receive and also because the price for refusing is very high. Palestinian women who refuse to move to their husbands' homes risk being condemned by society and foiling their marriages. As one of the participants said, "The moment you insist, and try to convince him otherwise, he says that you're not the right wife for him and that he'll seek a wife who will come and live with him and his family."

Family obligations are gendered; the son is seen as keeping the family name and carrying it forward, while the daughter is considered destined to marry and join a different family (Sa'ar, 2001; Sharabi, 1990). Sons benefit the family and daughters are a burden to it. The daughter can be as loved as the son, but she ultimately belongs to a different group. The family pushes the girl, even if in subtle ways, to feel that she is a guest in their house from an early age (Sharabi, 1990: 31). Suha from Nazareth-'Ilut related that "The daughter is taught, from an early age, that she will get married and leave her home, so from a certain age they treat her as a burden at home. They will allow her to study, and they'll invest in her, but they always tell her that she's a guest in that house. Even if she's a physician, they'll continue to hint to her that she is a guest in their home up until a certain age, and then they expect her to move. . . . Thus, they'll ensure that the home remains for the son. . . ." In addition, the gendered division of labor within the family confines women to the limited roles of marrying and raising children, and keeps them from participating in public life (Haj-Yahia, 2005). Women's status in the family, both when single and when married, limits their choices and opportunities in the private and public spheres.

The centrality of the family in the Arab world has important ramifications for gender relations, since Arab families are generally patriarchal (Joseph, 1996; see also NCHALAI, 2006). Patriarchy bestows privileges on men and older people (including older women), and justifies these privileges in kinship terms (Joseph, 1996: 195). After she spoke about love, culture, and customs, May from Nazareth-'Iksal comes to the following conclusion: "The truth is that the man chooses to live where his parents are, because in our case, there was in fact land in other places, farther from his parents' home. But his father decided to build on the land next to his home, so that his sons would be close to him. And aside from that, my father-in-law is the type who wants his sons next to him and won't let his sons or their wives move [a step] without knowing where they're going." The considerations that guided the Arab village household in Israel in determining the location of a house were primarily those of land ownership and availability of the plot for construction, which can significantly lower the cost (Khamaisi, 1994a). Since the 1990s, however, with the diminishing ratio of land to population caused by expropriation and population growth, ownership of the land as a factor determining location of a house has been losing significance. The family consideration, by contrast, is still strong, and in cases where there is no land available for the sons, the parents build a multilevel structure with an apartment for each son (ibid.: 122; see also Abou-Tabickh, 2008: 37–58). In both cases, of a new home in a new location or above the parents' home, the man is the owner—and controller.

Reem, who moved from Haifa to Shafa 'Amir twenty years ago, describes the family's role in the following way:

> Look, I was twenty-one, twenty-two. I loved him a lot and sac-rificed a great deal for him. . . . I moved because of and for him. Aside from which, you see your sisters around you, your friends and neighbors, and each one of them moves somewhere else. From a young age, they teach you that the woman from the west moves to the east, and no one knows where she'll end up. . . . I have a sister who got married to Majd al-Krum and the second to Jish and the third to Nazareth, and I to Shafa 'Amir, and only one stayed in Haifa. We don't ask. It's clear, and goes without saying. I agreed to move to him. I had to. . . . I have to move to the place of the man I've chosen. That's the way parents educate you, to the point where we don't even ask those questions. The man doesn't leave his home and community. He's close to his parents and his broth-ers, to his land, to people in the community. The Arab man won't shake loose. It's very comfortable for him here and he would suffer if he moved to a different community. It is known that the woman sacrifices herself all her life. And if you insist, then he'll say that you're not the right wife for him, and that he wants a girl who will come here to live with him and his family.

Economic Constraints

The significances and functions of the patrilocal residence rule are manifold. The rule reflects not only personal, familial, and cultural motivations and interests, but political and economic forces as well. Based on interview analysis, it is clear that the custom of patrilocal living and that of building a house before the wedding encompass ways of dealing with a myriad of economic conditions. Despite the fact that the map of residences before the establish-ment of the state indicates preference for living close to the extended family, the practice of building on top of the parents' home developed primarily as a result of lack of land in Arab towns and villages (Adalah et al., 2006; Bashir, 2004; Yiftachel, 1999b). Many Arab men build above their parents' home due to economic considerations. These are shaped by the fact that the Arab workforce is the lowest paid in Israel and Arabs are employed in the least-skilled and least-prestigious types of work (Haidar, 2005c: 187–197; see also Shihadeh, 2004). Only 59.1 percent of Arab men were employed in 2001. Fifteen to twenty Arab villages and towns head the rankings of unemployment in the state. Moreover, data from 2001 shows that women accounted for only 18.6 percent of the Arab workforce and received the lowest salaries (Haidar, 2005c: 186–197). As a result, the economic resources available to Arab women are very meager. This together with institutional discrimination in housing assistance (HRA, 2005) contribute to limiting their opportunities and access.

The Arab family and its sense of mutual obligation in some cases takes the place of the state's refusal to provide equal resources and infrastructure (Bishara, 1998; al-Haj, 1995). Internal electoral, economic, and religious disputes cause men to prefer living close to their families, so as to enjoy their protection (al-Haj, 1987). The feeling by national minorities in a majority culture that they are foreigners (Khamaisi, 1998, 2000), especially in the aftermath of October 2000, reinforces this preference as well. These factors contribute to the maintenance of the practice of living close to the extended family.

Building above the husband's parents' apartment is a relatively inexpensive cost-saving option for the young couple. Nevertheless, Arab men who want to sell or rent their apartments in Arab communities are frequently unable to do so. The location of the apartment in the family's building limits the possibilities, and turns it into a "dead asset," in the words of Nagham, who lives in a three-story building into which considerable expense was invested. When she considered moving elsewhere, she understood that she had an expensive but dead asset with no buyers, making it difficult for her to purchase another home.

The Unnamed Role of the State

The policy of Judaization and land segregation in Israel enables the establishment of settlements intended for Jewish residents only, and does not leave a lot of living choices for Palestinians (ACRI, 2005; Bashir, 2004; Shafir, 2004; Yiftachel and Kedar, 2003: 29; Ziv and Shamir, 2003: 89–91). The housing shortage in Arab communities is expected to become more acute in the next decade. Some 61 percent of Arab families will require at least one additional housing unit in the next decade, and 44 percent were sure that they would not be able to build or purchase a new house, due to lack of resources or lack of land on which to build (Sultany, 2005).

The state created an ethnocratic regime in part through land legislation, which permits the Judaizing of Israel's geographic landscape and ghettoizes Arab citizens (Yiftachel, 1999b). The latter basically cannot purchase land in 80 percent or more of the country and cannot settle in 88 percent of its 902 Jewish rural settlements (Adalah, 2007a, b, c, 2006; Yiftachel, 1999b). Arab citizens of the state who want to rent or buy an apartment in a Jewish city are often rejected and discriminated against because they are Arabs. In a study conducted in 2007, it was found that 75.3 percent of Jews are not willing to have Arabs live in their neighborhood (ACRI, 2007; see also Sultany, 2005). The only alternative residence to the husbands' villages that came up in the interviews was the city of Haifa. Discrimination against Arab couples attempting to purchase houses in Jewish urban areas makes Haifa one of the few options available. Patrilocal residence is a complex phenomenon that requires an understanding of all aspects of women's lives, including those produced by the state.

Interestingly, the women I interviewed did not name the state per se as a factor in their migrations. They mentioned the scarcity of land in Arab towns and villages, the fact that parents build apartments above their own for their sons, but did not directly mention the state. Some researchers assert that "the state is never absent, unless it has been learned through deep experience that it cannot be a reference point that can be depended on. Yet it is absent essentially because the expectations of it are humble" (Ghanim, 2005: 202).

CONCLUSION

Palestinian women do not call their moves migration. Nonetheless, those who try to discuss it find themselves silenced by society and by their families and husbands. Palestinian women migrate as individuals. But many of them migrate, and therefore this is a collective phenomenon. It is an extraordinary event of migration in that there are no written laws or clear terms. As Fatin, who migrated from Tur'an to Jaffa of Nazareth fifteen years ago, described it: "We have no interest in moving to another community. None whatsoever, quite the contrary! We move because he won't. He won't move because he has an interest [in staying]. And we don't think and don't ask at all. . . . We go, and we lose a lot as a result." Sana', who migrated from Haifa to Sakhnin fourteen years ago, added: "Over time, I convinced myself that it had been my choice, but as I said, during the same period I never, never, thought about why I had to change my place of residence, and didn't suggest that we live somewhere else. . . . Because I felt that this was a natural, regular thing and that it didn't really matter to me."

The migration experiences of many married women in Turkey, Latin America, and Africa to cities was liberating because it enabled them to escape from oppressive customs and traditions, and to challenge the authority of their husbands and the burden of social and public obligations. Moving away from their husbands' extended families in the village and establishing their nuclear families in the city can be significant in enhancing the women's positions in their families (Herzog, 2007; Ehrenreich and Hochschild, 2006; Thai, 2006; Schaeffer-Grabiel, 2004; Erman, 1998; Foner, 1978; Whiteford, 1978; Behrman and Wolfe, 1984; Little, 1976). The findings of the interviews discussed in this chapter indicate that, in contrast to movements of population in much of the rest of the world, the migration of the study participants upon their marriage, for the most part, brought about deterioration in their economic and social status, and did not change the patriarchal authority. Their migration led them to reside among the patrilineal family of their spouses, subjecting them to limiting sociocultural norms, as well as restricting their ability to accumulate economic resources (Abou-Tabickh, 2008: 59–97).

Palestinian women's migration with marriage is not openly forced migration, but it is not done out of free will either since women have no real option to refuse. It is actually a masked and forced migration (see Abou-Tabickh, 2008: 55–58). A woman who refuses to migrate to the man's settlement risks separation, exclusion, and a bad name. In the words of Ahlam, who migrated from Kufur Kanna to Rayneh twenty years ago: "I convinced myself that it was my choice and I could have refused to move to his place, but then I would have lost him. That's what I thought at that time, that the man and the place are intertwined. That's the way we all thought." Ahlam thus illustrates the intricate connection between the gendering of both place and social relations.

The migration of Palestinian women is not pushed by economic reasons in the sense of migration from villages to urban centers. Women migrate from every place to every place. The ubiquity of the patrilocal residence minimizes their ability to evaluate and measure the costs and benefits of moving to different locations. No search for a place to live or comparison of rents in other places can be seen in their pattern of migration. The place in which they will live is simply determined by their husband's place of origin. The patrilocal residence rule maintains women's subservience. It creates a social reality that masks the power relationship between genders within the household, determines the migration of women and makes it invisible, and limits women's rights to choose the location of their homes. It is a practice in which men bestow assets on each other, using cultural customs, and so continue to define space as owned by them.

Not all Palestinian women in Israel migrate with marriage. There are definitely women who choose together with their husband a third place, far from both families, to live in. There are also some men who choose to live near their wife's family or in her locality. From conversations with young women elsewhere, I have learned that more and more educated and independent women are aware of the limitations that will be imposed upon them in their new place of residence, and are conscious of the power that their spouse's family would have over them. These women talk about how difficult it is to persuade their future spouses to leave their patrilineal residence. They know that they pay a price, but are not willing to compromise. In many cases, they are forced to break off relationships with men, because the men are not willing to relocate. Not only do these women refuse to live in their husband's villages or towns, but they refuse to live in a home that he's already prepared for them. They are seeking spouses with whom they can begin a joint life as equals.

NOTES

This chapter is based on my master's thesis, "Migrants within Their Nation: How Do Palestinian Women in Israel Experience Their Migration with Marriage?" (University of Bar-Ilan, Israel). I wish to express my heartfelt gratitude to my thesis advisor Dr. Orna Sasson-Levy for her dedicated guidance and support.

1. The real names of the study participants as well as the locales of origin and destination have been changed.

2. Patrilocal residence: a pattern whereby the family lives with or near the patrilineal family.

3. Virilocal dwelling: similar to patrilocal residence in practice, whereby a married couple moves to the husband's kin's residence upon marriage, while lacking the patrilineal origin.

4. Amnon Be'eri Zulitzeanu contends that "the traditional reality in which the Arab public lives within the narrow confines of the Arab villages in the Galilee, the Sharon Triangle region and the Negev is rapidly disappearing and boundaries are fading" as more and more predominantly Jewish cities are becoming more mixed, such as Karmi'el, Safad, Bir al-Sabi', Nahariyya, and Yeruham. This is in addition to the official seven "mixed cities" in which at least 10 percent of the residents are Arab: Acre, Haifa, Ramleh, Lydd, Ma'alot-Tarshiha, Upper Nazareth, and Jaffa. Roughly 100,000 Arabs live in these cities—9 percent of Israel's entire Arab population (Be'eri Zulitzeanu, 2009).

5. The average age of marriage among Muslim women is 22.1; Christians 24.4; Druze 21.5.

6. For more on this, see Abou-Tabickh (2008: 45–48).

TWELVE

EMIGRATION PATTERNS AMONG
PALESTINIAN WOMEN IN ISRAEL

Ibtisam Ibrahim

INTRODUCTION

The growing phenomenon of women's emigration from developing countries to developed countries has received wide attention in most recent studies of emigration movements (e.g., Martin, 2004; Staab, 2004; Zlotnik, 2003; ILO, 1998). Arab women's emigration is the least-covered phenomenon in such studies despite the fact that 37 percent of the world's skilled and expert worker migrants come from Arab and African countries (AIPU, 2003). This chapter presents a case of female emigration, that of educated Palestinian women from Israel to Western countries in pursuit of advancing their studies or careers. The study focuses on ethnographic evidence from in-depth interviews that I conducted with sixteen women, combined with personal observations and related scholarly literature.

There is little published research about emigration from the Palestinian Occupied Territories of the West Bank, Gaza Strip, and East Jerusalem. One study from 1991 focuses on emigration from Palestinian refugee camps in the Gaza Strip as a result of an UNRWA policy encouraging emigration (Elnajjar, 2003). An earlier study by Lafi Jaafari discussed the migration of educated and skilled Palestinians and Jordanians to North America based on a survey conducted in 1970 among students in American universities (Jaafari, 1973). Jaafari concluded that Palestinian emigration to the United States for young men (90 percent of the migrants) and women was short-term and closely linked to education and occupational training (Jaafari, 1973).

In the scholarship on Palestinian citizens of Israel, studies on emigration are extremely rare.[1] One possible explanation is that Palestinian citizens of Israel do not emigrate in substantial numbers because they strongly resist leaving. Palestinians who survived the 1948 war see their presence in Israel as protecting the remaining Palestinian lands now included within the borders of the State of Israel. This is particularly true of the Galilee and Triangle regions, where Palestinians have maintained a foothold in their traditional homes. Their state-enforced segregation from the Jewish population and the national homogeneity of the surviving Arab villages and towns, ghettoized as they may be, preserved their Palestinian Arab identity as a national indigenous population. This strong sense of belonging to the land enhanced resistance to emigration.

Meanwhile, following the 1967 and 1973 wars, their compatriots in the West Bank and Gaza began to emigrate to join male family members who had left earlier to work in the Gulf or neighboring countries (Hilal, 1977). Hilal estimates that 1967 wartime émigrés number between 170,000 to 200,000 from the West Bank alone (Hilal, 1977). Initially, those male migrants had viewed their move for employment as temporary. But as economic pressures mounted and as the Israeli occupying authorities placed tremendous barriers on their mobility, both geographic and economic, within and outside the occupied area, the families of the earlier migrants felt forced to join their male members who had moved to work in oil-producing countries. Unsurprisingly, Israeli policy has facilitated "such moves—and [has tried] to make them irreversible" (Abu-Lughod, 1983). Israeli depopulation policies aimed at Palestinians in the West Bank and Gaza Strip caused another estimated 141,000 persons to emigrate or be expelled by 1974, in addition to the wartime émigrés. The majority who were forced to leave were skilled men not able to find employment either in the Occupied Territories or in Israel (Hilal, 1977).

A higher level of repression contributes to higher rates of family emigration from the Palestinian Occupied Territories. Since the start of the al-Aqsa Intifada, there appears to have been a rise in the number of Palestinians, many of them highly educated young men and women, who have left the Occupied Territories to move to Western countries. The dehumanizing conditions of occupation and "the continuous confiscation of land, military roadblocks and the separation wall coupled with restrictions on mobility and access give the impression that people are living in a cage" and are primary factors for Palestinian emigration (Assad, 2007). There are, however, no exact figures concerning the number of people leaving. According to human rights activists, the "emigration phenomenon is a well-kept secret . . . [because] from a national point of view, that story shouldn't be given publicity" (Shavit and Bana, 2001).[2]

THE MIGRATORY MOVEMENT OF PALESTINIANS FROM ISRAEL

Migration trends among residents of the West Bank and Gaza contrast sharply with those among Palestinians in Israel. Although they have continuously encountered the threat of transfer by the Israeli authorities and have suf-fered from Israel's discriminatory policies (Hajjar, 1998; Adalah, January 2, 2007; *Haaretz*, March 27, 2007), Palestinian citizens of Israel exhibit only a low rate of long-term emigration. The emigration rate is generally higher, however, among Christian Palestinian citizens. According to a survey by Sabeel, the emigration of Palestinian Christians from Israel, especially the youth, is mostly due to better living conditions abroad (Assad, 2007).[3]

During the 1970s and 1980s, several hundred young Palestinian men as well as numerous women from Israel left temporarily (for four to seven years) for the sake of university education and training abroad because Israeli universities had restricted the absorption of young Arab applicants.[4] Initially, these young people turned to the Communist bloc countries, where they went on educational grants from the Israeli Communist Party, mostly focusing on professional education in medicine, engineering, and law. Only a small percentage of those grantees were female, and all of them, males and females, returned to their hometowns and villages after they completed their education. Special qualifying exams, such as *bhinot staj* (internship exams) for physicians and state license exams for other professions, were developed to make it harder for these returning graduates to practice their professions. A large percentage of current Palestinian female and male physicians and lawyers in Israel received their educations in the Soviet bloc.

Since the demise of the Soviet Union in the late 1980s, Palestinians in Israel lost the Communist Party educational grants, but they did not stop seeking higher education in these countries. Families continued to send their sons and daughters to study abroad because the doors of Israeli higher educa-tion—particularly medical and law schools—continued to block Palestinian citizens. One of the obstacles facing Palestinian students applying to Israeli universities for admissions is the requirement of the psychometric examina-tions. The test is usually translated from Hebrew to Arabic. According to a committee established by the Council for Higher Education in Israel in 2002, the test is not sensitive to Palestinian culture or the Arabic language, and therefore Palestinian students are at a disadvantage when taking it (WGR, 2005). Another obstacle is that "Israeli universities regularly set the minimum age of admission based on the assumption that applicants have completed mandatory military service thus forcing non-serving Arab students to wait up to three years after high school before becoming eligible to apply" (Kanaaneh, 2009: 41). This enrollment age does not apply to Jew-ish students who are usually given the opportunity to defer their military service in order to study (HRA, 2005: 57).

Families began to take full responsibility for financing their children's studies abroad, often with great difficulty. Most favored sending their sons to study especially in Eastern Europe, Germany, or Italy. Daughters, on the other hand, were more commonly sent to study in Israeli universities such as the University of Haifa or, for families in the Galilee, to colleges closer to home such as Western Galilee, Yizraeel Valley, Sakhnin, and Oranim. The latter colleges are cheaper options and as commuter colleges potentially allow parents to exercise more control over their daughters' lives. Families in the Triangle prefer to send their daughters to study in nearby Beit Berl College or Tel Aviv University to get teaching credentials. Although the Palestinian minority makes up approximately 20 percent of Israel's total population, the percentage of Palestinians among university students in Israel is 8.3 percent of the student body (Haaretz, December 2, 2007).

Recently, there has been an increase in the number of young Arab men and women pursuing higher education and professional degrees in Jordanian universities. A new study estimates that the number of Palestinian students from Israel enrolled in Jordanian universities is about 3,500 (Arar and Haj-Yehia, 2007). Many students study pharmacology, medicine, and law in the universities of 'Amman and 'Irbid. There are about thirty medical students from the village of Kufur Qari' alone, and about one-third of them are women (Haaretz, October 13, 2007).

There is still a small percentage of Palestinian women from the Galilee and the Triangle region who attend major universities such as the Hebrew University in Jerusalem, Tel Aviv University, and Ben Gurion University in Bir al-Sabi'. Some female graduates from these universities have secured employment in the major cities where they studied and chose to stay rather than return to their home villages or towns. Sharing a flat or renting an apartment alone in East Jerusalem is a recent and now widespread phenomenon among Palestinian women from the Galilee and the Triangle. New opportunities for professional careers in the larger cities, particularly in Jerusalem, have allowed more independence for these female graduates. Furthermore, the distance from home villages and towns and from daily surveillance by their parents and fellow villagers enhanced these women's independence concerning marriage options. Their perceptions of the low probability for educated Arab women to find compatible husbands in their hometowns or villages, coupled with intolerable family pressure on single women, intensify the desire among these women to seek their personal freedom. Such freedom is sought through either further studies for a higher degree or job opportunities in urban areas. Indeed, many of these women have remained single while focusing on their careers or continuing their studies, usually toward a master's degree. The trend of internal migration of young single Palestinian women from Israel between the ages of twenty-five and forty-six who move from their home villages and settle in East Jerusalem could in fact be considered the first step in their migration abroad. Meanwhile, many of their male peers who have either studied abroad or in Israeli universities return to their towns and villages after their graduation as their families have secured housing and financed their marriages to local women.

PATTERNS OF EMIGRATION AMONG PALESTINIANS IN ISRAEL

In the spring of 1992, the American Embassy in Tel Aviv introduced a new Israeli-Arab Scholarship Program (IASP) for Palestinian citizens of Israel, annually providing four to six grants for two years of advanced graduate studies in U.S. universities. This new program contributed not only to the rise of Palestinian doctoral scholars and scientists but also to the rise of Palestinian women studying abroad. The selection process of applicants secured grantees across gender and religious lines. As a result, twenty-six of those grantees were women, mostly single, who chose to pursue their doctoral studies in American universities. According to U.S. Embassy data, sixty-four young Arab men and women grantees under this program received their master's and doctoral education from American universities from 1992 through 2005 (AMIDEAST, 2007).

Some of these women returned home after their graduation only to face a lack of employment opportunities in their fields. The status of Palestinians in Israel as a national minority in a Jewish state places their citizenship in constant conflict with their national identity, with powerful ramifications at multiple levels. As a national minority in the Israeli state, Palestinian citizens, Christians, Muslims, and Druze alike "are subject to various political and administrative restrictions and, in effect, they regularly experience discrimination and unequal opportunity in a broad range of public-governmental as well as private-individual issues" (Weingrod and Manna, 1998). They have never been fully accepted as Israeli citizens although formally granted citizenship. This discrimination based on national identity created conditions that restricted opportunities for Palestinians in Israeli academia, civil service, and professional jobs. Recently, the accounting track was canceled at one academic institution because "too many Arab students enrolled" (AIC 2009; Nana10, 2009). A *Haaretz* report suggests that "Arabs are kept out of high-tech due to security concerns, and lack of connections makes getting jobs in the private sector more difficult. Those who don't want to be teachers travel abroad to work" (*Haaretz*, December 2, 2007). It was noted in the same report that "Jewish society is closed to educated Arabs and the employment mobility of a young Arab has a very low ceiling. You can only exploit your potential in Arab society, which is not developed in high tech, infrastructure and investments" (*Haaretz*, December 2, 2007). The impact of the political and economic reality in Israel is at least as harsh, if not more so, for Palestinian women as for men.

If Palestinian citizens of Israel face varying degrees of discrimination on grounds of their nationality, Palestinian women citizens also face varying degrees of discrimination on the grounds of gender. It has been noted that governmental cutbacks hit Palestinian women the hardest and that there is a significant feminization (as well as Palestinianization) of poverty in Israel

(Ittijah, 2005). According to a report by the Arab Association for Human Rights (HRA, 2003: note 5), Arab women are the most disadvantaged population group in Israel. They are "the poorest, least paid, least educated portion of the community who are subject to forms of legal abuse, with inadequate protection by the courts." In terms of income levels, "80% of Arab women of working age did not work outside the house (compared to 45.8% nationwide)" in 1997 and most of the women who do work occupy the bottom rung on the employment ladder in Israel with about 61% of them receiving "less than the legal minimum wage, 72% work[ing] without legal contracts, and only 35% receiv[ing] payment for any kind for overtime they work" (HRA, 2003).[5]

Two of the early female graduates funded by the IASP found full-time teaching positions in an Israeli university and a college. Three male graduates were also hired for computer science, law, and political science teaching positions in Israeli universities and colleges. However, as more female graduates returned home with PhD degrees in hand looking for work in Israeli universities, the likelihood of being hired tended to be zero. Israeli universities give preference in hiring to new Jewish immigrants from the former Soviet Union through an institutionalized preferential policy that has been enforced in academic institutions since early 1990 (Immigrant Absorption Planning and Research, 2000).[6] As a result, skilled Palestinians have been pushed even farther to the margins; this compounds the employment problem for Palestinian female academics. As previously noted, only two women former grantees of the American Embassy Scholarship Program have been hired in Israeli universities since the establishment of this program.

One-year, post-graduate doctoral positions were offered to some of the men and women who had completed their degrees under the program, including the author of this chapter. These grants were for training in Israeli universities after the return of the graduates from the United States. Based on conversations with grantees, it appears that many were told that they might be offered a full-time teaching position in one of the Israeli universities following their training year.[7] However, grantees were routinely informed that university budget cuts left no hope to hire them on a full-time basis the following year. New PhD graduates are also routinely advised by Israeli academics to apply for postdoctoral positions or search for a job in the United States.

Highly educated Palestinian men and women from Israel were much more welcome at the Palestinian universities in the West Bank and East Jerusalem. However, intensified restrictions on mobility in and out of the West Bank since the recent intifada were serious obstacles for residents of Israel to work in Palestinian universities. Some of the early IASP graduates both male and female took part-time teaching positions in community colleges in Israel and some took temporary jobs in Palestinian NGOs, mainly in Jerusalem. But, for example, wandering between adjunct positions at two or three different colleges was a burden on these young academics. As a result of the scarcity of employment, a female graduate with a PhD degree in public administration took a job at the National Insurance Institute. A male graduate with an MBA is working with the International Committee of the Red Cross and another male PhD graduate in economics has returned to the United States after failing to find a teaching job in his field (AMIDEAST, 2007). The author of this chapter took a few freelance jobs with NGOs in East Jerusalem during the academic year 2004–2005 as she planned to settle close to her family. Stories about these difficult circumstances circulated widely among doctoral students abroad. The message was: "Refrain from returning; home has no place for you." This has led many men and women with graduate degrees to emigrate or remain abroad, seeking better opportunities in the United States, Canada, and Europe.

HIGHLY EDUCATED PALESTINIAN WOMEN LEAVING HOME

Based on conversations with my wide social network of educated Palestinian women, there appears to be a recent increase in the number of highly educated and skilled Palestinian women, originally educated at one of the Israeli universities or at Birzeit University in the West Bank, who then emigrate to the United States, Canada, or Europe. They go there seeking PhD programs, postdoctoral training, or better employment opportunities in their profession. Many of those who left for PhD programs are single, aged between twenty-five to forty-six years old. Making the decision to pursue a higher academic degree abroad in that age range is the functional equivalent of making the decision not to marry, or at least, not to be bothered by being unmarried at this stage. Having a higher education level and living alone outside the family home may be a cause or an effect of their being unmarried. Traditionally, most single Arab men and women live with their parents until marriage. In this context, single professional women crave a greater degree of independence than society normally grants them.

The question is: what drives these highly educated women to live abroad? A UN report says that Arab women migrate at the lowest rate of all international migrants (UNFPA, 2006). Generally, research on emigration refers to factors that repel or push people out of one place toward others that exert a positive attraction such as a high standard of living or job opportunities. One study on Moroccan emigration to the Netherlands identified four different motivations for female emigration (Heering et al., 2004). These include women seeking better employment opportunities and better earning power to help their families. For example, in the cases of Asian, Moroccan, and Mexican women, labor migration is encouraged by informal social networks, resulting in chain migration (Heering et al., 2004). The presence of a family network abroad has a positive effect on the migration intentions of women who have not yet migrated. For example, and according to ILO/SEAPAT's report,

> social networks have determined the self-sustaining and cumula-
> tive nature of Asian women migration flows. Asians are known
> for maintaining strong social relationships and networks of obliga-
> tions, and it was through these that information was transmitted,
> contacts established, employment opportunities for new migrants
> created and grasped, and social supports provided. Women, especially
> young women, are more likely to move as a result of chain migra-
> tion. They also rely more than men on informal social networks.
> (ILO/SEAPAT, 1996)

Other motivations include trailing spouses, where wives follow their husbands abroad. Other female emigrants seek a way out of a life with a dependent status and away from cultural barriers that limit their geographic, economic, and social mobility. Finally, Heering et al. also found that educated women were migrating because the cultural barriers to women working and living outside their own societies have become eroded and the women who migrate have internalized their roles as independent. All four motivations Heering et al. found for Moroccan women to emigrate to the Netherlands seem to apply to Palestinian women moving to the United States, Canada, and Europe as well, though the chain migration pattern is less relevant.

WHAT MAKES PALESTINIAN WOMEN CITIZENS OF ISRAEL EMIGRATE—RESULTS

To examine the motivations that drive Palestinian women in Israel to emi-grate either to the United States, Canada, or Europe, I conducted online or face-to-face interviews with eighteen Palestinian women, sixteen of whom currently live in the United States, Canada, and Europe, and two women living in their hometowns in the Galilee. One of these women was processing the paperwork for her departure to start a teaching and research career at an American academic institution the following year. The other had studied in the United States but has returned to live in the Galilee. Thirteen of these women live in the United States, one in Canada, and two in Europe. Ten of the eighteen women have PhD degrees, six from U.S. universities, three from Israeli universities, and one woman received her degree in Germany but has lived in Canada since 2000. One of the PhD graduates from the United States has recently moved to Europe. Three other interviewees are currently PhD students in the United States. Three other interviewees hold BAs from Israeli universities, with two of those continuing their MA studies after they moved with their families to the United States. A well-known artist who lived and developed her professional career in Jerusalem recently migrated to Europe for career purposes rather than studies.

The majority of these women have earned their BA degrees, and a few their MA degrees, from Israeli universities. One woman received her BA from a Palestinian university, one from the United States, and another one from Europe. Four of them arrived in the United States as "followers" or "trailing spouses," joining their husbands abroad. Nine of the women emigrated alone (including the woman who is processing her emigration visa). A few have chosen to settle down after a teaching career materialized in a U.S. university; others hope to gain teaching training in the United States after their graduation.

I DON'T HAVE A GREEN CARD

Almost half of the interviewees confessed that they had not yet decided whether to stay after they complete their studies or go home. What is common among most of these women, especially the single and recent arrivals, is that they consider their stays temporary. Most stressed that they would like to go back home. One of the PhD interviewees resists being considered in the category of émigrés. "I am a PhD student here and I hope to return one day. So, in that sense I did not emigrate and would like to think I did not leave, just temporarily went away, but maybe it's just semantics." Based on her experience as an undergraduate student in an Israeli university, this interviewee argued that freedom of expression and diverse opinion is not respected or welcomed in Israeli universities, especially if it comes from an Arab-Palestinian student or scholar, even for the sake of academic research. "I wanted to work on Palestinians and knew that I did not want to do that in Israeli universities after my undergraduate experience of how conservative they were and how negative the atmosphere was. I wanted to be in a place were I did not fear (or feared less) that my political opinion, which is a part of my academic project, would harm my opportunities."

Similarly, another PhD student in a U.S. university reported that the lack of freedom of speech in Israeli universities was a primary factor in her decision to leave. "I was an MA student [in an Israeli university]. At some point I was bored with my graduate studies and knew that there [was] something more that I could not achieve there. I felt that I have something important to say, but it would not be heard. People around me were not interested in hearing it, so I decided to apply to study abroad." Among those who arrived in the United States alone to pursue MA and then PhD studies is a woman who has been residing there for thirteen years but who insisted that she never decided to emigrate. "I still do not have a green card," she insisted. Although she has secured a tenure-track teaching position in a U.S. university, she is still not sure if she will stay here for the long term. "I find my situation in a constant state of transition," she confesses. The interviewee refused to buy a house or, in her words, seek a "permanent" relationship with the United States. This reflects a strong connection to home while living in exile. Another two married interviewees who arrived recently to pursue postgraduate training and PhD studies have also stressed that they have not migrated. They came to the United States just to pursue their PhDs and postgraduate training and after they complete their studies, they plan to go back home. The postgraduate student acknowledged that she "might stay, but I also would like to go back home. However, thinking about staying is always on our mind. Until now we are hesitant to go home. The political situation makes us concerned about returning, especially since my spouse is from the Occupied Territories and he doesn't carry an Israeli ID and he will have a problem living with me outside the Occupied Palestinian Territories."

The ongoing Israeli-Palestinian political and military conflict has a powerful impact on people's lives, including those who carry an Israeli ID card. The 2003 Nationality and Entry into Israel Law bans Palestinians from the West Bank and Gaza from obtaining residency status or citizenship in Israel through marriage to an Israeli citizen solely, thereby preventing them from living in Israel with their spouses (Adalah, 2005). This law has already harmed thousands of married couples and their children living in Israel, as well as newly married couples.

Despite the fact that she went through a second emigration when she moved from Europe to Canada, the earlier émigré to Europe still considered herself unsettled even after twenty years of living abroad: "I refuse to buy a home or any property as I plan to go back to Palestine one day. Yes, my thoughts are more related to going back and pursuing my career in Palestine. Israel is not an option, at least not for now." The discourse of this interviewee changed after her recent visit to Palestine/Israel and after she was promoted to a permanent position at her workplace. In a recent meeting with her, she admitted that she has begun searching for a house to buy instead of continuing to pay rent.

Most of the interviewees were aware of the lack of opportunities for Arab academics in the Israeli job market or universities and most of them referred to this aspect as a cause of their leaving to gain better education and not returning home right after their graduation. Two of the married interviewees, both of whom met their husbands during the time they were still students either in the United States or Europe, stressed that in case they did return home, their intention was to work in Palestinian universities or institutions rather than in Israel. According to one of the interviewees who considered herself settled in Europe after earning her PhD from a U.S. university: "Being a foreigner in the West is better than being an Arab Palestinian in Israel."

The availability and likelihood of receiving scholarships in Western countries was also a reason behind making the decision to come to study in the United States. As one interviewee made it clear, "The West offers more fellowships than Israel and it has excellent universities and resources." For another interviewee, the opportunity to study the field that she liked most was not possible in Israel because of her identity: "I wanted to study computer engineering and at that time it was very difficult for Arabs to enter into this field in Israeli universities. Thus I thought that I wanted to go abroad to study."

It is important to recognize that in addition to the educational and political constraints that restricted these women's opportunities, they face social constraints as well. A married interviewee, who arrived in the United States trailing her spouse but also to pursue her own graduate studies, emphasized the interconnection between the political and social constraints saying:

> I know that I also left and many others did because we have a problem with the national political constraints as well as social constraints on women. I always felt they were related. The fact that I was always treated as a stranger/outsider and a second-class citizen contributed to my decision to leave but even more to my intention not to go back. I ask myself why didn't I go back? The answer has to do with the political and social atmosphere. When I had my daughter, I decided not to raise her there because I didn't want her to be exposed to the inequalities, exploitation of women, and sexism that exists in Israel among both Arabs and Jews.

STRANGERS IN OUR LAND

The feeling of being a stranger in your land was expressed by most of the women I interviewed. One woman who built her career together with a group of artists from the Occupied Territories described the situation there as living in prison. She said she stopped being able to materialize her professional dream there anymore since she could not meet with her colleagues due to military checkpoints.[8] "With time, my need for a bigger space, or a more free space/zone just increased . . . in parallel the imprisonment in Occupied Territories in all its forms increasingly hardened . . . thus I decided to add more terrain to my personal geographical map, to include some spots in Europe: where I could feel a kind of ease on certain levels, without giving up on the Occupied Palestinian Territories." Indeed, women, like men, "change their priorities according to situations and moments of time" (Sizoo, 1997: 228). The aforementioned interviewee had spent most of her career in the same location, the Occupied Palestinian Territories, until she recently began to perceive that location differently.

According to Amal, another interviewee who had earned her PhD in the 1980s from a U.S. university but had returned home and worked there for many years, the major reasons for the emigration of Palestinian women of the 1948 area are "purely political and economic." Indeed, most of the women interviewed referred to the fact that the whole Palestinian population in Israel, men and women, suffers from institutionalized discrimination because of their national identity. According to Amal, their emigration derived from their status as "a national minority whose citizenship is in constant conflict with its nationality, and because of everything that is related to that reality, from discrimination to very limited opportunities." Lisa Hajjar points out that Arab women share structural discrimination and political marginalization with the men of their community (Hajjar, 1998: 5). According to Amal, "The effect of this political-economic reality is twice as harsh on women as it is on men."

One common factor that pushes some of these women to emigrate is personal freedom. "Seeking personal freedom and the desire to be oneself is as important a reason behind women's emigration as seeking professional opportunity," Amal explained. Once a single woman in Palestinian society is beyond her twenties, she is unlikely to get married.

> Our highly educated women have a difficult time finding compatible and understanding partners. This coupled with the cultural and religious requirements of celibacy puts a lot of pressure on our women. So, it seems at this point in history, our women have one of two possibilities: 1) become religious and live in harmony with the new reality, which makes it easy to find a husband, allow for freedom of movement and a job within the society while attending religious colleges, or working in local schools; or 2) emigrate outside the country to the U.S. and Europe or migrate inside the country to Jerusalem.

One of the PhD interviewees who refused to emigrate and returned to her hometown and her family commented that "for single women who are thirty years or older, the chance of finding a husband is low, so they don't have anything to lose and prefer to leave that society that does not accept single women with academic careers." In support of this perspective, Salma, a PhD student in the United States confessed that "It felt that now that I received my MA, then that's it. I reached the limit of opportunities and that I basically had to be in a state of waiting. Waiting for what? I don't know . . . just to wait for things to get better, maybe for a husband, or just *faraj* [relief]. I think that because I did not want to face reality; it was always safe to be in the university and to be involved in my studies."

This sense of escape from particular gendered limitations by pursuing PhD studies abroad strongly echoes Heering et al.'s observations on the migration of women who have internalized their role as independent. Salma said:

> Part of me always wanted to experience living abroad and I am glad that things happened this way. I think that the big decision is not so much about coming here as much as going back there, especially now that I have developed a different political consciousness. I don't think that I have emigrated as much as I took a break from life there in order to maintain my sanity. I just needed to recharge my intellectual and emotional energies that got wasted with every kilometer I drove. I used to drive to get everywhere, whether it was work, school, or to get a cup of coffee!

In the same context, another PhD interviewee argued:

> I wanted to get away from the region hoping to get some critical distance that would help me understand and analyze things more clearly. I wanted to get away in order to have a life and some sanity, to do something else and to allow myself the possibility of advancing, something I knew was limited in Israel. While I was there I was engaged with nonstop political activism that started to feel like it was not advancing the cause I aspired for nor was it going anywhere other than driving me crazy.

I DO CONSIDER MYSELF SETTLED HERE

Among the skilled married women who arrived as "followers" or "trailing spouses" there are a few women for whom the experience of reestablishing their career has been delayed until their husbands and children settle in new schools and jobs. For those in that category, migration continues to represent a challenge to women's economic and family roles, as well as in the pattern of relations with their husbands. Among this group of women were five interviewees who admitted that the purpose of their migration was "to seek education and to accompany my husband" or "accompanying my husband who had the grant to do his doctoral program . . . sure enough I did take advantage of the situation and pursued my education." Although these two interviewees pursued their PhD studies after they arrived here accompanying their husbands, a third one stressed that the reason "for coming here is my husband's career (I consider it our career) and I don't think that I would be here even for my own education because I can reach my goals back home while being close to my extended family." Another interviewee who came to the United States due to a purely marital reason similarly saw her emigration as being for her husband: She emigrated to marry a man she met while she was on a few weeks' educational visit to the United States. "I was visiting here and met [my husband] who came to this country from Lebanon to study . . . and half a year later, we got married and I moved here." The personal reason to emigrate for a fifth married interviewee was quite strong as well. She stressed that "the main reason was personal [accompanying her husband who arrived to pursue his PhD studies in a U.S. university] . . . however, I emigrated in order: 1) to live in a more liberal society; 2) to have the opportunity to go to graduate school; and 3) to give my kids a better life."

All five married women noted that they considered themselves settled in the United States; their stay here is not temporary. As one of them emphasized: "With four kids who feel that they belong so much here, it is hard to go back now or in a few years, but I want to go back home some day."

A different perspective was noted among three women who had arrived recently seeking academic training, namely, in a postdoctoral position, an annual contract to teach in an American academic institution, and studying for a PhD degree. These women explain that their moves to the United States were in order to pursue their personal careers and that their husbands were the "followers" or "trailing spouses." The husbands in the three cases were supportive and encouraged the wives to come and pursue their academic careers in the United States. A strong example of this was the case of one interviewee who emphasized how her husband was very supportive and proud. "He never hesitated and took a leave of absence from his job. He also arranged the financial support I needed to travel by selling a piece of land for that purpose. There were times that I hesitated to come, especially since I was a mother of a newly born child when I started the process. He was behind me and encouraged me." However, not all of the interviewees perceived the husbands who follow their career wives in their emigration to the United States or Europe as pillars of support. The graduate who returned to settle in the Galilee said: "I have trouble believing these men leave everything or leave good careers for their wives." She understood the husband's trailing as that of someone who does not have a serious career to give up.

CONCLUSION

A wave of migration to the United States, Canada, and Europe is taking place among independent, highly educated Palestinian women in Israel. There are diverse motives for their migration but they are different than the usual motives for migration of Palestinian women from the West Bank and Gaza Strip or of women in other developing countries. What is common among most of the Palestinian women who left Israel is their extensive educational background. Most of them have one or two degrees from Israeli universities and the majority of them worked for Israeli institutions or organizations, but they could no longer endure the conditions of being unequal citizens to the majority of their coworkers and colleagues, who were

Jewish. Or they could no longer tolerate the political unrest resulting from Israel's occupation of the Palestinian Territories. They left for the sake of further progress in their academic careers by either seeking PhD degrees or looking for new challenges in their professions. Most of the single women have realized considerable social, political, and economic independence.[9] Significantly unique, their migration differs from that of other women émigrés because they prepare for their migration by themselves, while female migration from other developing countries tends to be facilitated by family or work networks in the countries of destination.

Many of the women referred to their lives in "exile." Though they were not directly forced to leave their Palestinian villages and towns, and there is certainly a strong degree of choice involved in their decisions, the push factors do produce some element of coercion in their departures. Political unrest in the region and institutionalized discriminatory policies sharpen the desires of these Palestinian women to leave. Lack of opportunities in their home region and the feeling of being strangers in their own land were strong impetuses for these women to seek an alternative residential area. For these women, living in exile seemed better than staying home where they can accomplish or gain little. Although they do enjoy a great deal of independence, these educated Palestinian women emigrants still want to avoid cultural or political barriers that may block their progress.

NOTES

1. The emigration of Palestinian citizens of Israel to the United States was mentioned briefly in two papers by Yinon Cohen, "Palestinian and Jewish Israeli-born Immigrants in the United States," IMR 28, 2 (Summer 1994), and Yinon Cohen and Yitchak Haberfeld, "The Number of Israeli Immigrants in the United States in 1990," *Demography* 34, 2 (May 1997): 199–212. Most research about Palestinian emigration, as suggested in Lilian Abou-Tabickh's chapter (chapter 11) in this volume, discusses internal rural-urban migration. Rassem Khamaisi, for example, studies the statistically marginal migration of Palestinians to cities like Jerusalem, Nazareth, and Haifa (Khamaisi, 1998: 155).

2. A few additional studies on Palestinian migration have appeared very recently (Hilal, 2007; Lubbad, 2008a, 2008b).

3. Sabeel, a Palestinian-Christian nongovernmental organization, conducted a survey in summer 2006 of 1,500 Christian residents of the West Bank and East Jerusalem and residents of Israel exploring their reasons for emigration.

4. It is important to note that education at the primary and high school levels is highly unequal in Israel. The Ministry of Education severely underfunds Arab schools in Israel. According to statistics published in 2004, the "combined public and private investment in Palestinian school students stood at an average of New Israeli Shekels (NIS) 862 per student, compared with NIS 4,935 per Jewish student for the academic year 2000–2001" (WGR, 2005). At the level of higher education, Nimer Sultany points out that Arab students in the Israeli universities make up less than 10 percent of BA students and less than 1 percent of MA students (Sultany,

2002). Rhoda Kanaaneh argues that Israeli universities give preferential treatment to Israeli-Jewish students who have completed or will soon complete their military service (Kanaaneh, 2009: 41).

5. A report of the Arab Association for Human Rights on "Palestinian Arab Women in Israel" published in the Mediterranean Women's website in December 2003 (http://www.mediterraneas.org/article.php3?id_article=148).

6. A report published by Israel's Ministry of Immigrant Absorption identifies the government's wide variety of programs created with the aim of enabling many skilled Jewish immigrants from the former Soviet Union to obtain training and find suitable employment in their fields. One of the most successful was the program for immigrant scientists and R&D engineers, originally created in the early seventies to aid immigrant scientists who arrived from the Soviet Union then and continued to serve the 14,000 scientists and R&D engineers who arrived during the last decade. According to this report, some 80 percent of these immigrants were able to find initial employment in their fields of specialization. This program heavily subsidized the salaries of the scientists for three to four years and provided research funding.

7. In the summer of 1999, I was invited by the chair of the Sociology Department at Tel Aviv University to apply for a one-year post-doctorate in her department. One of the incentives offered to me was the possibility of being hired to a full-time teaching position the year after. However, after one month from my arrival at Tel Aviv University, I was told by the same chair that there was no chance of being hired at the university the following year. Her explanation was that I was still a new graduate with no publications and that the department was suffering from a budget shortage. She suggested I look for better opportunities somewhere else, especially abroad. In particular, she suggested I look for work in the United States since there were more opportunities there than in Israel. At least two of the latest female graduates from the Hebrew universities similarly report being advised by their Israeli mentors to look for teaching opportunities in the United States.

8. Although she is an Israeli citizen, she developed her professional career in Palestine and lived and worked only there prior to her emigration to Europe.

9. Abusharaf's (2001) research on Sudanese women émigrés to the United States and Canada presents a case similar to that of Palestinian women émigrés, with one major difference: most Sudani émigrés moved to the United States as green card lottery winners while Palestinian women moved to the United States on either a J-1 exchange visitor/researcher visa, J-2 spouse of J-1 holder visa, or F student visa.

WORKS CITED

Abdo, Nahla. 1994. "Nationalism and Feminism: Palestinian Women and the Inti-fada—No Going Back." In *Gender and National Identity: Women and Politics in Muslim Societies*. Valentine Moghadam, ed. Pp. 148–170. London: Zed Books.

Abdo, Nahla. 1999. "Gender and Politics under the Palestinian Authority." *Journal of Palestinian Studies* 28(2): 38–51.

Abdo, Nahla. 2004. "Honour Killing, Patriarchy, and the State: Women in Israel." In *Violence in the Name of Honour: Theoretical and Political Challenges*. Shahrzad Mojab and Nahla Abdo, eds. Pp. 57–90. Istanbul: Istanbul Bilgi University Press.

Abdo, Nahla, and Nira Yuval Davis. 1995. "Palestine, Israel and the Zionist Settler Project." In *Unsettling Settler Societies: Articulations of Gender, Race, Ethnicity and Class*. Daiva Stasiulis and Nira Yuval Davis, eds. Pp. 291–322. London: Sage Publications.

Abou-Tabickh, Lilian. 2008. "Migrants within Their Nation: How Do Palestinian Women in Israel Experience Their Migration with Marriage?" MA thesis, Program in Gender Studies, Bar-Ilan University.

Abu-Baker, Khawla. 1998. *A Rocky Road: Arab Women as Political Leaders in Israel*. Beit-Berl: The Institute for Israeli Arab Studies. (Hebrew)

Abu El-Asal, Reham. 2006. *Palestinian Feminist Associations in Israel: Theoretical Frameworks and Strategies*. Nazareth: al-Tufula Center and Education Action Internatioanl-UK. (Arabic)

Abu El-Haj, Nadia. 2001. *Facts on the Ground: Archaeological Practice and Territorial Self-Fashioning in Israeli Society*. Chicago: University of Chicago Press.

Abu-Lughod, Janet. 1983. "Demographic Consequences of the Occupation." *MERIP Reports* 115, The Palestinian Dilemma: 13–17.

Abu-Lughod, Lila. 1989. "Zones of Theory in the Anthropology of the Arab World." *Annual Review of Anthropology* (18): 267–306.

Abu-Lughod, Lila. 2002. "Do Muslim Women Really Need Saving? Anthropological Reflections on Cultural Relativism and Its Others." *American Anthropologist* 104(3): 783–790.

Abu-Lughod, Lila, and Ahmad Sa'di. 2007. "Introduction: The Claims of Memory." In *Nakba: Palestine, 1948 and the Claims of Memory*. Ahmad Sa'di and Lila Abu-Lughod, eds. Pp. 1–26. New York: Columbia University Press.

Abu Murad, Fathi M. 2004. *Al-Ramz al-fanni fi shi'r Mahmud Darwish*. Amman. (Arabic)

Abu-Oksa, Suheir Dauod. 2003. Political Representation of Palestinian Women in Municipal Politics in Israel 2003. Electronic document, http://www.mossawa-center.org/he/reports/2003/12/031214.html

Abu-Oksa, Dauod Suheir. 2005. "The Representation of Palestinian Women in Municipal Governing in Israel 1950–2003." *Journal of Palestine Studies* 16(62): 100–122. (Arabic)

Abu Rabi'a, Sarab. 2005. "Coping from Puddles: Three Generations of Bedouin Women in the Negev." In *Women in the South: Space, Periphery and Gender.* Henriette Yanai, Nitza Yanai, and Nitza Berkowitz, eds. Pp. 86–107. Beer Sheva: Hazuut Sfarim of Ben Gurion University. (Hebrew)

Abusharaf, Rogaia Mustafa. 2001. "Migration with a Feminine Face: Breaking the Cultural Mold." *Arab Studies Quarterly* 23(2): 61–86.

Abu-Sitta, Salman H. 2004. *Atlas of Palestine 1948.* London: Palestine Land Society.

Accad, Evelyn. 1978 (reprinted 2004). "Sexuality and Sexual Politics: Conflicts and Contradictions for Contemporary Women in the Middle East." In *Women and Sexuality in Muslim Societies: A Publication of Women for Women's Human Rights (WWHR).* Pinar Ilkkaracan, ed. Pp. 51–88. Damascus: Dar Almada for Culture and Publishing. (Arabic)

Accad, Evelyn. 1978 (reprinted 2004). "Sexuality and Sexual Politics: Conflicts and Contradictions for Contemporary Women in the Middle East." In *Women and Sexuality in Muslim Societies: A Publication of Women's Human Rights (WWHR).* Pinar Ilkkaracan, ed. Pp. 37–50. New Ways: Women for Women's Human Rights.

ACRI (Association for Citizens Rights in Israel). 2001. "Nazareth is to get a larger assistance in house acquisition." Electronic document, http://www.acri.org. il/Story.aspx?id=278

ACRI. nd. ACRI's Annual Report on the State of Human Rights. Electronic document, http://www.acri.org.il/eng/Story.aspx?id=399 (accessed June 17, 2009).

ACRI. 2007. Human Rights in Israel—An Overview 2007. Electronic document, http://www.acri.org.il/pdf/tmunat2007.pdf

Adalah: The Legal Center for Arab Minority Rights in Israel. 2004. Appeal Against Town of Kamoun and Planning Authorities for Refusing to Issue Building Permit to Arab Family Living on Their Privately Owned Land in Caravan, Which Is Surrounded by Villas of Jewish Families. *Adalah Electronic Newsletter* 4, September 2004. (Hebrew)

Adalah: The Legal Center for Arab Minority Rights in Israel. 2005. After Seven-Year Legal Struggle, Land and Planning Appeals Committee Grants Permit to Arab Bedouin Family to Build Home on their Privately Owned Land in the Galilee. *Adalah Electronic Newsletter* 15, July 2005. http://www.adalah. org/newsletter/eng/jul05/1.php

Adalah. nd. Adalah's Report: The Accused. Electronic document, http://www.adalah. org/ara/publications/theAccused-a.pdf (accessed June 17, 2009). (Arabic)

Adalah and the Center for Alternative Planning. 2006. Land Scarcity and Housing Shortage—Position Paper. Adalah, December 12, http://www.adalah.org/features/land/land_position_paper.pdf

Adalah: The Legal Center for Arab Minority Rights in Israel. 2007a. Adalah and Broad Coalition of NGOs Petition Supreme Court Demanding Cancellation of Selection Committees in Community Towns as They Illegally Exclude Arab Citizens, Mizrahi Jews, Single Parents and Gays. *Adalah Electronic Newsletter* 40, September 2007. (Hebrew)

Adalah: The Legal Center for Arab Minority Rights in Israel. 2007b. Selection Committees Find Arabs 'Socially Unsuitable' for Jewish Community Towns. *Adalah Electronic Newsletter* 43, December 2007. http://www.adalah.org/eng/hrw.php (Hebrew)

Adalah: The Legal Center for Arab Minority Rights in Israel. 2007c. Jewish National Fund Excludes Arab Citizens from 13% of 'Israel Lands.' *Adalah Electronic Newsletter* 43, December 2007. http://www.adalah.org/eng/hrw.php (Hebrew)

Adalah: The Legal Center for Arab Minority Rights in Israel. 2007d. Adalah's Report to the UN CERD ICERD (The International Convention on the Elimination of All Forms of Racial Discrimination) in Response to the List of Issues Presented to Israel, February 1, 2007. http://www.adalah.org/eng/intl07/adalah-cerd-Feb07.pdf

Adalah: The Legal Center for Arab Minority Rights in Israel. n.d. Special Report: The Jewish National Fund, Challenging the Discriminatory Land Policies of the Jewish National Fund (JNF). Electronic document, http://www.adalah.org/eng/jnf/php (accessed April 2, 2008).

Adalah. 2009a. Special Report: Ban on Family Unification. Electronic document, http://www.adalah.org/eng/famunif.php (November 28, 2007).

Adalah. 2009b. National Labor Court Upholds Suspension of Arab Employee for Participating in a Demonstration. Adalah News Update, February 15, 2009. Electronic document, http://www.adalah.org/eng/pressreleases/pr.php?file=09_02_15_1 (accessed June 15, 2009).

Afsaruddin, Asma. 1999. "Introduction: The Hermeneutic of Gendered Space and Discourse." In *Hermeneutics and Honor: Negotiating Female "Public" Space in Islamic/ate Societies*. Asma Afsaruddin, ed. Pp. 1–28. Cambridge: Harvard University Press.

Ahmed, Leila. 2000. "Arab Culture and Writing Women's Bodies." In *Women and Sexuality in Muslim Societies*. Pinar Ilkkaracan, ed. Pp. 51–66. Istanbul, Turkey: Women for Women's Human Rights (WWHR).

Ahmed, Sara. 2000. *Strange Encounters: Embodied Others in Post-Coloniality*. New York: Routledge.

Ahronot, Yediot. 2009. Senior Nurse Who Demonstrated Against IDF Will Stay at Home. Ynetnews, February 12. Electronic document, http://www.ynet.co.il/articles/1,7340,L-3670868,00.html (accessed June 15, 2009). (Hebrew)

al-Ali, Nadje. 2007. *Iraqi Women: Untold Stories from 1948 to the Present*. London: Zed Books.

'Ali, Nihad. 2004. "The Islamic Movement in Israel: Between Religion, Nationality, and Modernity. In *Maelstrom of Identities: A Critical Look at Religion and Secularity in Israel*. Yossi Yonah and Yehuda Goodman, eds. Pp. 132–164. Jerusalem: Van Leer Jerusalem Institute and Hakibbutz Hameuchad Publishing House. (Hebrew)

al-'Ard (Arabic)

"Arab nationalism." *Hadhih al-'Ard*. October 5, 1959. p. 2.

al-Khazin, Shukri. "The Problems of High School Education for Arabs in Israel." *Hadhih al-'Ard*. October 5, 1959, p. 4.

Editorial. *Ghayth al-'Ard*. January 4, 1960, p. 1.

"The Military Governor." *Ghayth al-'Ard*. January 4, 1960, p. 2.

Editorial. *Sir al-'Ard.* October 30, 1959, p.1.

"Oh, Police." *Nada al-'Ard.* January 25, 1960, p. 1.

Editorial. *Akhbar al-'Ard.* October 17, 1965, p.1.

Jabur Jabur. "Factionalism between Arab Citizens of Israel." *Shadha al-'Ard.* November 28, 1959, p. 2.

"The Goals of the Darkness System in Repressing Al-'Ard." *Wihdat al-'Ard.* January 16, 1960, p. 4.

Alternative Information Center (AIC). 2009. The Carmel Academic Center in Haifa Closes Academic Track as too Many Palestinian Students Registered. May 27, 2009. Electronic document, http://www.alternativenews.org/english/1950-carmel-academic-center-closes-academic-tract-as-too-many-palestinian-students-registered-.html (accessed June 4, 2009).

Altoma, Salih. 1972. *Palestinian Themes in Modern Arabic Literature, 1917–1970.* Cairo: Anglo-Egyptian Bookshop.

AMIDEAST. 2007. Celebrating 15 Years of the Israeli-Arab Scholarship Program. Electronic newsletter, January. http://www.amideast.org/programs_services/exchange_programs/iasp/IASP%20Winter%202006-2007%20Master.pdf (accessed June 8, 2009).

Amun, Hasan, Uri Davis, and San'Allah Nasr Dakhl-Allah. 1981. *The Palestinian Arabs in Israel-Deir al-Assad: The Destiny of an Arab Village in the Galilee.* Ahmad al-Shihabi, trans. Beirut: Dar al-Kalimah lil-Nahsr. (Arabic)

Arab Association for Human Rights (HRA). 2004. By All Means Possible: A Report on the Destruction by the State of Crops of Bedouin Citizens in the Naqab (Negev) by Aerial Spraying with Chemicals. Electronic document, http://www.arabhra.org/HraAdmin/UserImages/Files/CropDestructionReportEnglish.pdf (accessed April 2, 2008).

Arab Association for Human Rights (HRA). 2005a. On the Margins: Annual Review of Human Rights Violations of the Arab Palestinian Minority in Israel 2005. Electronic document, www.arabhra.org/HRA/SecondaryArticles/SecondaryArticlePage.aspx?SecondaryArticle=1339 (accessed February 14, 2008).

Arab Association for Human Rights (HRA). 2005b. On the Margins: Annual Review of Human Rights Violations of the Arab Palestinian Minority in Israel 2005. www.arabhra.org. (Hebrew)

Arab Association for Human Rights (HRA). 2005c. HRA Position toward Reforms in the Israeli Land Administration Structure. HRA. Electronic document, www.acri.org.il/hebrew-acri/engine/printfactory.asp?id=929

Arab Inter-Parliamentary Union (AIPU). 2003. "Brain Drain from African and Arab Countries and Its Consequences." The 10th Afro-Arab Parliamentary Conference, Addis Ababa, January 8–10, 2003.

Arabrap.net (accessed November 15, 2006).

Arabs48. 2007. Decline in the Percentage of Arab Bedouin Recruitment in the Military by 20% from Last Year. April 5. Electronic document, http://www.arabs48. com/display.x?cid=19&sid =57&id = 44330 (accessed April 10, 2007). (Arabic)

Arabs48. 2009. Regional Work Court Approves the Suspension of an Arab Employee Because of Her Participation in a Demonstration. Arabs48, February 12. Electronic document, http://www.arabs48.com/print.x?cid=6andid=60635, accessed June 15. (Arabic)

Arar, Khalid, and Kais Haj-Yehia. 2007. "Arab Students from Israel in Jordanian Universities: Issues and Dilemmas." In *Academics and Higher Education among Arabs in Israel: Trends and Issues*. Khalid Arar and Kais Haj-Yehia, eds. Pp. 36–51. Tel Aviv: Ramot. (Hebrew)

Arens, Moshe. 1998. "The Wages of a Non Policy." *Jerusalem Post*, April 10.

Arieli, Shual, Doubi Schwartz, and Hadas Tagari. 2006. *Injustice and Folly: On the Proposals to Cede Arab Localities from Israel to Palestine*. Jerusalem: The Floersheimer Institute for Policy Studies. (Arabic)

Aronoff, Myron. 1991. "Myths, Symbols and Rituals of the Emerging State." In *New Perspectives on Israeli History: The Early Years*. Laurence Silberstein, ed. Pp. 175–192. New York: New York University Press.

Asad, Talal. 1975. "Anthropological Texts and Ideological Problems: An Analysis of Cohen on Arab Villages in Israel." *Economy and Society* 4(3): 251–282.

Assad, Samar. 2007. Easter in the Holy Land: Christians in the Occupied Land. *Palestine Center Information Brief* 151.

Association for Human Rights (HRA) in Israel. 2003. "Palestinian Arab Women in Israel." A paper published for The Mediterranean Women. December 30, 2003. http://www.mediterraneas.org/article.php3?id_article=148 (accessed December 16, 2009).

Aswat (Palestinian Gay Women). www.aswatgroup.org (accessed June 23, 2009).

Athamneh, Nawaf. 2007. In 90% of the Cases, Women Waive Their Rights in Inheritance. *Mahsom*, February 20, 2007. Electronic document, http://212.179.113.235/mahsom/article.php?id=4758 (accessed June 15, 2009).

Bachelard, Gaston. 1969. *The Poetics of Space*. Maria Jolas, trans. Boston: Beacon Press.

Bader-'Arraf, Kamilia. 1995. "The Arab Woman toward the 21st Century." In *Arab Citizens of Israel toward the 21st Century*. Yacob M. Landau, Assad Ganem, and Aluf Hareven, eds. Pp. 213–218. Jerusalem: Magnes. (Hebrew)

Baker, Alison. 1998. *Voices of Resistance: Oral Histories of Moroccan Women*. Albany: State University of New York Press.

Balibar, Etienne. 2002. *Politics and the Other Scene*. Christine Jones, James Swenson, and Chris Turner, trans. London and New York: Verso.

Ballinger, Pamela. 2002. *History in Exile: Memory and Identity at the Borders of the Balkans*. Princeton: Princeton University Press.

Barakat, Halim. 1993. *The Arab World: Society, Culture, and State*. Berkeley: University of California Press.

Bardenstein, Carol. 1998. "Threads of Memory and Discourses of Rootedness: Of Trees, Oranges and Prickly-Pear Cactus in Israel/Palestine." *Edebiyat* 8(1): 1–36.

Baransi, Saleh. 1981a. "All This Time We Were Alone." *MERIP Reports* 96: 16–21.

Baransi, Saleh. 1981b. "Oral History: The Story of a Palestinian under Occupation." *Journal of Palestinian Studies* 11(1): 3–30.

Bar-On, Dan. 1998. "Transgenerational Aftereffects of the Holocaust in Israel: Three Generations." In *Breaking Crystal: Writing and Memory after Auschwitz*. Efraim Sicher, ed. Pp. 92–118. Chicago: University of Illinois Press.

Bashir, Nabih. 2004. *Judaizing the Place: Misgav Regional Council in the Galilee*. Haifa: Mada El Carmel. (Arabic)

Basu, Amrita. 1995. "Introduction." In *The Challenge of Local Feminisms: Women's Movements in Global Perspective.* Amrita Basu, ed. Pp. 1–21. Boulder: Westview Press.

Bauml, Yair. 2001. "The Attitude of the Israeli Establishment toward the Arabs in Israel: Policy, Principles, and Activities: The Second Decade, 1958–1968." PhD dissertation, University of Haifa. Department of Middle Eastern History. (Hebrew)

Bauml, Yair. 2002. "The Military Government and the Process of Its Abolishment, 1958–1968." *The New East* 23: 133–156. (Hebrew)

Baxter, Diane. 2007. "Honor Thy Sister: Selfhood, Gender, and Agency in Palestinian Culture." *Anthropological Quarterly* 80(30): 737–775.

Be'eri-Zulitzeanu, Amnon. 2009. "A Coexistence-Policy Imperative." *Haaretz.* March, 15.

Behrman, Jere R., and Barbara L. Wolfe. 1984. Micro Determinants of Female Migration in a Developing Country: Labor Market, Demographic Marriage Market, and Economic Marriage Market Incentives. *Research in Population Economics* 5: 137–166.

Beinin, Joel. 1990. *Was the Red Flag Flying There?: Marxist Politics and the Arab-Israeli Conflict in Egypt and Israel, 1948–1965.* Berkeley: University of California Press.

Beinin, Joel. 2005. "Forgetfulness for Memory: The Limits of the New Israeli History." *Journal of Palestine Studies* 34 (2): 6–23.

Ben-Ari, Eyal, and Edna Lomsky-Feder. 1999. "Introduction: Cultural Constructions of War and the Military in Israel." In *The Military and Militarism in Israeli Society.* Edna Lomsky-Feder and Eyal Ben-Ari, eds. Pp. 1–36. New York: State University of New York Press.

Ben-Artsi, Yosi, and Maxim Shoshami. 1986. "Arabs of Haifa 1972–1983: Demographic and Spatial Changes." In *Residual Patterns and Internal Migration Among Arabs in Israel: Patterns of Social Geography.* Pp.7–31. University of Haifa: Arab-Jewish Centre, Institute for Middle East Research Centre, Gostab Heighnman. (Hebrew)

Benjamin, Orly. 2003. "The Power of Unsilencing: Between Silence and Negotiation in Heterosexual Relationships." *Journal for the Theory of Social Behavior* 33(1): 1–19.

Benvenisti, Meron. 2000. *Sacred Landscape: The Buried History of the Holy Land Since 1948.* Berkeley: University of Californian Press.

Ben-Yehuda, Nachman. 1999. "The Masada Mythical Narrative and the Israeli Army." In *The Military and Militarism in Israeli Society.* Edna Lomsky-Feder and Eyal Ben-Ari, eds. Pp. 57–88. New York: State University of New York Press.

Benziman, Uzi, and Atallah Mansour. 1992. *Subtenants—the Arabs in Israel: Their Status and the Policy toward Them.* Jerusalem: Keter. (Hebrew)

Berkovitz, Niza. 2001. "Motherhood and Citizenship: The Status of Women in Israel." In *Israel: From Mobilized to Civil Society?* Yoav Peled and Adi Ophir, eds. Pp. 206–243. Tel Aviv: The Van Leer Jerusalem Institute/Hakibbutz Hemeuchad Publishing House. (Hebrew)

Bhabha, Homi. 1994. "Remembering Fanon: Self, Psyche, and the Colonial Condition." In *Colonial Discourse and Post-Colonial Theory: A Reader.* Patrick Williams and Laura Chrisman, eds. Pp. 112–123. New York: Columbia University Press.

Birth, Kevin. 1990. "Review of Reading and the Righting of Writing Ethnographies." *American Ethnologist* 17: 549–557.

Bishara, Azmi. 1998. *The Ruptured Political Discourse and Other Studies*. Ramallah, Palestine: MUWATIN—The Palestinian Institute for the Study of Democracy. (Arabic)

Bishara, Azmi. 2001. "Reflections on October 2000: A Landmark in Jewish-Arab Relations in Israel." *Journal of Palestine Studies* 30(3): 54–67.

Bishara, Azmi. 2002. *The Ruptured Discourse and other Studies*. Ramallah: MUWATIN-the Palestinian Institute for the Study of Democracy. (Arabic)

ha-Boker Tel Aviv (Hebrew)
 ha-Boker, July 13, 1964
 ha-Boker, July 24, 1964
 ha-Boker, December 1, 1964

Bourdieu, Pierre. 1977. *Outline of a Theory of Practice*. Cambridge: Cambridge University Press.

Bourque, Susan C., and Jean Grossholtz. 1984. "Politics an Unnatural Practice: Political Science Looks at Female Participation." In *Women and the Public Sphere: A Critique of Sociology and Politics*. Janet Siltanen and Michelle Stanwith, eds. Pp. 103–121. New York: St. Martin's Press.

B'Tselem. n.d. Defense (Emergency) Regulations. Electronic document, http://www. btselem.org/english/Legal_Documents/Emergency_Regulations.asp (accessed June 19, 2009).

Central Bureau of Statistics (CBS). 2006. Internal Migration Balance in Israel, Based on Sex and Locality. Electronic document, http://gis.cbs.gov.il/website/Localities_2006/viewer.htm (accessed June 15, 2009).

Cockburn, Cynthia. 2004. "The Continuum of Violence: A Gender Perspective on War and Peace." In *Sites of Violence: Gender and Conflict Zones*. Winona Giles and Jennifer Hyndman, eds. Pp. 24–44. Berkeley: University of California Press.

Cohen, Abner. 1965. *Arab Border Villages in Israel: A Study of Continuity and Change in Social Organization*. Oxford: University of Manchester Press.

Cohen, Hillel. 2000. *Absentees Attendants: The Palestinian Refugees in Israel Since 1948*. Jerusalem: Van Leer Institute. (Hebrew)

Cohen, Hillel. 2006. *Good Arabs: The Israeli Security Services and the Israeli Arabs*. Jerusalem: Ivrit Hebrew Publishing House. (Hebrew)

Cohen, Yinon. 1997. "Palestinian and Jewish Israeli-born Immigrants in the United States." *International Migration Review* 28(2): 243–255.

Cohen, Yinon, and Yitchak Haberfeld. 1997. "The Number of Israeli Immigrants in the United States in 1990." *Demography* 34(2): 199–212.

Collins, John. 2004. *Occupied by Memory: The Intifada Generation and the Palestinian State of Emergency*. New York: New York University Press.

Collins, Patricia Hill. 1990. *Black Feminist Thought: Knowledge, Consciousness, and the Politics of Empowerment*. New York: Routledge, Chapman and Hall.

Colors from Palestine. 2008. Calendar. Electronic document, http://www.resistanceart. com/2008_Front_Back_Covers.htm (accessed May 7, 2009).

Cook, Jonathan. 2009. "Loyalty Oath" to Keep Arabs Out of Galilee Town. *The National*, June 8. Electronic document, http://www.thenational.ae/ article/20090608/FOREIGN/706079808/1002 (accessed June 15, 2009).

D'Amico, Francine. 2000. "Citizen-Soldier? Class, Race, Gender, Sexuality and the US Military." In *States of Conflict: Gender, Violence, and Resistance*. Susie Jacobs, Ruth Jacobson, and Jen Marchbank, eds. Pp. 105–122. London: Zed Books.

DAM. 2006. Dedication. London: Red Circle Music. Electronic reference, www. dampalestine.com (accessed June 5, 2009).

Das, Veena. 2000. "The Act of Witnessing: Violence, Poisonous Knowledge, and Subjectivity." In *Violence and Subjectivity*, Veena Das, Arthur Kleinman, Mamphela Ramphele, and Pamela Reynolds, eds. Pp. 205–225. Berkeley: University of California Press.

Davar Tel Aviv
    Davar, July 13, 1964

Davies, Brown, and Rom Harre. 1990. "Positioning: The Discursive Production of Selves." *Journal for the Theory of Social Behavior* 20(1): 43–63.

Dirbas, Sahira. 1992. *Al-Birweh: Unforgotten Homeland*. N.p. (Arabic)

Dirks, Nicholas. 1997. "The Policing of Tradition: Colonialism and Anthropology in Southern India." *Comparative Studies in Society and History* 39(1): 182–212.

Dowty, Alan. 1991. "Minority Rights, Jewish Political Traditions and Zionism." *Shafar* 10(1): 23–48.

Eber, Dena Elisabeth, and Arthur Neal. 2001. "Introduction: Memory, Constructed Reality, and Artistic Truth." In *Memory and Representation: Constructed Truths and Competing Realities*. Dena Elisabeth Eber and Arthur Neal, eds. Pp. 3–20. Bowling Green: Bowling Green State University Popular Press.

Ehrenreich, Barbara, and Arlie Russell Hochschild. 2006. "Introduction." In *Global Woman: Nannies, Maids, and Sex Workers in the New Economy*. Barbara Ehrenreich and Arlie Russell Hochschild, eds. Pp. 7–23. Tel Aviv: Babel Publishing. (Hebrew)

Ehrlich, Avishai. 1993. "Society in War: The National Conflict and the Social Structure." In *Israeli Society, Critical Aspects*. Uri Ram, ed. Pp. 253–274. Tel Aviv: Brirot Hotsa Laour. (Hebrew)

Elazar, Daniel, and Haim Kelkheim. 1987. "The Municipal Level of the Government and Politics in Israel." In *The Municipal Government in Israel*. Daniel Elazar and Haim Kelkheim, eds. Jerusalem: Jerusalem Center for Public and State Affairs. (Hebrew)

Elnajjar, Hassan. 2003. "Planned Emigration: The Palestinian Case." *International Migration Review* 27(1): 34–50.

Ember, Melvin, and Carol R. Ember. 1971. "The Conditions Favoring Matrilocal versus Patrilocal Residence." *American Anthropologist* 73: 571–594.

Enloe, Cynthia. 1980. *Ethnic Soldiers: State Security in Divided Societies*. Athens: University of Georgia Press.

Enloe, Cynthia. 2000. *Maneuvers: The International Politics of Militarizing Women's Lives*. Berkeley: University of California Press.

Erman, Tahire. 1998. "The Impact of Migration on Turkish Rural Women: Four Emergent Patterns." *Gender and Society* 12(2): 146–167.

Espanioly, Hala, Arabiya Mansour, and Areen Hawari. 1997. Education. WGR: NGO Alternative Pre-Sessional Report on Israel's Implementation of the United Nations Convention on the Elimination of all Forms of Discrimination Against Women (CEDAW). Pp. 71–86. Submitted in Jan 2003 to the Pre-Sessional Working Group. (Arabic)

Eyal, Gil. 1996. "The Discursive Origins of Israeli Separatism: The Case of the Arab Village." *Theory and Society* 25: 389–429.

Falah, Ghazi. 1985. "How Israel Controls the Bedouin in Israel." Special Issue, The Palestinians in Israel and the Occupied Territories. *Journal of Palestine Studies* 14(2): 32–51.

Falah, Ghazi. 1989a. *The Forgotten Palestinians: The Arab of the Naqab 1906–1986.* Tayiba: Arab Heritage Center. (Arabic)

Falah, Ghazi. 1989b. "Israeli 'Judaization' Policy in Galilee and Its Impact on Local Arab Urbanization." *Political Geography Quarterly* 8(3): 229–253.

Falah, Ghazi. 1989c. Israeli State Policy toward Bedouin Sedentarization in the Negev. *Journal of Palestine Studies* 18(2): 71–91.

Falah, Ghazi. 1996. "The 1948 Israeli-Palestinian War and Its Aftermath: The Transformation and De-Signification of Palestine's Cultural Landscape." *Annals of the Association of American Geographers* 86(2): 256–285.

Fanon, Frantz. 1990. *The Wretched of the Earth.* New York: Penguin.

Farah, Ja'far. "The Other Side of Judaizing the Galilee." *Zafon1-Karmi'el,* May 14. 15–17. (Hebrew).

Feldman, Illana. 2006. "Home as a Refrain: Remembering and Living Displacement in Gaza." *History and Memory* 18(2): 10–47.

Ferguson, Kathy. 1995. *Kibbutz Journal: Reflections on Gender, Race and Militarism in Israel.* California: Trilogy Books.

Firro, Kais. 2001. "Reshaping Druze Particularism in Israel." *Journal of Palestine Studies* 30(3): 40–53.

Fleischmann, Ellen. 2003. *The Nation and Its "New" Women: The Palestinian Women's Movement 1920–1948.* Berkeley: University of California Press.

Foner, Nancy. 1978. *Jamaica Farewell: Jamaican Migrants in London.* Berkeley: University of California Press.

Foucault, Michel. 1979. *Discipline and Punish: The Birth of the Prison.* New York: Vintage Books.

Furani, Khaled. 2004. "When Poets Go to Sleep: An Anthropological Inquiry into Modernizing Arabic Poetic Forms." PhD Dissertation, The Graduate Center of the City University of New York. Department of Anthropology.

Furman, Mirta. 1999. "Army and War: Collective Narratives of Early Childhood in Contemporary Israel." In *The Military and Militarism in Israeli Society.* Edna Lomsky-Feder and Eyal Ben-Ari, eds. Pp. 141–168. New York: State University of New York Press.

Garcia, Alma. 2004. *Narratives of Mexican American Women: Emergent Identities of the Second Generation.* California: AltaMira Press.

General Assembly of the United Nations. 1948. Universal Declaration of Human Rights. Adopted and proclaimed by General Assembly Resolution 217 A (III) of 10 Dec 1948. Electronic document, http://www.un.org/Overview/rights.html

General Committee of the Arab Locales in Israel. 2006. Future Vision for the Arab-Palestinians in Israel. Nazareth. (Hebrew)

Gertz, Nurith, and George Khleifi. 2008. *Palestinian Cinema: Landscape, Trauma, and Memory.* Bloomington: Indiana University Press.

Ghanem, As'ad. 1998. "State and Minority in Israel: The Case of Ethnic State and the Predicament of Its Minority." *Ethnic and Racial Studies* 21(3): 428–448.

Ghanem, As'ad. 2000. "The Palestinian Minority in Israel: The 'Challenge' of the Jewish State and Its Implications." *Third World Quarterly* 21(1): 87–104.

Ghanem, As'ad. 2001. *The Palestinian Arab Minority in Israel, 1948–2000: A Political Study*. Albany: State University of New York Press.

Ghanem, As'ad. 2004. "The Palestinian Arab Minority in Israel." In *Israel: A General Survey, 2004*. Camille Mansour, ed. Pp. 237–294. Beirut: Institute for Palestine Studies. (Arabic)

Ghanem, As'ad, Nadim Rouhana, and Oren Yiftachel. 1998. "Questioning 'Ethnic Democracy': A Response to Sammy Smooha." *Israel Studies* 3(2): 253–267.

Ghanem, As'ad, and Sarah Ozacky-Lazar. 1999. *The Arab Vote to the 15th Knesset*. Giv'at-Haviva: The Institute for Peace Studies. (Hebrew)

Ghanem, As'ad, and Sarah Ozacky-Lazar. 2003. "The Status of the Palestinians in Israel in an Era of Peace: Part of the Problem but Not Part of the Solution." *Israel Affairs* 9 (1/2): 263–289.

Ghanim, Honaida. 2004. "The Role and Function of the Palestinian Intellectual in Israel." PhD dissertation, The Hebrew University, Jerusalem. (Hebrew)

Ghanim, Honaida. 2005. *Attitudes Toward the Status and Rights of Palestinian Woman in Israel*. Nazareth: Women Against Violence. (Arabic)

Ghanim, Honaida. 2007. "Life in the Shadow of Emergency in Palestine." In *The Partition Motif in Contemporary Conflicts*. Smita Tewari Jassal and Eyal Ben-Ari, eds. Pp. 283–296. New Delhi: Sage Publications.

Giddens, Anthony. 1984. *The Constitution of Society*. Cambridge: Polity Press.

Gil, Eyal. 2005. *The Disenchantment of the Orient: Expertise in Arab Affairs and the Israeli State*. Jerusalem: Van Leer Institute and Hakibbutz Hameuchad Publishing House. (Hebrew)

Gill, Lesley. 1997. "Creating Citizens, Making Men: The Military and Masculinity in Bolivia." *Cultural Anthropology* 12(4): 527–550.

Ginat, Joseph. 1982. *Women in Muslim Rural Society: Status and Role in Family and Community*. New Brunswick: Transaction Books.

Ginat, Yousef. 1989. "Voting Patterns and Political Behavior in the Arab Sector." In *The Arab Sector in Israel and Parliament Elections*. Jacob Landau, ed. Pp. 3–21. Jerusalem: The Jerusalem Institute for Israel Studies. (Hebrew)

Gocek, Fatma Muge, ed. 2002. *Social Constructions of Nationalism in the Middle East*. New York: State University of New York Press.

Gojanski, Tamar. 1987. *The Development of Capitalism in Palestine*. Hanna Ibrahim, trans. Nazareth: The Library. (Arabic)

Golan, Galia. 1997. "Militarization and Gender: The Israeli Experience." *Women's Studies International Forum* 20(5/6): 581–586.

Gonen, Amaram, and Rasem Khamaisi. 1992. *Trends in the Spatial Distribution of the Arabs in Israel*. Jerusalem: Florsheimer Institute for Policy Research. (Hebrew)

Gorkin, Michael, and Rafiqa Othman. 1996. *Three Mothers, Three Daughters: Palestinian Women's Stories*. Berkeley: University of California Press.

Gough, Kathleen. 1971. "The Origin of the Family." *Journal of Marriage and the Family* 33 (November): 760–771.

Gramsci, Antonio. 1971. *Selections from the Prison Notebook*. London: Lawrence and Wishart.

Granott, Abraham. 1952. *The Land System in Palestine: History and Structure*. London: Eyre and Spottiswoode.

Granqvist, Hilma. 1931. *Marriage Conditions in a Palestinian Village*. Helsinki: Societas Scientiarum Fennica.

Granqvist, Hilma. 1931–1935. *Marriage Conditions in a Palestinian Village II*. Helsingfors: Akademische Buchhandlung.

Grinberg, Lev. 2000. "Introduction." In *Contested Memory: Myth, Nationalism and Democracy—Studies in the Aftermath of the Rabin Assassination*. Lev Grinberg, ed. Pp. 27–41. Beer Sheva: Ben-Gurion University, Hubert Humphrey Institute for Social Research. (Hebrew)

Griffiths, Morwenna. 1995. *Feminisms and the Self: The Web of Identity*. London: Routledge.

Groag, Shmuel, and Shuli Hartman. nd. Planning Rights in Arab Communities in Israel: An Overview. Electronic document,www.bimkom.org/dynContent/articles/PLANNING%20RIGHTS.pdf, (accessed May 6, 2009).

Haaretz (Hebrew) Tel Aviv

Haaretz, November 25, 1964.

Haaretz, July 24, 1964.

Haaretz, December 4, 1964.

Haaretz. 2002. "Ephraim Sneh's Plan: Um al-Fahm and Villages in the Triangle Will Be Transferred to the Palestinians, in Exchange for Concentrating the Settlements in the Territories." *Haaretz*, March 22.

Haaretz. 2007. "Haaretz Editorial: A Jewish and a Racist State." *Haaretz*, July 2. (Hebrew)

Haaretz. 2008. Livni: National Aspirations of Israel's Arabs Can Be Met by Palestinian Homeland. *Haaretz*, December 11. Electronic document, www.haaretz.com/hasen/objects/pages/PrintArticleEn.jhtml?itemNo=1045787 (accessed June 15, 2009).

Haaretz. 2009. Israel Moves Closer to Banning Mourning of Its Independence. *Haaretz*, May 25. Electronic document, http://www.haaretz.com/hasen/spages/1087792.html (accessed June 22, 2009).

Haidar, Aziz. 1997. *The Palestinians in Israel and the Oslo Agreement*. Beirut: Institute for Palestine Studies.

Haidar, Aziz. 2005a. "Demography." In *Arab Society in Israel 1: Populations, Society and Economy*. Aziz Haidar, ed. Pp. 25–50. Jerusalem: Van Leer Institute and Hakibbutz Hameuchad Publishing. (Hebrew)

Haidar, Aziz. 2005b. "Introduction." In *Arab Society in Israel 1: Populations, Society and Economy*. Aziz Haider, ed. Pp. 145–148. Jerusalem: Van Leer Institute and Hakibbutz Hameuchad Publishing. (Hebrew)

Haidar, Aziz. 2005c. "The Arab Economy in Israel: A Policy That Produces Dependence." In *Arab Society in Israel 1: Populations, Society and Economy*. Aziz Haidar, ed. Pp. 171–200. Jerusalem: Van Leer Institute and Hakibbutz Hameuchad Publishing. (Hebrew)

al-Haj, Majid. 1987. *Social Change and Family Processes: Arab Communities in Shefar-A'm*. Boulder: Westview Press.

al-Haj, Majid. 1988. "The Arab Internal Refugees in Israel: The Emergence of a Minority within the Minority." *Immigrants and Minorities* 7(2):149–165.

al-Haj, Majid. 1995. "Kinship and Modernization in Developing Societies: The Emergence of Instrumentalized Kinship." *Journal of Comparative Family Studies* 26(3): 311–328.

al-Haj, Majid, and Henry Rosenfeld. 1990. *The Arab Local Government in Israel.* Giv'at-Haviva: The Institute for Arab Studies. (Hebrew)

al-Haj, Majid, and Avner Yaniv. 1983. "Uniformity of Diversity: A Reappraisal of Voting Behavior of the Arabs Minority in Israel." In *The Elections in Israel—1981.* Asher Arian, ed. Pp. 139–164. New Brunswick: Transaction.

The Hajj, Smadar Lavie, and Forest Rouse. 1993. "Notes on the Fantastic Journey of the Hajj, His Anthropologist, and Her American Passport." *American Ethnologist* 20(2): 363–384.

Haj-Yahia, Muhammad. 2005. On the Characteristics of Patriarchal Societies, Gender Inequality, and Wife Abuse: The Case of Palestinian Society. *Adalah Electronic Newsletter* 20, November 2005. (Hebrew)

Haj-Yihia, Qussay, and Khalid Arar. 2007. *Arabs and Higher Education in Israel.* Tel Aviv: Ramot. (Hebrew)

Hajjar, Lisa. 1998. "Between and Rock and a Hard Place: Arab Women, Liberal Feminism and the Israeli State." *Middle East Report* 207.

Hajjar, Lisa. 2005. *Courting Conflict: The Israeli Military Court System in the West Bank and Gaza.* Berkeley: University of California Press.

Halperin-Kaddari, Ruth. 2004. *Women in Israel: A State of Their Own.* Philadelphia: University of Philadelphia Press.

Hamdan, Hanaa. 2005. Policy of Settlement and "Judaizing the Space" in the Negev. *Adalah Electronic Newsletter*, March 11, 2005. http://www.adalah.org/newsletter/heb/mar05/ar2.pdf (accessed June 16). (Hebrew)

Hammami, Rema. 1995. "Between Heaven and Earth: Transformations in Religiosity and Labor Among Southern Palestinian Peasant Refugee Women (1920–1993)." PhD thesis, Temple University.

Hammami, Rema. 2004. "Gender, Nakba and Nation: Palestinian Women's Presence and Absence in the Narration of 1948 Memories." *Annual Review of Women's and Gender Studies* (Institute of Women's Studies, Birzeit University) 2: 26–41.

Harding, Sandra. 1991. *Whose Science? Whose Knowledge? Thinking from Women's Lives.* Ithaca: Cornell University Press.

Harris, Ron. 2001. "Arab Politics in a Jewish State: al-'Ard Movement and the Supreme Court." *Plilim, the Multi-Disciplinary Journal of Public Law, Society and Culture* 10: 107–155. (Hebrew)

Hart, Jason. 2008. "Introduction." In *Years of Conflict: Adolescence, Political Violence and Displacement.* Jason Hart, ed. Pp. 1–20. New York: Berghahn Books.

Hasan, Manar. 1999. "The Politics of Honor: Patriarchy, the State and Honour Killing." In *Sex, Gender and Politics.* Dafna N. Izraeli, Ariella Friedman, Henriette Dahan-Kalev, Sylvie Fogiel-Bijaoui, Hanna Herzog, Manar Hasan, Hannah Naveh, eds. Pp. 267–305. Tel Aviv: Hakibbutz Hameuchad Publishing. (Hebrew)

Hasso, Frances. 1998. "The 'Women's Front': Nationalism, Feminism, and Modernity in Palestine." *Gender and Society* 12(4): 441–465.

Hasso, Frances. 2000. "Modernity and Gender in Arab Accounts of the 1948 and 1967 Defeats." *International Journal of Middle East Studies* 32(4): 491–510.

Hasso, Frances. 2001. "Feminist Generations? The Long-Term Impact of Social Movement Involvement on Palestinian Women's Lives." *American Journal of Sociology* 107(3): 586–611.

Havakook, Ya'acov. 1998. *Footprints in the Sand: The Bedouin Trackers in the IDF.* Tel Aviv: Israeli Ministry of Defense. (Hebrew)

Hawkesworth, Mary. 2006. *Globalization and Feminist Activism.* Lanham: Rowman and Littlefield Publishers.

Heering, Liesbeth, Rob van der Erf, and Leo van Wissen. 2004. "The Role of Family Networks and Migration Culture in the Continuation of Moroccan Emigration: A Gender Perspective." *Journal of Ethnic and Migration Studies* 30(2): 323–337.

Helman, Sara. 1999. "Militarism and the Construction of the Life-World of Israeli Males: The Case of the Reserves System." In *The Military and Militarism in Israeli Society.* Edna Lomsky-Feder and Eyal Ben-Ari, eds. Pp. 191–221. Albany: State University of New York Press.

Helman, Sara. 2001. "Citizenship, Regime, Identity and Peace Protest in Israel." In *Military, State, and Society in Israel: Theoretical and Comparative Perspectives.* Daniel Maman, Eyal Ben-Ari, and Zeev Rosenhek, eds. Pp. 295–318. New Brunswick: Transaction.

Henry, Astrid. 2005. *Not My Mother's Sister: Generational Conflict and Third-Wave Feminism.* Bloomington: Indiana University Press.

Hertzler, Joyce O. 1965. *A Sociology of Language.* New York: Random House.

Herzog, Hanna. 1998. "Homefront and Battlefront: The Status of Jewish and Palestinian Women in Israel." *Israel Studies* 3(1): 61–84.

Herzog, Hanna. 2004a. "'Both an Arab and a Woman:' Gendered, Racialised Experiences of Female Palestinian Citizens of Israel." *Social Identities* 10(1): 53–82.

Herzog, Hanna. 2004b. "Family-Military Relations in Israel as a Gendering Social Mechanism." *Armed Forces and Society* 31(1): 5–30.

Herzog, Hanna. 2007. "Mixed Cities as a Place of Choice: The Palestinian Women's Perspective." In *Mixed Towns, Trapped Communities: Historical Narratives, Spatial Dynamics, Gender Relations and Cultural Encounters in Palestinian-Israeli Towns.* Daniel Monterescu and Dan Rabinowitz, eds. Pp. 243–257. Hampshire, England, and Burlington, Vt.: Ashgate.

Herzog, Hanna, and Taghreed Yahia-Younis. 2007. "Men's Bargaining with Patriarchy: The Case of Primaries within Hamulas in Palestinian-Arab Communities in Israel." *Gender and Society* 21(4): 579–602.

Hilal, Jamil. 1977. "Class Transformation in the West Bank and Gaza." *Journal of Palestine Studies* 6(2): 167–175.

Hilal, Jamil. 2007. Assessing the Impact of Migration on Palestinian Society in the West Bank and Gaza. CARIM Research Reports 2007/02. San Domenico di Fiesole, Italy: Robert Schuman Centre for Advanced Studies, European University Institute. Electronic document, http://www.eui.eu/RSCAS/e-texts/CARIM-RR_2007_02.pdf (accessed June 3, 2008).

al-Hizmawi, Mohammad. 1998. *Land Ownership in Palestine 1918–1948.* Akka: al-Aswar Institute. (Arabic)

Hodgkin, Katharine, and Susannah Radstone. 2003. "Remembering Suffering: Trauma and History." In *Contested Pasts: The Politics of Memory.* Katharine Hodgkin and Susannah Radstone, eds. Pp. 99–103. London: Routledge.

hooks, bell. 1989. *Talking Back: Thinking Feminist, Thinking Black*. Boston: South End Press.

Horowitz, Dan, and Moshe Lisk. 1990. *Trouble in Utopia: The Overburdened Polity of Israel*. Tel Aviv: Am Oved Publishers Ltd. (Hebrew)

Hourany, Faysal. 2003. Roots of Palestinian Rejection 1918–1948. Ramallah: MUWA-TIN—The Palestinian Institute for the Study of Democracy. (Arabic)

Human Rights Watch (HRW). 2001. Second Class: Discrimination against Palestinian Arab Children in Israel's Schools. Electronic document, http://www.hrw.org/reports/2001/israel2/, accessed December 16, 2004.

Humphries, Isabelle, and Laleh Khalili. 2007. "Gender of Nakba Memory." In *Nakba: Palestine, 1948 and the Claims of Memory*. Ahmad Sa'di and Lila Abu-Lughod, eds. Pp. 207–228. New York: Columbia University Press.

Ibrahim Abu Lughod Institute. 2004. *Between the Archival Forest and the Anecdotal Trees: A Multidisciplinary Approach to Palestinian Social History: Selected Papers Presented at the 9th International Conference*. Birzeit University.

Ilkkaracan, Pinar. 2002/2003. "Women, Sexuality and Social Change in the Middle East and the Maghreb." *Al-Raida* 10(99): 12–22.

Iluz, Eva. 2002. *The Romantic Utopia: Between Love and Consumption*. Haifa: Haifa University Publishing and Zimora-Beitan. (Hebrew)

International Crisis Group (ICG). 2004. Identity Crisis: Israel and Its Arab Citizens. Amman/Brussels: International Crisis Group. Electronic document http://www.crisisgroup.org/home/index.cfm?id=2528&l=1 (accessed on January 18, 2010).

International Labor Organization (ILO) and South East Asia and the Pacific Multidisciplinary Advisory Team (SEAPAT). 1996. Women in Migration: Women's Migration in Asia. Online Gender Learning and Information Module.

International Labor Organization (ILO). 1998. http://www.ilo.org/public/english/region/asro/mdtmanila/training/unit2/asiamign.htm#keyissues (accessed December 16, 2009).

Immigrant Absorption Planning and Research. 2000. Immigration and Integration Policies in Israel in the Nineties. May 2000. Electronic document, http://moia.gov.il/NR/rdonlyres/99D88E6F-AE86-4A10-90D4-5C0172AE7DA8/0/policies.pdf (accessed June 8, 2009). (Arabic)

al-Ittihad 1959–1966 Haifa

Ittijah: Union of Arab Community Based Organizations. Fact Sheets: Palestinian NGOs. Electronic document, http://www.ittijah.org/inside/ngos.html (accessed April 1, 2008).

Ittijah: Union of Arab Community Based Organizations. 2005. Palestinian Women Citizens of Israel, in the Israeli Economy. Statement presented to the United Nations' Economic and Social Council on February 17, 2005. Electronic document, http://old.ittijah.org/press/womeneconomy.pdf (accessed June 8, 2009).

Jaafari, Ibrahim Lafi. 1973. "The Brain Drain to the United States: The Migration of Jordanian and Palestinian Professionals and Students." *Journal of Palestine Studies* 3(1): 119–131.

Jabareen, Hassan. 1999. On the Oppression of Identities in the Name of Civil Equality. *Adalah's Review, Politics, Identity and Law* 1:26–27.

Jacoby, Tami. 1999. "Gendered Nation: A History of the Interface of Women's Protest and Jewish Nationalism in Israel." *International Feminist Journal of Politics* 1(3): 382–402.

Jad, Islah. 1996. "The Palestinian Feminist Movement and the National Elections." *Nablus: Center for Palestinian Researchers and Studies* 10: 19–40. (Arabic)

Jakubowska, Longina. 1992. "Resisting 'Ethnicity': The Israeli State and Bedouin Identity." In *The Paths to Domination, Resistance and Terror*. Carolyn Nordstrom and Jo Ann Martin, eds. Pp. 85–105. Berkeley: University of California Press.

Jakubowska, Longina. 2000. "Finding Ways to Make a Living: Employment Among Negev Bedouin." *Nomadic Peoples* 4(2): 94–105.

Jamal, Amal. 2002. "Abstention as Participation: The Labyrinth of Arab Politics in Israel." In *The Elections in Israel 2001*. Asher Aryan and Mikhal Shamir, eds. Pp. 55–103. Jerusalem: Israel Democracy Institute.

Jamal, Amal. 2003. Ethnic Nationalism, Native People and Civic Equality: On Collective Rights in Israel. Paper presented at the Conference on the Legal and Socio-Economic Status of Arab Citizens in Israel, New York University, April 3.

Jamal, Amal. 2007a. "Strategies of Minority Struggle for Equality in Ethnic States: Arab Politics in Israel." *Citizenship Studies* 11(3): 263–282.

Jamal, Amal. 2007b. "Nationalizing States and the Constitution of 'Hollow Citizenship': Israel and Its Palestinian Citizens." *Ethnopolitics* 6(4): 471–493.

Jamal, Amal. 2008. "The Counter-Hegemonic Role of Civil Society: Palestinian Arab NGOs in Israel." *Citizenship Studies* 12(3): 283–306.

Jansson, Maria. 2004. "Bedouin Soldiers—Loyal 'Israelis'?: A Study on Loyalty and Identification Among a Minority Group in a Nation Building Process." MA thesis, Department of Political Science, Gothenburg University, Sweden.

Jayawardena, Kumari. 1986. *Feminism and Nationalism in the Third World*. London: Zed Books.

Jayyusi, Lena. 2007. "Interability, Cumulativity, and Presence: The Relational Figures of Palestinian Memory." In *Nakba: Palestine, 1948, and the Claims of Memory*. Ahmad Sa'di and Lila Abu-Lughod, eds. Pp. 107–133. New York: Columbia University Press.

Jerusalem Post November 25, 1964.

Jiryis, Sabri. 1966. *The Arabs in Israel*. Haifa: al-Ittihad. (Hebrew)

Jiryis, Sabri. 1973. *The Arabs in Israel*. Beirut: Institute of Palestine Studies. (Arabic)

Jiryis, Sabri. 1976. *The Arabs in Israel*. New York and London: Monthly Review Press.

Jiryis, Sabri. 1981. "Domination by the Law." *Journal of Palestine Studies* 11(1): 67–92.

Jiryis, Sabri. 2005. Interview by Leena Dallasheh. August 13. Fasuta.

Joseph, Suad. 1996. "Gender and Family in the Arab World." In *Arab Women: Between Defiance and Restraint*. Suha Sabbagh, ed. Pp. 194–202. New York: Olive Branch Press.

Joseph, Suad. 1999. *Intimate Selving in Arab Families: Gender, Self and Identity*. New York: Syracuse University Press.

Joseph, Suad. 2000. "Gendering Citizenship in the Middle East." In *Gender and Citizenship in the Middle East*. Suad Joseph, ed. Pp. 3–30. New York: Syracuse University Press.

Kabaha, Mustafa. 2004. The Palestinian Arab National Minority in Israel and Its Relationship to the Majority State and Its Institution. Published on December 22, 2004. Electronic document, http://www.aljazeera.net/NR/exeres/16E623F6-5238-428E-BE47-DE3B12CCEFB7.htm (accessed June 4, 2009). (Arabic)

Kama, Blanche. 1984. *The Status of Arab Women in Israel*. The Office of the Prime Minister, the Bureau of the Counselor for Arab Affairs.

Kanaaneh, Rhoda. 1995. "We'll Talk Later." *Cultural Anthropology* 10(1): 125–135.

Kanaaneh, Rhoda. 2002. *Birthing the Nation: Strategies of Palestinian Women in Israel*. Berkeley: University of California Press.

Kanaaneh, Rhoda. 2005. "Boys or Men? Duped or 'Made'?: Palestinian Soldiers in the Israeli Military. *American Ethnologist* 32(2): 260–275.

Kanaaneh, Rhoda. 2009. *Surrounded: Palestinian Soldiers in the Israeli Military*. Stanford: Stanford University Press.

Kanafani, Ghassan. 1972. *The 1936–1939 Revolt in Palestine*. Ghassan Kanafani Educational Association. (Arabic)

Kandiyoti, Deniz. 1977. "Sex Roles and Social Change: A Comparative Appraisal of Turkey's Women." *Signs: Journal of Women in Culture and Society* 3: 57–73.

Kandiyoti, Deniz. 1988. "Bargaining with Patriarchy." *Gender and Society* 2(3): 274–290.

Karkabi, Zahi. 1994. *The Land, the Motherland and Survival*. Haifa: Emile Touma Institute for Social and Political Studies. (Arabic)

Karni, Gil. 1998. *Tuba and Migdal*. 45 min. (Hebrew)

Katz, Shiela Hannah. 1996. "Adam and Adama, 'Ird and Ard: En-gendering Political Conflict and Identity in Early Jewish and Palestinian Nationalisms." In *Gendering the Middle East: Emerging Perspectives*. Deniz Kandiyoti, ed. Pp. 85–106. New York: Syracuse University Press.

Katz, Sheila. 2003. *Women and Gender in Early Jewish and Palestinian Nationalism*. Orlando: University Press of Florida.

Keinan, Tamar, and Dorit Bar. 2007. Mobility Among Arab Women in Israel. Tagreed Alahmad, ed. Haifa: Kayan Feminist Organization. Electronic document, http://www.kayan.org.il/Public/Mobility%20Among%20Arab%20Women%20Report.pdf (accessed June 5, 2009).

Kelly, Liz. 2000. "Wars Against Women: Sexual Violence, Sexual Politics and the Militarized States." In *States of Conflict: Gender, Violence and Resistance*. Susie Jacobs, Ruth Jacobson, and Jennifer Marchbank, eds. Pp. 45–65. London: Zed Books.

Kemp, Adriana. 1997. "Talking Borders: The Construction of Political Territory in Israel 1949–1957." PhD dissertation, Tel Aviv University. (Hebrew)

Kemp, Adriana. 1999. "The Mirror Language of the Border: Territorial Borders and the Construction of National Minority in Israel." *Israel Sociology* 2(1): 319–349. (Hebrew)

Khalidi, Rashid. 1997. *Palestinian Identity: The Construction of Modern National Consciousness*. Berkeley: University of California Press.

Khalidi, Rashid. 1998. "Attainable Justice: Elements of Solution to the Refugees Issue." *International Journal* 53: 233–252.

Khamaisi, Rassem. 1994. "Centrifugal Factors and Their Effect on the Structure of Arab Localities." In *The Arab Localities in Israel: Geographical Processes*. David Grossman and Avinoam Meir, eds. Pp. 114–127. Jerusalem: Magnes Press. (Hebrew)

Khamaisi, Rassem. 1995. "The Consequence of Land Ownership on Creating Housing Spaces." *Horizons in Geography* 40–41: 43–56.

Khamaisi, Rassem. 1998a. "Towards a Policy of Building New Towns in the Formation of a New Nation-State: Palestine." *Third Town Planning Review* 20(3): 285–308.

Khamaisi, Rassem. 1998b. "The Small Arab Localities in Israel: From Village to Suburb." *Horizons in Geography* 48–49: 111–130.

Khamaisi, Rassem. 2000. "Something Went Wrong on the Way to Town." *Panim* 13: 78–83. (Hebrew)

Khamaisi, Rassem. 2003. "The Mechanisms of Controlling Land and Judaizing Space in Israel." In *In the Name of Security: The Sociology of Peace and War in Israel in Changing Times*. Majid al-Haj and Uri Ben Eliezer, eds. Pp. 421–447. Haifa: Haifa University Press and Pardes Publishing House.

Khamaisi, Rassem. 2006. "Environmental Policies and Spatial Control: The Case of the Arab Localities Development in Israel." *Arab Studies Quarterly* 28(1): 33–54.

Khamis, Samar. 2005. Twofold Discrimination: The Status of the Arab Woman as an Individual and as a Member of a National Collective Struggling for Its Rights. Adalah Electronic Newsletter, November 20, 2005. http://www.adalah. org/newsletter/heb/nov05/ar2.pdf (accessed June 15, 2009).

Kimmerling, Baruch. 2001. *The Invention and Decline of Israeliness: State, Society and the Military*. Berkeley: University of California Press.

Kimmerling, Baruch. 2004. *Immigrants, Settlers, Natives: Israel Between Plurality of Cultures and Cultural Wars*. Tel Aviv: Am Oved. (Hebrew)

Kimmerling, Baruch. 2005. *The Invention and Decline of Israeliness: State, Society and the Military*. Berkeley: University of California Press.

Kosaifi, George. 1980. "Demographic Characteristics of the Arab Palestinian People." In *The Sociology of the Palestinians*. Khalil Nakhleh and Elia Zureik, eds. Pp. 13–46. London: Croom Helm.

Krahulik, Karen. 2005. "Aswat (Voices): An Interview with Rauda Morcos." *Peace and Change* 30(4): 492–520.

Khleifi, Michel. 1985. *Ma'lul Celebrates Its Destruction*.

Kretzmer, David. 1990. *The Legal Status of the Arabs in Israel*. Boulder: Westview Press.

Kuttab, Eileen. 1993. "Palestinian Women in the Intifada: Fighting on Two Fronts." *Arab Studies Quarterly* 15(2): 95–123.

Lahav, Pnina. 1997. *Judgment in Jerusalem: Chief Justice Simon Agranat and the Zionist Century*. Berkeley: University of California Press.

Lakoff, Robin T. 1975. *Language and Women's Place*. New York: Harper and Row.

Lal, Jayati. 1996. "Situating Locations: The Politics of Self, Identity, and 'Other' in Living and Writing the Text." In *Feminist Dilemmas in Fieldwork*. Diane L. Wolf, ed. Pp. 185–214. Boulder: Westview Press.

Landau, Jacob. 1969. *The Arabs in Israel: A Political Study*. London: Oxford University Press.

Landau, Jacob. 1993. *The Arab Minority in Israel, 1967–1991: Political Aspects*. Oxford: Clarendon Press.

Lang, Sharon. 2005. *Sharaf Politics: Honor and Peacemaking in Israeli-Palestinian Society.* New York: Routledge Press.

Lentin, Ronit. 2000. *Israel and the Daughters of the Shoah: Reoccupying the Territories of Silence.* Oxford: Berghahn Books.

Lesch, Ann, and Ian Lustick, eds. 2005. "The Failure of Oslo and the Abiding Question of the Refugees." In *Exile and Return: Predicaments of Palestinians and Jews.* Pp. 3–16. Philadelphia: University of Pennsylvania Press.

Levi-Strauss, Claude. 1960. "The Family." In *Man, Culture and Society.* Harry L. Shapiro, ed. Pp. 261–285. New York: Oxford University Press.

Levi-Strauss, Claude. 1969. *The Elementary Structures of Kinship.* London: Eyre and Spottiswoode.

Lewin-Epstein, Noah, and Moshe Semyonov. 1993. *The Arab Minority in Israel's Economy: Patterns of Ethnic Inequality.* Boulder: Westview Press.

Liebman, Charles, and Don-Yehia Eliezer. 1983. *Civil Religion in Israel: Traditional Judaism and Political Culture in the Jewish State.* Berkeley: University of California Press.

Little, Kenneth. 1976. "Women in African Towns South of the Sahara: The Urbanization Dilemma." In *Women and World Development.* Irene Tinker and Michele Bramsen, eds. Pp. 78–87. Washington, DC: Overseas Development Council.

Lipsitz, George. 1990. *Time Passages: Collective Memory and American Popular Culture.* Minneapolis: University of Minnesota Press.

Lipshitz, Gabriel. 1991. "Ethnic Differences in Migration Patterns: Disparities among Arabs and Jews in the Peripheral Regions of Israel." *Professional Geographer* 43(4): 456–464.

Lockman, Zachary. 1996. *Comrades and Enemies: Arab and Jewish Workers in Palestine 1906–1948.* Berkeley: University of California Press.

Louër, Laurence. 2007. *To Be an Arab in Israel.* New York: Columbia University Press.

Lubbad, Ismail. 2008a. Palestinian Migration: Any Circularity? Demographic and Economic Perspectives. *CARIM Research Reports* 2008/36. San Domenico di Fiesole, Italy. Robert Schuman Centre for Advanced Studies, European University Institute. Electronic document, http://cadmus.eui.eu/dspace/bitstream/1814/8389/1/CARIM_ASandN_2008_36.pdf (accessed May 29, 2008).

Lubbad, Ismail. 2008b. Irregular Migration, the Palestinian Case: Demographic and Socioeconomic Perspectives. Euro-Mediterranean Consortium for Applied Research on International Migration, Irregular Migration Series. Electronic document, http://hdl.handle.net/1814/10115 (accessed June 4, 2009).

Lustick, Ian. 1980. *Arabs in the Jewish State: Israel's Control of a National Minority.* Austin: University of Texas Press.

Ma'ariv Tel Aviv July 23, 1964.

Mada al-Carmel. 2007 The Haifa Declaration. Electronic document, http://www.mada-research.org/archive/haifaenglish.pdf (accessed April 3, 2008).

Ma'adi, Zainab. 2004. *The Feminine Body and the Dream of Development: Visions of the Feminine Body in the Shawia Region.* Casablanca: Fanak Publishing. (Arabic)

Macleod, Arlene Elowe. 1991. *Accommodating Protest: Working Women, the New Veiling, and Change in Cairo.* New York: Columbia University Press.

Mahsom. 2005a. Electronic document, http://www.mahsom.com/article.php?id=660 (accessed on November 29, 2007).

Mahsom. 2005b. Haifa University Discriminates against Arab Student in Dormitory Services. Electronic document, http://212.179.113.235/mahsom/article.php?id=1790 (accessed June 16, 2009). (Hebrew)

Maira, Sunaina. 2008. " 'We Ain't Missing': Palestinian Hip Hop—A Transnational Youth Movement. CR: The New Centennial Review 8(2): 161–192.

Mana', Adel. 1999. The History of Palestine at the Late Ottoman Period, 1700–1918: A New Reading. Beirut: Institute for Palestine Studies. (Arabic)

Mana', Adel. 2006. "Memory and the History of the Nakba: The Model of Majd al-Kroum." In Towards Contextualizing a Historical Narrative of al-Nakba: Problems and Challenges. Mustafa Kabaha, ed. Pp. 173–207. Haifa: Mada al-Carmel. (Arabic)

Mannheim, Karl. 1952. "The Problem of Generations." In Essays on the Sociology of Knowledge. Paul Kecskemeti, ed. Pp. 276–320. London: Routledge and Kegan Paul.

al-Marashli, Ahmad, Hashem Abdelhadi, and Anis Sayigh. 1984. The Palestine Encyclopedia, vol. 1. Damascus: The Palestinian Encyclopedia Board.

Martin, Susan Forbes. 2004. Women and Migration, a Paper Prepared for the United Nations—Division for the Advancement of Women Consultative Meeting on Migration and Mobility and How This Movement Affects Women. CM/MMW/2003/WP.1 January 14, 2004.

Marx, Karl, and Friedrich Engels. 1955–1959. Selected Writings. Merhavia: Sifriyat Poalim. (Hebrew)

Masalha, Nur. 1997. A Land Without a People: Israel, Transfer and the Palestinians, 1949–1996. London: Faber and Faber.

Masarweh, Maram. 2009. The Man's Dubious Honour. Haaretz, February 1. Electronic document, http://www.haaretz.co.il/hasite/spages/1060494.html?more=1 (accessed June 16, 2009). (Hebrew)

Massad, Joseph. 1995. "Conceiving the Masculine: Gender and Palestinian Nationalism." Middle East Journal 49(3): 467–483.

Massad, Joseph. 2006. The Persistence of the Palestinian Question: Essays on Zionism and the Palestinians. London: Routledge.

Mauss, Marcel. 2005. [1923–1924] Essai sur le don. Tel Aviv: Resling. (Hebrew)

Mazali, Rela. 1998. "Parenting Troops: The Summons to Acquiescence." In The Women & War Reader. Lois Ann Lorentzen and Jennifer Turpin, eds. Pp. 272–286. New York: New York University Press.

Mazurana, Dyan, Angela Raven-Roberts, and Jane Parpart, eds. 2005. Gender, Conflict, and Peacekeeping. New York: Rowman & Littlefield Publishers.

McClintock, Anne. 1995. Imperial Leather: Race, Gender, and Sexuality in the Colonial Contest. New York: Routledge.

McDonald, David. 2006. "My Voice Is My Weapon: Music, Nationalism, and the Poetics of Palestinian Resistance." PhD dissertation, University of Illinois Urbana Champaign, Department of Anthropology.

Me'ari, Muhammad. 2005. Interview by Leena Dallasheh. August 8. Haifa.

Meehan, Maureen. 1998. "Israeli Forces Open Fire on Arab Citizens of Israel Protesting Land Confiscations Inside Israeli Borders." http://www.um-elfahem.net/forums/viewtopic.php?f=2andt=410 (accessed May 31, 2010).

Melamed, Shoham. 2004. "Motherhood, Fertility and the Construction of the "Demographic Threat" in the Marital Age Law." *Theory and Criticism* 25: 69–96. (Hebrew)

Memmi, Albert. 1991. *The Colonizer and the Colonized*. Boston: Beacon Press.

Mernissi, Fatima. 2004. "Virginity and Patriarchy." In *Women and Sexuality in Muslim Societies: A Publication of Women for Women's Rights (WWHR)*. Pinar Ilkka-racan, ed. Pp. 241–254. Damascus: Dar Almada for Culture and Publishing. (Arabic)

Meyer-Brodnitz, Michael. 1983. "Rural-Urban Migration of Arabs in Israel: A Case Study of Residential Choice and Planning Policy." PhD dissertation, University of London.

Meyer, Lawrence. 1982. *Israel Now: Portrait of a Troubled Land*. New York: Delacorte Press.

Mitchell, Timothy. 2002. *Rule of Experts: Egypt, Techno-Politics, Modernity*. Berkeley: University of California Press.

Moghadam, Valentine. 1994. "Introduction and Overview." In *Gender and National Identity: Women and Politics in Muslim Societies*. Valentine Moghadam, ed. Pp. 1–17. London: Zed Books.

Mohanty, Chandra Talpade. 2003. *Feminism Without Borders: Decolonizing Theory, Practicing Solidarity*. Durham: Duke University Press.

Moore-Gilbert, Bart. 1997. *Postcolonial Theory: Contexts, Practices, Politics*. London: Verso.

Morris, Benny. 2004. *The Birth of the Palestinian Refugee Problem Revisited*. Cambridge: Cambridge University Press.

Morris, Benny. 2005 [1991]. *The Birth of the Palestinian Refugee Problem, 1947–1949*. Tel Aviv: Am Oved. (Hebrew)

Muhammad, Jibril, and Wasif Nazzal. 1990. *The Palestinians of 1948 Continuing Struggle 1948–1988*. Jerusalem: Alzahra Center for Studies and Research. (Arabic)

Muhawi, Ibrahim, and Sharif Kanaana. 1989. *Speak Bird, Speak Again: Palestinian Arab Folktales*. Berkeley: University of California Press.

Murdock, George P. 1949. *Social Structure*. New York: The Free Press.

Murdock, George P., and Suzanne F. Wilson. 1980. "Settlement Patterns and Community Organization: Cross-Cultural Codes 3." In *Cross Cultural Samples and Codes*. Barry Herbert III and Alice Schlegel, eds. Pp. 75–99. Pittsburgh: University of Pittsburgh in Cooperation with Ethnology.

Nahmias, Roe. 2007. GDP Per Capita of Arab Israelis Third of That of Jews. Ynet-news, January 18. Electronic document, www.ynetnews.com/articles/0,7340,L-3354260,00.html (accessed April 18, 2007).

Najjar, Orayb Aref. 2003. "Still 'A Difficult Journey Up the Mountain'? Palestinian Women's National versus Gender Politics 1919–2002." In *Sing, Whisper, Shout, Pray! Feminist Visions for a Just World*. M. Jacqui Alexander, Lisa Albrecht, Sharon Day, and Mab Segrest, eds. Pp. 181–211. Canada: Edge Work Books.

Nana10. 2009. Center Decided to Close Academic Track because "it's for Arabs." May 24, 2009. Electronic document, http://news.nana10.co.il/Article/?ArticleID=638903andTypeID=1andsid=126 (accessed June 4, 2009).

Naples, Nancy. 2002. "Changing the Terms: Community Activism, Globalization, and the Dilemmas of Transnational Feminist Praxis." In *Women's Activism and*

Globalization: Linking Local Struggles and Transnational Politics. Nancy Naples and Manisha Desai, eds. Pp. 1–14. New York: Routledge..

Nashat, Guity, and Judith Tucker. 1999. *Women in the Middle East and North Africa: Restoring Women to History.* Indianapolis: Indiana University Press.

Nassar, Maha T. 2006. "Affirmation and Resistance Press, Poetry and the Formation of National Identity Among Palestinian Citizens of Israel, 1948–1967." PhD thesis, Department of Near Eastern Languages and Civilizations, University of Chicago.

National Committee for the Heads of the Arab Local Authorities in Israel (NCHALAI). 2006. *The Future Vision of the Palestinian Arabs in Israel.* Electronic document, http://www.alternativenews.org/news/english/the-future-vision-of-the-palestinian-arabs-in-israel-20070109.html (accessed April 3, 2008).

Natur, Salman. 1985. *The Story Is Not Yet Over.* Haifa: al-Ittihad. (Arabic)

Natur, Salman. 1995. *The Chaos in the Time of Immigration.* Haifa: al-Ittihad. (Arabic)

el-Okbi, Nuri. 2004. *Waiting for Justice: The Story of the Elokbi Tribe in Israel.* NP. (Arabic and English)

Otterbein, Keith, and Charlotte S. Otterbein. 1965. "An Eye for an Eye: A Tooth for a Tooth: A Cross-Cultural Study of Feuding." *American Anthropologist* 67: 1470–1482.

Ozacky-Lazar, Sarah. 2002. "The Military Government as an Apparatus of Control of Arab Citizens: The First Decade, 1948–1958." *The New East* 23: 103–131. (Hebrew)

Ozacky-Lazar, Sarah, and As'ad Ghanem. 1994. *The Elections for Arab Municipalities, November, 1993: Results and Analysis.* Giv'at-Haviva: The Institute for Peace Studies. (Hebrew)

Ozacky-Lazar, Sarah, and As'ad Ghanem. 1996. *The Arab Vote to the 14th Knesset.* Givat-Haviva: The Institute for Peace Studies. (Hebrew)

Panet. 2009. Adalah's Statement on the Suspension of Johayna Hussein from Her Job. *Panet*, February 13. Electronic document, http://www.panet.co.il/online/articles/1/2/S-178066,1,2.html (accessed June 15, 2009). (Arabic)

Panet. 2009. A Nurse from Dayr Hanna Is Suspended from Her Job for Demonstrating in Umm al-Fahim. *Panet*, February 12. Electronic document, http://www.panet.co.il/online/articles/1/2/S-177983,1,2.html (accessed June 15). (Arabic)

Pappe, Ilan. 2006. "Post-Zionist Scholarship in Israel." In *The Struggle for Sovereignty: Palestine and Israel, 1993–2005.* Joel Beinin and Rebecca Stein, eds. Pp. 151–161. Stanford: Stanford University Press.

Pappe, Ilan. 2007. *The Ethnic Cleansing of Palestine.* Oxford: Oneworld Publications.

Parsons, Laila. 2001. "The Druze and the Birth of Israel." In *The War for Palestine: Rewriting the History of 1948.* Eugene L. Rogan and Avi Shlaim, eds. Pp. 60–78. Cambridge: Cambridge University Press.

Peled, Alon. 1998. *A Question of Loyalty: Military Manpower Policy in Multiethnic States.* Ithaca: Cornell University Press.

Peretz, Don. 1991. "Early State Policy Towards the Arab Population, 1948–1955." In *New Perspectives on Israeli History: The Early Years of the State.* Laurence Silberstein, ed. Pp. 82–102. New York: New York University Press.

Perry, Imani. 2004. *Prophets of the Hood: Politics and Poetics in Hip Hop.* Durham: Duke University Press.

Peteet, Julie M. 1991. *Gender in Crisis: Women and the Palestinian Resistance Movement*. New York: Columbia University Press.

Peteet, Julie. 1999. "Gender and Sexuality: Belonging to the National and Moral Order." In *Hermeneutics and Honor: Negotiating Female "Public" Space in Islamic/ate Societies*. Asma Afsaruddin, ed. Pp. 70–88. Cambridge: Harvard University Press.

Peteet, Julie. 2000. "Male Gender Rituals of Resistance in the Palestinian Intifada: A Cultural Politics of Violence." In *Imagined Masculinities: Male Identity and Culture in the Modern Middle East*. Mai Ghoussoub and Emma Sinclair-Webb, eds. Pp. 103–126. London: Saqi Books.

Peteet, Julie. 2002. "Icons and Militants: Mothering in the Danger Zone." In *Gender, Politics, and Islam*. Therese Saliba, Carolyn Allen, and Judith Howard, eds. Pp. 133–160. Chicago: The University of Chicago Press.

Peteet, Julie. 2005. *Landscape of Hope and Despair: Palestinian Refugee Camps*. Philadelphia: University of Pennsylvania Press.

Peterson, J. E. 1989. "The Political Status of Women in Arab Gulf States." *Middle East Journal* 43(1): 34–50.

Portelli, Alessandro. 1981. " 'The Time of My Life': Function of Time in Oral History." *International Journal of Oral History* 2(3): 162–180.

Qahwaji, Habib. 1972. *The Arabs in the Shadow of Israeli Occupation since 1948*. Beirut: PLO Research Center. (Arabic)

Qahwaji, Habib. 1978. *The Full Story of the Movement al-'Ard*. Al-Quds: Manshorat al-'Araby. (Arabic)

al-Qattan, Omar. 2006. "Challenges of Palestinian Filmmaking: 1991 to 2003." In *Dreams of a Nation: On Palestinian Cinema*. Hamid Dabashi, ed. Pp. 110–130. New York: Verso Press.

Rabinowitz, Dan. 1998. *Anthropology and the Palestinians*. Israel: The Institute for Israeli Arab Studies. (Hebrew)

Rabinowitz, Dan, and Khawla Abu-Baker. 2005. *Coffins on Our Shoulders: The Experience of the Palestinian Citizens of Israel*. Berkeley: University of California Press.

Raiter, Izlah, and Reuben Aharoni. 1993. *The Political World of the Arabs in Israel*. Biet Berl: The Institute for Israeli Arab Studies, Israel. (Hebrew)

Ransel, David. 2000. *Village Mothers: Three Generations of Change in Russia and Tataria*. Bloomington: Indiana University Press.

Reiker, Martina. 1992. Constructing Palestinian Subalternity in the Galilee: Reflections on Representations of the Palestinian Peasantry. Electronic document, http://humwww.ucsc.edu/CultStudies/PUBS/Inscriptions/vol_6/Reiker.html (accessed June 8, 2009).

Rekhess, Elie. 1986. "The Arab Village in Israel: A New Political Center." In *Horizons in Geography*. Micha Klein, ed. Pp. 145–160. (Hebrew)

Rekhess, Elie. 1991. "Initial Israeli Policy Guidelines Towards the Arab Minority, 1948–1949." In *New Perspectives on Israeli History: The Early Years of the State*. Laurence Silberstein, ed. Pp. 103–123. New York: New York University Press.

Rekhess, Elie. 1993. *The Arab Minority in Israel: Between Communism and Arab Nationalism 1965–1991*. Tel Aviv: University of Tel Aviv. (Hebrew)

Rekhess, Elie. 2006. The Arabs in Israel and the War in the North. The Konard Adenauer Program for Jewish-Arab Cooperation. Special Issue. August 14.

Electronic document, http://www.dayan.org/kapjac/files/War_North1_EN.pdf (accessed April 1, 2008).

Rekhess, Elie. 2007. "The Evolvement of an Arab-Palestinian National Minority in Israel." *Israel Studies* 12(3): 1–28.

Reuben, Paz. 1989. *The Islamic Movement in Israel after the Municipal Elections.* Tel Aviv: Dian Center, Tel Aviv University. (Hebrew)

Robben, Antonius. 1995. "The Politics of Truth and Emotion among Victims and Perpetrators of Violence." In *Fieldwork under Fire: Contemporary Studies of Violence and Survival.* Carolyn Nordstrom and Antonius Robben, eds. Pp. 91–103. Berkeley: University of California Press.

Robinson, Shira. 2003. "Local Struggle, National Struggle: Palestinian Responses to the Kfar Qasim Massacre and Its Aftermath, 1956–1966." *International Journal of Middle East Studies* 35(3): 393–416.

Robinson, Shira. 2005. "Occupied Citizens in a Liberal State: Palestinians Under Military Rule and the Colonial Formation of Israeli Society, 1948–1966." PhD dissertation, Department of History, Stanford University.

Rose, Tricia. 1994. *Black Noise: Rap Music and Black Culture in Contemporary America.* Hanover: University of New England Press.

Rosenfeld, Henry. 1964. *They Were Peasants: Reviewing Social Development of the Arab Village in Israel.* Tel Aviv: Hakibbutz Hameuchad. (Hebrew)

Rosenhek, Zeev. 1999. "The Exclusionary Logic of the Welfare State: Palestinian Citizens in the Israeli Welfare State." *International Sociology* 14(2): 195–215.

Rouhana, Nadim. 1989. "The Political Transformation of the Palestinians in Israel: From Acquiescence to Challenge." *Journal of Palestine Studies* 18(3): 38–59.

Rouhana, Nadim. 1997. *Palestinian Citizens in an Ethnic Jewish State: Identities in Conflict.* New Haven: Yale University Press.

Rouhana, Nadim. 2005. "Truth and Reconciliation: The Right of Return in the Contact of Past Injustice." In *Exile and Return: Predicaments of Palestinians and Jews.* Ann Lesch and Ian Lustick, eds. Pp. 261–278. Philadelphia: University of Pennsylvania Press.

Rouhana, Nadim, and Areej Sabbagh-Khoury. 2009. *Palestinians' Conception of the Right of Return-Analysis of Survey.* Haifa: Mada al-Carmel—The Arab Center for Applied Social Research.

Rouhana, Nadim, and Nimer Sultany. 2003. "Redrawing the Boundaries of Citizenship: Israel's New Hegemony." *Journal of Palestine Studies* 33(1): 5–22.

Rouhana, Nadim, Nabil Saleh, and Nimer Sultany. 2003. *The Palestinian Minority in the Israeli Parliamentary Elections 2003.* Haifa: Mada al-Carmel—The Arab Center for Applied Social Research. (Arabic)

Rouhana, Nadim, Nabil Saleh, and Nimer Sultany. 2004. *Voting Without Voice: The Palestinian Minority in the Israeli Parliament Elections 2003.* Haifa: Mada Center. (Arabic)

Sa'di, Ahmad. 1996. "Minority Resistance to State Control: Towards a Re-analysis of Palestinian Political Activity in Israel." *Social Identities* 2(3): 395–412.

Sa'di, Ahmad. 2003. "Social Conceptions, Citizenship Rights and Protest: The Road to the October Events." In *The Or Commission Testimonies: Seven Professional*

Assessments Submitted to the Or Commission. Sarah Ozacky-Lazar and As'ad Ghanem, eds. Pp. 184–206. Jerusalem: Keter.

Sa'di, Ahmad. 2003. "The Incorporation of the Palestinian Minority by the Israeli State, 1948–1970: On the Nature, Transformation, and Constraints of Collaboration." *Social Text* 75(21,2): 75–94.

Sa'di, Ahmad. 2006. "Memory and Identity." In *Toward Constructing Historical Narrative on Nakba: Issues and Challenges.* Mustafa Kabaha, ed. Pp. 57–79. Haifa: Mada al-Carmel. (Arabic)

Sa'di, Ahmad, and Lila Abu-Lughod, eds. 2007. *Nakba: Palestine, 1948, and the Claims of Memory.* New York: Columbia University Press.

Sa'di, Ahmad, Michael Shalev, and Yitzhak Schnell. 2000. "Development and Employment." In *After the Rift: New Directions for Government Policy Towards the Arab Population in Israel.* Dan Rabinowitz, As'ad Ghanem, and Oren Yiftachel, eds. Pp. 45–54. An Emergency Report by an Inter-University Research Team submitted to Mr. Ehud Barak, Prime Minister of Israel.

Sa'ar, Amalia. 2001. "Lonely in Your Firm Grip: Women in Israeli-Palestinian Families." *Journal of the Royal Anthropological Institute* 7(4): 723–739.

Sa'ar, Amalia. 2004. "On the Sexuality of Single Women in the Palestinian Community in Israel." *Theory and Criticism* 25: 13–25.

Sa'ar, Amalia. 2007. "Contradictory Location: Assessing the Position of Palestinian Women Citizens of Israel." *Journal of Middle East Women's Studies* 3(3): 45–74.

Sabbagh, Suha. 1996. "The Debate on Arab Women." In *Arab Women: Between Defiance and Restraint.* Suha Sabbagh, ed. Pp. i–xxvii. New York: Olive Branch Press.

Sabbagh-Khoury, Areej. 2006. "Between the 'Law of Return' and the Rights of Return: Reflections on Palestinian Discourse in Israel." MA thesis, Department of Sociology and Anthropology, Tel Aviv University.

Sahlins, Marshall. 1968. *Tribesmen.* Englewood Cliffs, N.J.: Prentice-Hall.

Said, Edward. 1978. *Orientalism.* New York: Vintage.

Said, Edward W., and David Barsamian. 1994. *The Pen and the Sword: Conversations with David Barsamian.* Monroe: Common Courage Press.

Said, Nader. 1999. *Palestinian Women and Elections.* Ramallah: MUWATIN—The Palestinian Institute for the Study of Democracy.

Salah, Ra'id. 2007. Interview by Jamil Dakwar, May 28, 2006. "The Islamic Movement inside Israel by Shaykh Ra'id Salah." *Journal of Palestine Studies* 142: 66–76.

Salloum, Jackie, dir. 2008. *Slingshot Hip Hop.* 94 min. (Arabic, English, and Hebrew)

Sanbar, Elias. 2001. "Out of Place, Out of Time." *Mediterranean Historical Review* 16(1): 87–94.

Sasson-Levy, Orna. 2003. "Feminism and Military Gender Practices: Israeli Women Soldiers in 'Masculine' Roles." *Sociological Inquiry* 73(3): 440–465.

Sayigh, Rosemary. 1979. *Palestinians: From Peasants to Revolutionaries.* London: Zed Books.

Sayigh, Rosemary. 1980. *Palestinian Peasants from Expulsion to Revolution.* Beirut: Arab Studies Association. (Arabic)

Sayigh, Rosemary. 1993. "Palestinian Women and Politics in Lebanon." In *Arab Women Between Defiance and Restraint.* Suha Sabbagh, ed. Pp. 175–192. New York: Olive Branch Press.

Sayigh, Rosemary. 1996. "Researching Gender in a Palestinian Camp: Political, Theoretical and Methodological Problems." In *Gendering the Middle East: Emerging Perspectives*. Deniz Kandiyoti, ed. Pp. 145–168. Syracuse: Syracuse University Press.

Sayigh, Rosemary. 1998. "Palestinian Camp Women as Tellers of History." *Journal of Palestinian Studies* 27(2): 42–58.

Sayigh, Rosemary. 2002. "Remembering Mothers, Forming Daughters: Palestinian Women's Narratives in Refugee Camps in Lebanon." In *Women and the Politics of Military Confrontation: Palestinian and Israeli Gendered Narratives of Dislocation*. Nahla Abdo and Ronit Lentin, eds. Pp. 56–71. New York: Berghahn Books.

Sayigh, Rosemary. 2007. "Women's Nakba Stories: Between Being and Knowing." In *Nakba: Palestine, 1948, and the Claims of Memory*. Ahmad Sa'di and Lila Abu-Lughod, eds. Pp. 135–158. New York: Columbia University Press.

Sayigh, Yazid. 1997. *Armed Struggle and the Search for State: The Palestinian National Movement, 1949–1993*. New York: Clarendon Press and Oxford University Press.

Schaeffer-Grabiel, Felicity. 2004. "Cyberbrides and Global Imaginaries: Mexican Women's Turn From the National to the Foreign." *Space and Culture* 7(1): 33–48.

Scholch, Alexander. 1988. *Palestine in Transformation (1856–1882): Studies in Social, Economic and Political Development*. Amman: Jordanian University. (Arabic)

Scott, Joan. 1988. *Gender and the Politics of History*. New York: Columbia University Press.

Segev, Tom. 1986. *1946: The First Israelis*. New York: The Free Press.

Sered, Susan. 2000. *What Makes Women Sick? Maternity, Modesty, and Militarism in Israel*. Hanover: Brandeis University Press.

Shadmi, Erella. 2000. "Between Resistance and Compliance, Feminism and Nationalism: Women in Black in Israel." *Women's Studies International Forum* 23(1): 23–34.

Shafir, Gershon. 2004. "Introduction to the New Edition on Land, Work and the Israeli-Palestinian Conflict 1882–1914." In *Colonization and Post Colonization*. Yehouda Shenhav, ed. Pp. 461–469. Jerusalem: Van Leer Institute and Hakibbutz Hameuchad Publishing. (Hebrew)

Shafir, Gershon, and Yoav Peled. 1999. "Citizenship and Stratification in an Ethnic Democracy." In *Israeli and Palestinian Identities in History and Literature*. Kamal Abdel-Malek and David C. Jacobson, eds. Pp. 87–110. New York: St. Martin's Press.

Shamir, Ronen. 1996. "Suspended in Space: Bedouins under the Law of Israel." *Law and Society Review* 30(2): 231–257.

Sharabi, Hisham. 1988. *Neopatriarchy: A Theory of Distorted Change in Arab Society*. New York: Oxford University Press.

Sharabi, Hisham. 1990. *Introduction to the Study of the Arab Society*. Beirut: Dar Al-Taila. (Arabic)

Sharoni, Simona. 1994. "Homefront as Battlefield: Gender, Military, Occupation and Violence Against Women." In *Women and the Israeli Occupation: The Politics of Change*. Tamar Mayer, ed. Pp. 121–137. London: Routledge.

Sharoni, Simona. 1996. "Gender and the Israeli-Palestinian Accord: Feminist Approaches to International Politics." In *Gendering the Middle East: Emerging*

Perspectives. Deniz Kandiyoti, ed. Pp. 107–126. New York: Syracuse University Press.

Shavit, Uriya, and Jalal Bana. 2001. "The Secret Exodus: Palestinian Emigration." http://www.kokhavivpublications.com/2001/israel/oct/05/0110050920.html (accessed May 31, 2010).

Shenhav, Yehouda. 2005. "Arab Jews, Population Exchange, and the Palestinian Right of Return." In *Exile and Return: Predicaments of Palestinians and Jews*. Ann Lesch and Ian Lustick, eds. Pp. 225–245. Philadelphia: University of Pennsylvania Press.

Shenhav, Yehouda, and Hanan Hever. 2004. "Trends in the Postcolonial Research Studies." In *Colonization and Post Colonization*. Yehouda Shenhav, ed. Pp. 189–200. Jerusalem: Van Leer Institute and Hakibbutz Hameuchad Publishing. (Hebrew)

Shihadeh, Mtanes. 2004. *Unemployment and Exclusion: The Arab Minority in the Israeli Labor Markets*. Haifa: Mada al-Carmel. (Hebrew)

Shihadeh, Mtanes, and Areej Sabbagh-Khoury. 2005. *Growing Dependency and Decreasing Space: Budget and Jurisdiction in Arab and Jewish Local Authorities in Israel*. Haifa: Mada al-Carmel. (Arabic)

Shohat, Ella. 2001. *Forbidden Memories: Towards Multicultural Thinking*. Tel Aviv: Bimat Kedem Publishing. (Hebrew)

Sigaut, Marion. 2001. *Mansur Kardosh: A Good Man from Nazareth*. Nazareth: al-Muassasah al-'Arabieh le-Huquq al-Insan. (Arabic)

Sikkuy. 2003. *Sikkuy Report 2002–2003*. Shalom (Shuli) Dicther ,and As'ad Ghanem, eds. Jerusalem.

Silberstein, Laurence. 2000. "Mapping, Not Tracing: Opening Reflection." In *Mapping Jewish Identities*. Laurence Silberstein, ed. Pp. 1–36. New York: New York University Press.

Sizoo, Edith. 1997. "How Women Change Places and Places Change Women." In *Women's Lifeworlds: Women's Narratives on Shaping Their Realties*. Edith Sizoo, ed. Pp. 221–240. London: Routledge.

Slyomovics, Susan. 1998. *The Object of Memory: Arab and Jew Narrate the Palestinian Village*. Philadelphia: University of Pennsylvania Press.

Slyomovics, Susan. 2007. "The Rape of Qula, A Destroyed Palestinian Village." In *Nakba: Palestine, 1948, and the Claims of Memory*. Ahmad Sa'di and Lila Abu-Lughod, eds. Pp. 27–51. New York: Columbia University Press.

Smith, Pamela Ann. 1984. *Palestine and the Palestinians 1876–1983*. New York: St. Martin's Press.

Smooha, Sammy. 1989a. *Arabs and Jews in Israel Vol I: Conflicted and Shared Attitudes in a Divided Society*. Colorado: Westview Special Studies on the Middle East.

Smooha, Sammy. 1989b. *The Orientation and Politicization of the Arab Minority in Israel*. Haifa: The Jewish Arab Center.

Smooha, Sammy. 1992. *Arabs and Jews in Israel Vol II: Change and Continuity in Mutual Intolerance*. Colorado: Westview Special Studies on the Middle East.

Smooha, Sammy. 1997. "Ethnic Democracy: Israel as an Archetype." *Israel Studies* 2(2): 198–241.

Smooha, Sammy. 1999. "The Advances and Limits of the Israelization of Israel's Palestinian Citizens." In *Israeli and Palestinian Identities in History and Literature*. Kamal Abdel-Malek and David Jacobson, eds. Pp. 9–33. New York: St. Martin's Press.

Sorek, Tamir. 2003. "Palestinian Nationalism Has Left the Field: A Shortened History of Arab Soccer in Israel." *International Journal of Middle East Studies* 35: 417–437.

Spivak, Gayatri Chakravorty. 1992. "Women in Differences: Mahasweta Devi's Douloti the Bountiful." In *Nationalisms and Sexualities*. Andrew Parker, Mary Russo, Doris Sommer, and Patricia Yeager, eds. Pp. 96–116. London: Routledge.

Spivak, Gayatri Chakravorty. 1994. "Can the Subaltern Speak?" In *Colonial Discourse and Post-Colonial Theory: A Reader*. Patrick Williams and Laura Chrisman, eds. Pp. 66–111. New York: Columbia University Press.

Srur, Roni. 2000. Attitudes of the Muslim Student Towards Women with an Emphasis on Women's Sexuality. Final qualifying paper in psychology. Jerusalem: The Hebrew University of Jerusalem. (Hebrew)

Staab, Silke. 2004. In Search of Work. International Migration of Women in Latin America and the Caribbean. Research prepared for Women and Development Unit—United Nations. ECLAC, Santiago, Chile.

Stendel, Ori. 1973. *The Minorities in Israel: Trends in the Development of the Arabs and Druze Communities 1948–1973*. Jerusalem: The Israel Economist.

Stendel, Ori. 1992. *The Arabs in Israel: Between Hammer and Anvil*. Jerusalem: Academon—The Hebrew University Students' Printing and Publishing House. (Hebrew)

Stendel, Ori. 1996. *The Arabs in Israel*. Brighton: Sussex Academic Press.

Stewart, Kenda. 2007. "Football for Peace": Palestinian and Jewish Citizens Search for a Common Ground. American Anthropological Association Annual Meeting. Washington, D.C.

Sultany, Nimer. 2002. Palestinian Arabs in Israeli Universities. July 15. Arab48.com. (Arabic)

Sultany, Nimer (ed.). 2003. *Israel and the Palestinian Minority*. Haifa: Mada al-Carmel.

Sultany, Nimer (ed.). 2004. *Israel and the Palestinian Minority*. Haifa: Mada al-Carmel.

Sultany, Nimer, ed. 2005. *Israel and the Palestinian Minority*. Haifa: Mada al-Carmel—Arab Center for Applied Social Research. (Hebrew)

Swedenburg, Ted. 1990. "The Palestinian Peasant as National Signifier." *Anthropological Quarterly* 63(1): 96–117.

Swedenburg, Ted. 1995. *Memories of Revolt: The 1936–1939 Rebellion and the Palestinian National Past*. Minneapolis: University of Minnesota Press.

Thai, Hung Cam. 2006. "Clashing Dreams: Highly Educated Overseas Brides and Low-Wage U.S. Husbands." In *Global Woman: Nannies, Maids, and Sex Workers in the New Economy*. Barbara Ehrenreich and Arlie Russell Hochschild, eds. Pp. 296–326. Tel Aviv: Babel Publishing. (Hebrew)

Tong, Rosemarie. 1989. *Feminist Thought: A Comprehensive Introduction*. Boulder: Westview Press.

Torstrick, Rebecca. 2000. *The Limits of Coexistence: Identity Politics in Israel*. Ann Arbor: University of Michigan Press.

Touma-Shukha, Sawsan. 2007. *On the Margin of the Margin: Women and Work*. Nazareth: Women against Violence. (Arabic)

Ueno, Chzuko. 2004. *Nationalism and Gender*. Melbourne: Trans Pacific Press.

United Nations General Assembly Resolution 194 (December 11, 1948). Electronic document, http://domino.un.org/unispal.nsf/361eea1cc08301c485256cf600606959/

c758572b78d1cd0085256bcf0077e51a!OpenDocument (accessed October 17, 2007).

United Nations Population Fund 2006 Migration by Region: The Arab States (UNFPA). Electronic document, http://www.unfpa.org/swp/2006/presskit/docs/factsheet_middle-east.doc (accessed May 22, 2009).

Universal Declaration of Human Rights (UDHR). 1948. Adopted and proclaimed by General Assembly Resolution 217 A (III) of December 10, 1948. http://www.un.org/Overview/rights.html (accessed June 4, 2009).

Vailer-Polak, Dana. 2009. A Website Published a Surfer's Letter: Should I Kill My Cousin Who Shamed Our Family? *Haaretz*, May 20. Electronic document, http://www.haaretz.co.il/hasite/spages/1086796.html (accessed June 16, 2009). (Hebrew)

Visweswaran, Kamala. 1994. *Fictions of Feminist Ethnography*. Minneapolis: University of Minnesota Press.

Wang, Lihua. 1999. "The Seeds of Socialist Ideology: Women's Experiences in Beishadao Village." *Women's Studies International Forum* 22(1): 25–35.

Warwar, Badea. 2002. "Beyond the Boundaries." In *Women and the Politics of Military Confrontation: Palestinian and Israeli Gendered Narratives of Dislocation*. Nahla Abdo-Zudi, and Ronit Lentin, eds. Pp. 111–118. New York: Berghahn Books.

Weingrod, Alex, and Adel Manna. 1998. "Living the Seam: Israeli Palestinian in Jerusalem." *International Journal of Middle East Studies* 30(3): 369–386.

Weiss, Yfaat. 2001. " 'The Monster and Its Creator'—or How the Law of Return Made Israel a Multi-Ethnic State." *Theory and Criticism* 19: 45–70. (Hebrew)

Wells, Julia. 2003. "The Sabotage of Patriarchy in Colonial Rhodesia, Rural African Women's Living Legacy to their Daughters." *Feminist Review* 75: 101–117.

Whiteford, Michael B. 1978. "Women, Migration and Social Change: A Colombian Case Study." *International Migration Review* 12(2): 236–247.

Wolf, Diane L., ed. 1996. *Feminist Dilemmas in Fieldwork*. Boulder: Westview Press.

Woollacott, Martin. 2000. War Comes Home: Israel's Killing of Its Own—Eight Israeli Arabs—Changes Everything. *The Guardian*, October 4. Electronic document, http://www.guardian.co.uk/Columnists /Column/0,5673,377059,00.html (accessed February 8, 2006).

Working Group on the Status of Palestinian Women Citizens of Israel (WGR). 2005. "The Status of Palestinian Women Citizens of Israel." NGO Alternative Pre-Sessional Report on Israel's Implementation of the United Nations Convention on the Elimination of All Forms of Discrimination against Women (CEDAW). Submitted in January 2005 to the Pre-Sessional Working Group.

Yacobi, Haim. 2003. "Routine Life in Lod: Power, Identity and Regional Protest in the Mixed City of Lod." *Jama'a* 10: 69–109. (Hebrew)

Yahia-Younis, Taghreed. 2001. "Strangers in Their Own Homes: Women's Vote Patterns in Municipal Elections in an Arab Locality in Israel." Master's thesis, Department of Sociology and Anthropology, Tel Aviv University. (Hebrew)

Yahia-Younis, Taghreed. 2006. "Strangeness, Gender and Politics: Women in Local Politics in Palestinian-Arab Society in Israel." PhD dissertation, Department of Sociology and Anthropology, Tel Aviv University. (Hebrew)

Yahia-Younis, Taghreed, and Hanna Herzog. 2005. "Gender and Kinship-Based Discourse: Primaries Held by Hamayil to Select Candidates for Local Authorities in Palestinian-Arab Locations." *State and Society* 5(1): 1077–1104. (Hebrew)

Yediot Ahronot Tel Aviv
  Yediot Ahronot, July 12, 1964.
  Yediot Ahronot, July 27, 1964.
  Yediot Ahronot, November 24, 1965.
Yiftachel, Oren. 1991. "State Policies, Land Control and an Ethnic Minority: The Arabs in the Galilee Region, Israel." *Society and Space* (9:3): 329–362.
Yiftachel, Oren. 1995. "The Dark Side of Modernism: Planning as Control of an Ethnic Minority." In *Postmodern Cities and Spaces*. Sophie Watson and Katherine Gibson, eds. Pp. 216–42. Cambridge: Basil Blackwell.
Yiftachel, Oren. 1999a. *"Ethnocracy" and "Glocality": New Approaches to Studying Society and Space in Israel*. Beer Sheva: Ben-Gurion University of the Negev.
Yiftachel, Oren. 1999b. "Land Day." *Theory and Critique* 12–13: 279–290. (Hebrew)
Yiftachel, Oren. 2006. "The Shrinking Space of Citizenship.' In *The Struggle for Sovereignty: Palestine and Israel, 1993–2005*. Joel Beinin and Rebecca Stein, eds. Pp. 162–174. Stanford: Stanford University Press.
Yiftachel, Oren, and Alexander Kedar. 2003. "On Land and Power: Territorial Regime in Israel." In *Space, Land, Home*. Yehouda Shenhav, ed. Pp. 19–51. Jerusalem: Van Leer Institute and Hakibbutz Hameuchad Publishing. (Hebrew)
Ynetnews. 2006. "155 victims of the war in the north." August 41, 2006. http://www.ynet.co.il/articles/0,7340,L-3288289,00.html (accessed June 2, 2010).
Ynetnews. 2007. "Arab Rappers vs. National Service," by Sharon Roffe-Ophir. November 7, 2007. http://www.ynetnews.com/Ext/Comp/ArticleLayout/CdaArticlePrintPreview/1,2506,L-3468843,00.html (accessed November 7, 2007).
Yonah, Yossi. 2004. "Israel's Immigration Policies: The Twofold Face of the 'Demographic Threat.' " *Social Identities* 10(2): 195–218.
Young, Elise G. 1992. *Keepers of the History: Women and the Israeli-Palestinian Conflict*. New York: Teachers College Press.
Yuval-Davis, Nira. 1987. "Front and Rear: The Sexual Division of Labor in the Israeli Army." In *Women, State and Ideology: Studies from Africa and Asia*. Haleh Afshar, ed. Pp. 186–204. New York: State University of New York Press.
Yuval-Davis, Nira. 1987. "The Jewish Collectivity." In *Women in the Middle East*. Magida Salman et al., eds. Pp. 60–93. London: Zed Books Ltd.
Yuval-Davis, Nira. 2001. "Nationalism, Feminism and Gender Relations." In *Understanding Nationalism*. Montserrat Guiberhau and John Hutchinson, eds. Pp. 12–141. Cambridge: Polity Press.
Zinger-Harouti, Roni. 2008. "In the morning I know that I will be dead." *Haaretz*, February 15, 2008, This Week: 5. (Hebrew)
Ziv, Neta, and Ronen Shamir. 2003. "Build Your House: Big Politics and Small Politics against Land Discrimination." In *Space, Land, Home*. Yehouda Shenhav, ed. Pp. 84–112. Jerusalem: Van Leer Institute and Hakibbutz Hameuchad Publishing. (Hebrew)
Zlotnik, Hania. 2003. The Global Dimensions of Female Migration. Migration Information Sources, March 2003. Electronic document, http://www.migrationinformation.org/feature/display.cfm?ID=109 (accessed June 8, 2009).
Zreik, Raef. 2003a. "The Palestinian Question: Themes of Justice and Power. Part 1: The Palestinians of the Occupied Territories." *Journal of Palestine Studies* 32(4): 39–49.

Zreik, Raef. 2003b. "The Palestinian Question: Themes of Justice and Power: Part 2: The Palestinians in Israel." *Journal of Palestine Studies* 33(1): 42–54.

Zuckerman, Alan S. 2005. *The Social Logic of Politics: Personal Networks as Contexts for Political Behavior.* Philadelphia: Temple University Press.

Zurayk, Qustantin. 1948. *The Meaning of Nakba.* Beirut: Dar al-Alam L'lmalayin. (Arabic)

Zureik, Elia. 1976. "Transformation of Class Structure among the Arabs in Israel: From Peasantry to Proletariat." *Journal of Palestine Studies* 6(1): 39–66.

Zureik, Elia. 1979. *The Palestinians in Israel: A Study in Internal Colonialism.* London: Routledge and Kegan Paul.

Zureik, Elia. 1999. Public Opinion and Palestinian Refugees. Ottawa: Report Submitted to the International Development Research Centre.

Zureik, Elia. 2003. "Demography and Transfer: Israel's Road to Nowhere." *Third World Quarterly: Journal of Emerging Areas* 24(4): 619–630.

ABOUT THE CONTRIBUTORS

Lilian Abou-Tabickh is a PhD candidate in Political Science and Women and Gender Studies at the University of Toronto. She received her MA in Gender Studies at Bar-Ilan University. Her thesis, "Migrants within Their Nation: How Do Palestinian Women in Israel Experience Their Move with Marriage," won the best research award by the Gender Studies Program at Bar-Ilan University in 2008. Her other publication is entitled "Collective National Rights, Civil Equality and Women's Rights: Palestinian Women in Israel and the Violation of Their Right to Free Choice of Residence." Lilian is a board member of Kayan–Arab Feminist Center, Haifa, and her research interests focus on the intersection of women's rights, social structures, and the State.

Lila Abu-Lughod is the Joseph L. Buttenwieser Professor of Social Science in the Department of Anthropology and the Institute for Research on Women and Gender at Columbia University in New York. She is the author of three ethnographies based on fieldwork in Egypt: *Veiled Sentiments: Honor and Poetry in a Bedouin Society*; *Writing Women's Worlds: Bedouin Stories*; and *Dramas of Nationhood: The Politics of Television in Egypt*. She is coeditor with Ahmad Sa'di of *Nakba: Palestine, 1948, and the Claims of Memory*.

Leena Dallasheh is a PhD candidate at the Department of Middle Eastern and Islamic Studies at New York University. Her research focuses on the social and political history of Nazareth from 1940 to 1966. She wrote her master's thesis at New York University about "Al-'Ard: A Pan-Arab Nationalist Movement in Israel in the Late 1950s and Early 1960s." She has an LLB from the Hebrew University of Jerusalem.

Amal Eqeiq is a native Palestinian born in the city of Al-Taybeh. She is a PhD candidate in Comparative Literature at the University of Washington, and teaches Arabic at the Department of Near Eastern Languages and Civilization. She was an IASP (Israeli-Arab Scholarship Program, Department of State) grantee from 2004–2006 at the University of Oregon, where she received her MA in Comparative Literature. Her research interests focus on modern Arab literature and popular culture, Palestinian studies, feminism, indigenous literature in Mexico, and Mexican/Chicano-Chicana literature.

Honaida Ghanim is the General Director of MADAR, the Palestinian Forum for Israeli Studies and a postdoctoral fellow at the Department of Sociology and Anthropology at the Hebrew University of Jerusalem. She received her PhD in Sociology from the Hebrew University focusing on the social role of Palestinian intellectuals in Israel, 1948–2002. Between 2005 and 2007, Honaida was a postdoctoral fellow at the Center for Middle Eastern Studies and Sociology Department at Harvard University. Before then, she was a visiting lecturer at Al-Quds University, Birzeit University, Bethlehem University, and the Hebrew University. Her research interests are in the fields of political and cultural sociology as well as gender studies, especially the dynamics of institutionalized power, subjectivity, and the formation of the political and cultural foundation of social life. Her book, *Intellectuals Reinventing a Nation: Israeli-Palestinian Persons-of-Pen Crossing Boundaries and Struggling Liminality*, is forthcoming.

Ibtisam Ibrahim is Assistant Professor of Sociology and the director of the Arab Studies Program at American University. Her research interests include the Arab World / Middle East studies focusing on national and ethnic identities of Palestinians, particularly the Palestinian minority in Israel, women and development, women in war and peace, democracy and Islam in the Arab World, and the Arab-Israeli Conflict. Ibtisam's research and publications include: "Status of Arab Women in Israel"; "Divisiveness along Religious Lines: Arab Minority in Israel"; "Debating Democracy in the Arab World"; "Palestinian Female Suicide Bombers: Equal Partners in the Struggle for Liberation"; and "The Past's Promises: Lessons from Peace Processes in Northern Ireland and the Middle East." She is currently working on "The Impact of Physical Boundaries Upon Inter-Group Conflict: A Comparative Study between Belfast and Jerusalem."

Rhoda Ann Kanaaneh has taught anthropology and gender and sexuality studies at New York University and American University in Washington, DC, and has held fellowships at Harvard, the European University Institute, and Columbia University. She is the author of the award winning book "Birthing the Nation: Strategies of Palestinian Women in Israel" (2002) and of *Surrounded: Palestinian Soldiers in the Israeli Military* (2009).

Fatma Kassem received her PhD from the Department of Behavioural Science at Ben-Gurion University. In 2007–2008, she was a fellow at the Europe in the Middle East—the Middle East in Europe program at the Department of Political Science at the Free University-Berlin. She is currently teaching at the Department of Sociology and Anthropology at Ben-Gurion University in the Naqab.

Lena Meari is a PhD candidate in the Department of Cultural Anthropology at the University of California-Davis. She is conducting her fieldwork on the interrogation encounter between Palestinian political activists and the Shabak (Israeli security service). She received her BA in Psychology and Interdisciplinary Studies from Haifa University, an MA in Clinical Psychology from Tel Aviv University, and an MA in Gender, Law, and Development from the Institute of Women Studies at Birzeit University. She worked at the institute as an instructor and took part in research on the ethnography of checkpoints and Palestinian families' coping strategies within the colonial context.

Isis Nusair is Assistant Professor of Women's Studies and International Studies at Denison University. She teaches courses on transnational feminism; feminism in the Middle East and North Africa; and gender, war, and conflict. Isis previously served as a researcher on women's human rights in the Middle East and North Africa at Human Rights Watch, and at the Euro-Mediterranean Human Rights Network. Her current research focuses on the impact of war and displacement on Iraqi women refugees in Jordan. Her other publications include "Gendered, Racialized, and Sexualized Torture at Abu-Ghraib" and "Gender Mainstreaming and Feminist Organizing in the Middle East and North Africa."

Areej Sabbagh-Khoury is a PhD candidate at the Department of Sociology and Anthropology at Tel Aviv University where she also completed her BA and MA degrees. Her MA thesis is entitled "Between the 'Law of Return' and the Right of Return: Reflections on Palestinian Discourse in Israel." Since 2002, she has worked as a project coordinator and researcher at Mada al-Carmel, Arab Center for Applied Social Research located in Haifa. Her fields of interest include Palestinians in Israel, discourses of the internally displaced, and the Israeli Zionist socialist left. *The Palestinians in Israel: A Guide to History, Politics, and Society*, coedited with Nadim N. Rouhana, is forthcoming from Mada al-Carmel.

Manal Shalabi is a feminist and political activist. She worked as the coordinator of the National Hotline for Battered Women in Haifa. She holds a BA in Social Work from Haifa University, and an MA in Gender Studies from Bar-Ilan University. She is currently the Outreach Program Coordinator for the Fulbright Foundation.

Taghreed Yahia-Younis is a political sociologist. She received her PhD from the Department of Sociology and Anthropology at Tel Aviv University. Her dissertation is entitled "Strangeness, Gender and Politics: Women in Palestinian Local Politics in Israel." She currently teaches at Tel Aviv University.

INDEX

Made in the USA
Middletown, DE
19 February 2015